BLACK POLITICS IN BRITAIN

Research in Ethnic Relations Series

Black Radicalism and the Politics of De-industrialisation
The Hidden History of Indian Foundry Workers
Mark Duffield

The Ghetto and the Underclass
Essays on Race and Social Policy
John Rex

The Politics of Community
The Bangladeshi Community in East London
John Eade

Race and Borough Politics
Frank Reeves

Ethnic Minority Housing:
Explanations and Policies
Philip Sarre, Deborah Phillips
and Richard Skellington

Reluctant Hosts: Europe and its Refugees
Danièle Joly and Robin Cohen

Democracy and the Nation State
Tomas Hammar

Antiracist Strategies
Alrick X. Cambridge and Stephan Feuchtwang

Black Politics in Britain

Edited by

HARRY GOULBOURNE

Senior Research Fellow
Centre for Research in Ethnic Relations
University of Warwick

Avebury

Aldershot · Brookfield USA · Hong Kong · Singapore · Sydney

Published by

Avebury

Gower Publishing Company Limited
Gower House, Croft Road, Aldershot
Hants. GU11 3HR, England

Gower Publishing Company
Old Post Road, Brookfield, Vermont 05036
USA

British Library Cataloguing in Publication Data
Black politics in Britain. - (Research in
ethnic relations series)
1. Great Britain. Race relations.
Political aspects
I. Goulbourne, Harry II. Series
323.141

ISBN 0-566-07148-7

Printed in Great Britain by Billing & Sons Ltd, Worcester

Contents

Preface

Nearly all the papers in this volume were first presented at a one day conference on Black people and British politics at Warwick University in November, 1987. The original idea of the conference came from Haris Beider, a postgraduate student at the Centre for Research in Ethnic Relations who is conducting research into Moslems and politics in Birmingham. Without Haris' dedication and hard work the conference may never have been held and special thanks are therefore due to him. The general aim of the conference was to bring together a number of black politicians from all parties, academics and community leaders to discuss a number of questions with which they are all concerned in one way or another. We were successful with this. Part of the original intention, however, was also to include some of the comments made by politicians and community spokespersons who attended and made the conference a success. Time and space have not permitted this. But, hopefully, we will have the opportunity for academics, politicians and community groups leaders to discuss together again aspects of the political experience of black people in Britain. And we should be able to do a better job the second time around.

The conference was partly financed by the Centre for Research in Ethnic Relations and partly by a generous grant from the Barrow & Geraldine S. Cadbury Trust in Birmingham for which I remain grateful.

Some contributors very kindly supplied their final papers on discs. The great bulk of the work involved in presenting the camera-ready manuscript for publication was done by the staff of the Centre, particularly Rose Goodwin to whom I am very grateful. I must also thank Sarbjit Chahal and Ann Bromiley for their patience and dedicated work at very short notice.

H.G.
Coventry
May, 1989.

List of participants at the Conference on Black People and British Politics, November 1987

Dr Muhammad Anwar, Commission for Racial Equality.

Mr Haris Beider, Centre for Research in Ethnic Relations, University of Warwick.

Dr Clark Brundin, Vice-Chancellor, University of Warwick.

Dr Raj Chandran, former Conservative parliamentary candidate for Preston.

Mr Alphanso Charles, Dominican Overseas National Association

Councillor Balraj Singh Dhesi, then Mayor of Royal Leamington Spa.

Ms Marian Fitzgerald, then, Research Fellow, Brunel University.

Ms Zerbano Gifford, former Liberal parliamentary candidate for Harrow.

Dr Harry Goulbourne, Centre for Research in Ethnic Relations, University of Warwick.

Mrs Selina Goulbourne, Lecturer, Inns of Court School of Law, Grays' Inn.

Mrs Noshiba Hussain, of the then Social Democratic Party.

Mr Avtar Johal, the Indian Workers' Association, Birmingham.

Dr Sasha Josephides, then of the Centre for Research in Ethnic Relations, University of Warwick.

Dr Michael Keith, Centre for Research in Ethnic Relations, University of Warwick.

Councillor Lloyd King, the Labour Party, Hackney.

Mr Horace Lashley, then Fellow, Department of Education, University of Warwick

Dr Zig Layton-Henry, Department of Politics, University of Warwick.

Dr Michel LeLohé, the European School, University of Bradford.

Mr Basil Lewis, former Conservative Haringay councillor.

Councillor G. Manku, Birmingham Labour Party.

Councillor Philip Murphy, Birmingham Labour Party.

Mr Mike Phillips, Polytechnic of Central London.

Professor John Rex, Centre for Research in Ethnic Relations, University of Warwick.

Dr Paul Rich, then of the Department of Politics, University of Warwick.

Ms Karen Ross, Centre for Research in Ethnic Relations, University of Warwick.

Mr Pyare Shivpuri, journalist.

Dr John Solomos, Birkbeck College, University of London.

Councillor John Taylor, Solihull Conservative Party.

Mr William Trant, Director, West Indian Standing Conference.

Mrs Charlotte Wellington, Centre for Research in Ethnic Relations, University of Warwick.

Mr Gus Williams, ACAFESS Ltd. & the then Birmingham Liberal Party.

Messrs Roy Evans (of the then SDP), Russell Proffitt (of the Labour Party) and Keith Vaz, M.P. (Labour) were, at the last moment, unable to attend the conference.

Notes on contributors

Muhammad Anwar is the Principal Research Officer with the Commission for Racial Equality, London. His main publications include *The Myth of Return (1979) and Race and Politics* (1986).

Marian Fitzgerald is a Researcher with the Home Office, London. Until 1988 she worked at Brunel University. She is the author of *Black People and Party Politics in Britain* (1987).

Harry Goulbourne is a Senior Research Fellow at the Centre for Research in Ethnic Relations, University of Warwick. He lectured in politics at the University of Dar es Salaam and the University of the West Indies (Mona) for over ten years. He has published extensively on East African and Commonwealth Caribbean politics. His main publications include *Politics and State in the Third World* (1979), *Teachers, Politics and Education in Jamaica, 1892–1972* (1988). His book, entitled *The Communal Option: Nationalism and Ethnicity in Post–Imperial Britain*, is due to be published soon.

Mark Johnson is a Senior Research Fellow at the Centre for Research in Ethnic Relations, University of Warwick. He has worked and published extensively on health, welfare and social services in inner city areas. His main publications include *Black Welfare and Local Government: Section 11 and Social Services Department* (1988); he has contributed several chapters on housing and social mobility in a number of well–received texts; he writes regularly on health and welfare in *New Community*.

Sasha Josephides now lives and works in Canada. Until 1989 she was a Research Fellow at the Centre for Research, University of Warwick. She has conducted research into, and written on, aspects of the Cypriot community in London as well as the Indian Workers' Associations in Britain. She is engaged in the writing of a book on these associations.

Michael Keith is a Research Fellow in the Centre for Research in Ethnic Relations, University of Warwick. He has conducted research into, and published articles on, police–community relations, particularly in London. His book on the subject, entitled *Lore and Disorder: Policing in a Multi–Racial Society*, is due to be published soon.

Zig Layton–Henry is a Senior Lecturer in Politics, University of Warwick. He has published extensively on race and British politics. He is author of *The Politics of Race in Britain* (1984) and is co–editor of *Race Government and Politics in Britain* (1986).

Michel LeLohé is a Senior Lecturer in the School for European Studies, University of Bradford. He has published numerous articles and reports on race and politics in Bradford, and writes regularly on the political situation with respect to race for the Commission for Racial Equality's journal *New Community*.

Everton Pryce is completing a Ph.D. Thesis in Politics for the University of Essex. He lectures in politics in the Department of Extra–Mural Studies, University of the West Indies (Mona) where he is also an administrator. He has published on aspects of both Caribbean and British politics in newspapers and academic journals.

Kalbir Shukra is completing a Ph.D. Thesis in Politics for the University of Kent. She also works for the London Borough of Greenwich. Her area of interest is the Black Sections movement in the Labour party.

1 Some introductory remarks

HARRY GOULBOURNE

Introduction

One major characteristic of British politics in the 1980s has been the audibility of a black voice in debates regarding the *res publica*. This is both distinctive and new. But the social base which provides the background for the new voice was, broadly speaking, established between 1948, with the landing of *SS Empire Windrush* from Jamaica, and the entry of Asians with formal/legal British connections from Malawi in 1976. The voice has been, in the main, one of protest. But the adoption of this weapon has been determined by the initial and continuing hostile reception of non-white minorities by the majority community, especially those small and discrete pockets made up of individuals and groups who are in a position to exercise social, economic and political power.

Any discussion, therefore, of black people and their relationship to the nation's politics must be set against the more general background of the changes Britain has been undergoing since the end of the war against fascism. In this respect, it is now commonplace to accept that the last forty years has witnessed a significant (although widely dispersed) change in the cultural and 'racial' or ethnic composition of Britain as a result of the entry, settlement and reproduction of non-white newcomers from Africa, Asia and the Caribbean. For much of this time the cares and concerns of the newcomers were excluded from the established mainstream political channels of British society. But the Britain of the late 1970s and the 1980s has been partly characterised by an apparent clarity of these groups' quite distinctive, and at the level of politics, harmonious voices. Moreover, increasingly in the 1980s a transition has been taking place from a predominantly *protest* mode of participation to one of *engagement* in mainstream politics and institutions. The essays in this volume discuss, in the distinctive voices of their authors, some important aspects of these politics in the life of the nation.

It is not necessary, therefore, to comment extensively on either the merits and demerits of the contributions. In a collection of this kind, such judgement or assessment must be carried out by the reader. I want, instead, to comment in a very general way on some aspects of the study of black people and politics in Britain. Few would disagree with the view that what one contributor refers to as the 'black factor' in British politics raises new and urgent questions for the future of democratic participation by individuals of both the majority and minority communities or groups. The latter are becoming more strident in an attempt to make themselves heard by an hitherto hostile, indifferent or reluctant host. Ultimately, it may be said that the challenge all those of us who have made Britain our home are asked to confront has to do with redefining or fashioning the model citizen for a *multi-coloured* and also *post-imperial* society. One point of departure in such an undertaking is an appraisal of the political relationship between black minorities and the state institutions and civil society which have been constructed by and for the white majority population, as the title of Gilroy's book - There Ain't No Black in the Union Jack - suggests (Gilroy, 1987).

The Study of Black People and Politics in Britain

This collection of essays represents what will perhaps become a general effort by students of politics to better understand the intonation and idiosyncrasies of the new voice and assess whether indeed it contributes a new tone or interpretation to the chorus - some might be tempted, irreverently, to say the cacophony - of British politics. The bringing together of a number of essays concentrating exclusively on some important aspects of black people and politics in Britain is a new perspective. But there is no intention here to make undue claims: without doubt there have been some serious attempts to describe and analyse important aspects of black people and politics in Britain.

It is true, nonetheless, to say that in general such attempts have been concerned principally to see black political engagements as the actions of the outsider, the stranger, largely from the perspective of the process of decision-making, or public policy. Earlier, black people featured in the post-war literature on British politics mainly as the football in a discourse about immigration. This might be a simple reflection of the wider sociological literature which portrays black people in Britain almost exclusively as *victims* of racism. Perhaps quite unintentionally, therefore, much of the extant literature tends to contribute to a largely one-sided description of the black situation in Britain and thereby helps in the construction of a widespread but rather distorted wisdom about black people and political action.

This emphasis is, of course, perfectly understandable. After all, the attention given to black people as victims of racism in housing, education, employment, the judicial system, indeed almost every area of life, has come about largely as a result of the creation of a space in the political arena through protest by black people themselves in order to secure for themselves a modicum of active participation in the political life of the nation. This, in turn, created and continues to create, the raw stuff from which social, but particularly *political*, analysis is made. It has been, therefore, the political action of black groups and individuals which has forced a change in the focus of analysis. In other words, a generation of observers has been encouraged to move away from looking at the diverse groups of newcomers from the former empire as so many curiosities or alien bodies to be fitted into the ostensibly homogeneous British social fabric and to see them as legitimate, even if not independent, agents of political perspectives and action.

Even so, there is still another hurdle for the academic. This is the need to begin to see the actors themselves and not only those who in the 1970s and 1980s *reacted* to perceived demands and needs, that is, the policy-makers and the implementors of policy. But in some quarters this will require or demand a radically new epistemological leap for researchers and analysts. To continue to concentrate on how large forces such as social, economic and political processes affect black people is obviously necessary and my remarks here are not meant to rubbish such efforts. These forces constitute the very context or determinants of social behaviour. But imbedded within this methodology is the view from *above* which desperately needs to be corrected or complemented by views from *below*. It would be expected, of course, that in most cases the view from below will drastically change the picture as seen from above. We desperately need to include black people's own interpretations of their reality and the action they have taken to change or modify their situations. The failure of much British 'race relations' research and writing to move into this gear runs the danger of developing and cementing a tradition of scholarship in which, to paraphrase Gordon Lewis, we see victimization but not the victim, we see the forces of anti-racism, but not the anti-racist, we see the processes of institutional change but not the groups and individuals who fight for such changes (Lewis, 1983).[1]

Worst of all perhaps, we tend to be too concerned to see black people and members of the white majority population who have sided with the causes of black people as a mere generality. For example, we have plenty of accounts of Enoch Powell's views about Britain's non-white population. But the critical and appreciative analyses of individuals such as Fenner Brockway and groups such as the League of Coloured Peoples are less well known. Individuals and groups such as these have contributed to the growing tradition of opposition to discrimination based on race, colour, gender and so forth in the past. And more recently individuals such as Tony Benn, Bernie Grant, the Lords Chitnis and Pitt have been amongst those who have continued in the same critical tradition. When we ignore the contributions which may be viewed in a positive light we quite unwittingly deny the most deserving contributors to a worthy tradition a place in the scheme of things whilst, paradoxically, ensuring that the views of the true enemies of the desirable and truly open society are given both circulation and longevity.

There are important considerations which qualify this general observation. In the first place there are some notable exceptions. These tend to be of two distinct kinds. On the negative side, there is Heineman's detailed study of the Campaign Against Racial Discrimination in the 1960s

(CARD) (Heineman, 1972). In this study many of the actors themselves appear on the stage, but such is the author's blinkered view of the non-white participants that the opposite failure looms high in the analysis – the wider processes to which the groups and individuals contributed are grossly misunderstood and the result is that the researcher concludes that the only success the group had was due to white individual contacts with decision-makers. Thus, whilst there are Asian and West Indian actors in Heineman's account, they are nonetheless portrayed as having only nuisance value in the total political game because they articulated views which ran counter to those of the liberal establishment with which the analyst agreed. On the positive side, however, there are new texts appearing which attempt to portray important aspects of black politics and to situate these within the general framework of the national political situation. Although it is largely only an *argument*, rather than an extensive *demonstration*, of the role of black people in British politics, Paul Gilroy's pioneering work is an outstanding example of the kind of *inclusive* account we need (Gilroy, 1987).

Of equal importance are the personal testimonies of observant actors, such as Learie Constantine in his *Colour Bar* (Constantine, 1953) or Trevor Carter in his *Shattering Illusions* (Carter, 1986). And it should be hoped and expected that in the coming years we will see several witnesses and testimonies like these from those who have made their way into the political parties and participated as councillors in local government and the Palace of Westminster as members of the popularly elected House of Commons. An example of the former may be a black woman council leader such as Merle Amory, former leader of Brent or the first Asian/Moslem Lord Mayor of Bradford in 1986/7, Councillor Ajeeb. In the case of parliamentarians the personal testimonies of the first four black members of the House of Commons – Diane Abbot, Paul Boateng, Bernie Grant and Keith Vaz, elected in June 1987 – will be invaluable. The free and open discussions between politicians from all the major parties who attended the one-day conference on Black people and British politics at Warwick University in November, 1987 indicate the wealth of experience they share which, when they are written up, will enrich the literature on politics in this country.

The second qualification is that researchers in the field are not entirely unaware of the institutional bias and there have been attempts to correct this imbalance. One major problem here, however, has been the mutual mistrust between researchers and activists (Jacob, 1986). In the past this was particularly true with respect to West Indian groups (see, for example, Rex & Tomlinson, 1979). More recently specific events, either in the Indian sub-continent (such as the murder of Mrs. Indira Gandhi and the Khalistan question) or events in Britain (such as the Rushdie Affair), have affected specific Asian groups in ways which would suggest that access for the researcher to some Sikh or Moslem groups may not be as easy as before. In the case of West Indians, it is impossible to read any monograph on this sector of the population without feeling the tension between the groups or individuals and the researcher. This is particularly the case where the researcher is from the white majority community.

It would seem that this tension is generated by what may be best described as a kind of *zoological* perspective of some of the research done on the black experience in post-imperial Britain. Essentially, black people are perceived, according to this perspective, in much the same way as a zoologist might observe captured animals in a zoo. And, sometimes it is almost as if the *social* zoologist has the same concern as the *animal* behaviouralist because there is the same sense of the utterly *other* which would do social Darwinism mightily proud. There is a kind of benignity displayed in not wishing to disturb the behavioural patterns of the observed so that these may be captured for certainty. In short, just as the observed subject of the zoologist is not expected to be active in the discussion about itself, so too is little expected of the perceived *inactive* black social or political actor. Not infrequently, therefore, the critical and uncooperative attitudes taken by black informants represents a kind of low-key resistance, or a refusal to have their reality treated in this manner.

This *zoologicism* in turn is continuing to have undesirable effects on the ways in which black people and politics are being discussed. The relative absence of black people in academic political discourses which concern them has meant that the black voice has had to surface almost exclusively outside the boundaries of the academy. With respect to black people themselves, therefore, this discourse is taking place almost exclusively within the political arena and the form of articulation that politics takes is appropriate to that forum.[2] For example, the media which is the transmission belt for these politics tends, though not necessarily intentionally, to distort the terms of the debate, and often the main points of debate themselves. One consequence of these occurrences is that there is, so to speak, an *over-politicisation* of all matters which touch upon the lives of black people. This, inevitably, leads to a highly charged ideological situation which, in turn, acts as a major ingredient in everything worth saying about black people and politics in Britain. This is true not only with respect to what members of the majority but also what members of the black minorities themselves have to say about relationships which in a less ideologically charged situation would not necessarily be seen as *political*.

A second disconcerting effect of the *zoological perspective* is the tendency for participants in discussions about political matters concerning black people in Britain to be active politicians themselves. This is rather reminiscent of the temporary blight which overcame political discourse in post-independent Africa for much of the 1960s-70s. In that situation not only active politics but also political discussion were deemed to be, in general, the preserve of those who had led the struggle for independence, but specifically the incumbent president. Subsequent, the study of politics in universities was demoted or restricted to the formalistic study of public administration or international institutions. The big political questions about the state and civil society were either left unstated or broached exclusively by the president.

Similarly, critical but sympathetic commentary on the political activities of black people in Britain has been either absent or highly formalistic. I would suggest that this is the result of seeing black people almost exclusively as victims incapable of doing much to change their own situation. A second contributing factor here may also be the feeling of illegitimacy on the part of many white researchers to comment on black political action. The preference, therefore, is to comment on the actions of the state and public institutions. An important aspect of this point, however, is the relative absence of black academics who ought not to suffer any *angst* with respect to legitimacy. The kind of *crisis* the black academic working in this sphere is likely to experience will, of course, be far more acute than that of the white academic. But it is this kind of crisis involving the relationship of the object and the subject which is likely to take us beyond the boundaries of the zoo.[3]

Beyond the Zoo and Victimology

This collection seeks to contribute to the growing literature on black people and politics in Britain by emphasizing the following two factors. First, the volume goes beyond *victimology* and the *zoological* perspective by seeing black people as *active* as distinct from *passive* actors in areas of public affairs which affect their lives as well as the well-being of the nation as a whole. Such participation has involved Britain's black population in something of a militant struggle in order to secure the minimum hearing in some high places and some quite lowly places too.

Since, however, the 'black community', like any other community (the majority white community itself not excluded) is divided in several ways, including colour, language and culture, class, gender, and so forth, it follows that this 'community', again like others, participates in aspects of the very process whereby it is dominated by others. Obviously, these factors of differentiation do not apply identically across communities. For example, racism acts as a powerful factor to hide much of the social divisions in the black communities in Britain. These divisions and their attendant processes of exploitation and subordination are not, however, major concerns of the essays in this volume.

Their absence here is not due to any underestimation of their increasing significance. But what remains of greater urgency and immediacy for the vast majority of non-white peoples in Britain is the daily experience of racism in almost every area of social life. Thus, although black people of all shades, cultural backgrounds, etc., have sought to participate in all aspects of the nation's life, they do so against a background of majority white hostility, sanctioned by the state and justified on the basis of apparent racial or colour difference. From this proposition it follows that the politics generated by this situation constitutes a proper focus for political analysis. It is to this end that the essays in this volume are brought together. And the volume is offered as a modest contribution towards sharpening this focus.

Secondly, the volume hopes to encourage the development of a wide and generous perspective on black political activity so that some of the most important and relevant aspects of these politics should not be abandoned by the creators of the *official* knowledge which will become the certainty and wisdom of tomorrow. This outlook has two important implications for the study of black people and politics in Britain. In the first instance, a wide and general outlook should dissuade us from concentrating exclusively on any one aspect of political life (say, immigration or police brutality) and the black population. Secondly, by trying to focus upon the specifically political dimensions of black experiences in Britain, we should eventually be better able to distinguish between those aspects which are indeed political and those which are not. The purpose, then, of this volume is to look at a number of aspects of what politics may mean for black people themselves.

The collection, therefore, draws attention to *aspects* – not the *totality* – of these politics at two levels. The first five essays by Anwar, Fitzgerald, Johnson, Layton–Henry and LeLohe are concerned about quantifiable political variables. Generally, these are to do with the voting behaviour of the black electorate, but specific questions, such as voting intention and turn–out, preference, perceptions of party political profiles and agendas, loyalty and potential shifts in party following, etc., are variously raised by these contributors. Unavoidably, there is a limited amount of overlapping because these writers tend to draw upon much the same sources and there is a certain uniformity of purpose. But there is also much internal debate about the recurring figures they employ and this difference in interpretation should be of interest to all students of British politics, particularly those concerned about the immediate future behaviour of the black vote.

The purpose of the essays in the first part of the collection, then, is to focus attention on the potential or actual strategic importance of the black vote in contemporary Britain because of the residential concentration of the black population. Expectedly, the importance of this on possible outcomes in elections is not lost on politicians, including black politicians, particularly those in the Labour party who were concerned to secure selection and election of black candidates in the 1987 general elections. This is likely to be of continuing importance as the juvenile black population matures into members of the electorate, especially in the neglected inner cities. The attempt by the Prime Minister, Margaret Thatcher, on her historic third consecutive victory at the polls in June, 1987 to steal the thunder from the Labour party about the blight of our inner cities, indicates that the Conservative party's leadership also has an eye on the black vote. In this respect, Layton–Henry's conclusion about the 'shift' other analysts perceive amongst Asians, makes interesting reading if only because it raises some pertinent questions about elections and black politics for the political parties in the near future.

There are, of course, several other points of contention here. But I believe the presence of contention is one of the few advantages of a collection over a one-author work: the reader is invited to listen to, or participate in, a vigourous debate which takes place between the same covers whereas the singular authorial voice can ill-afford an inflection of doubt let alone letting the reader know that there may be several, perhaps equally legitimate, perspectives on the same question. Another example, therefore, of disagreement and difference in these essays is over the degree of registration by Asians, Afro-Caribbeans and whites. In this regard the essays by Anwar, Johnson and LeLohe are of particular interest. One related question which is left unsatisfactorily treated, however, is how we are to account for the high level of political awareness and physical salience of Afro-Caribbeans in the political arena and its surrounds (such as the unions and the media) (see for example, Morris, in Ali, 1988, pp.142 ff.) and at the same time harbour a profound academic deprecation of their organizational and participatory capacities. The issue is, of course, implied throughout much of the discussion, but it is still only implied rather than explicitly and rigourously stated and treated. This is one point, then, in this collection, where at least one contributor comes dangerously close to revolving the discussion around the issue of ethnic *competition* between Britain's non-white minorities.

Overall, these essays seek to present the issues in terms which would be generally acceptable to all concerned about the welfare of those citizens caught in an ostensibly seamless and endless struggle to gain recognition and a place in the nation's political life. The essays are nearly all comparative in perspective and bring into focus the two main sets of non-white or black communities in Britain, people of African and Asian backgrounds who share a British colonial *past* and a post-imperial British *present* within the metropolis of a greatly reduced world power. The past glory has given way to doubts and a certain sapping of national confidence and therefore as a majority population white Britisher are caught-up with the fall-out of the country's loss and demotion in the world cominity of nation-states.

Whilst the essays in the first part of this collection may be said, then, to approach the subject of black people and British politics from a macro-analytical perspective, the essays in the second part introduces another level of analysis. Contributions by Josephides, Keith, Pryce, Shukra and myself reverses the process by drawing attention to some examples of the kinds of issues which exercise communities and spokespersons. Specific events and moments in Nottinghill and Brixton are, for example, related by Pryce and Keith in their contributions to broader political questions of the day as well as to some general ontological issues. Their essays describe situations in which different perspectives on leadership emerge and give way to a series of lively debates over means and ends. Shukra's paper draws our attention to the fight within the Labour party for the recognition of Black Sections and raises the crucial question of whether black parliamentary participation is to be preferred to black political mobilization over specific issues within specific communities. Josephides' essay concentrates on the long history of the Indian Workers' Associations which, from one account, originated in Coventry in 1938. My own piece is an attempt to sketch a general framework within which to situate black, particularly West Indian, groups in Britain since the last war.

The essays in both parts of this collection, therefore, attempt to bring into the chorus of British politics the voices of black people themselves. Now, there are severe limitations here. For one there is always the question of selection; and selection means exclusion. The topics covered, however, has been partly determined by preference, partly by availability of papers and individuals willing and able to work to a timetable, and partly – it has to be admitted – by the interests of individuals working on race relations matters in Britain. But the hope is that the stuff of which black politics are made can become more accessible to the general reader and students of British politics. Certainly, the attempt is made by the authors to incorporate material from groups themselves and to use a variety of sources, thereby making them more accessible to students. They also serve to open new avenues and perspectives on a set of questions which are likely to become more pertinent, if not more insistent, over the coming years.

Inevitably, however, there are some obvious absences here. There is little on the growing importance of the political dimension of Islam in Britain, particularly as expressed in the Rushdie Affair; nor is there anything specifically on the growing dynamics of diasporic politics such as the Khalistan question (see, Goulbourne, forthcoming). The media's portrayal of black politicians and politics and the black politician's use of the media are conspicuously absent. So too are the day-to-day experiences of black councillors and members of parliament who, since the late 1970s have been experiencing the travails and excitement of the pioneer in hostile territory. In particular, the emerging politics of minority-minority (as distinct from majority-minority) politics are absent, and perhaps correctly so. The relations between Britain's visible and salient minorities – the imperial category constructed in East and Southern African as 'Asians' and the new British creation of 'Afro-Caribbeans' – are distinctively under-theorized both in this volume and elsewhere (see, however, with respect to West Indians, Gilroy, 1987).

With one exception the papers, nonetheless, retain the uniformity of the notion that black means people with both African and Asian backgrounds in Britain. There is the assumption that Britain's non-white minorities, whether of African or Asian backgrounds, have enough in common to unite in order to overcome hurdles placed in their way. The word *black* is therefore used generally to denote people who experience discrimination based on their (non-white) colour. The problems and issues discussed affect both the 'Asian' and the 'Afro-Caribbean' to one degree or another – for example, Shukra's discussion of Black Sections. When, however, contributors wish to indicate the *differential* experiences of particular groups they do so unselfconsciously. Thus, the chapters by Josephides, Pryce, Keith and myself address specific instances in the lives of organizations and groups which may be found predominantly in one or the other community.

It is important to note, however, that the word *black* is returning to the traditionally contentious status it has long had in the West. For example, some Asians have expressed the view that they and their communities are distinctively not black (Madood, 1988). Some Asian journalists and politicians, wishing to retain the political unity of all Britain's non-white peoples, have argued that whilst they are not physically or *culturally* black they are black in a political sense. For still others – and no doubt the majority of politicians – *blackness* retains its unity as a construct against *whiteness* and its attendant cultural and ideological hegemony, and against its economic and political domination. People of Afro-Caribbean backgrounds in Britain, like Afro-Americans (Haskins, 1988), are also beginning to question the specific niche or category they ostensibly occupy within the British ethnic enclave. For example, whilst there is little or no sign of an attempt to abandon *blackness*, some individuals and groups feel that the term 'Afro-Caribbean' is less than adequate and that 'African-Caribbean' may be more appropriate.

I have argued elsewhere (Goulbourne, forthcoming (a)) that this discourse over *blackness* in some quarters relates, essentially, to a political point. In other words, it surely cannot be the case that those who wish to abandon the word black are seriously suggesting that it more properly describes, or is phenotypical of, the totality of people of African descent in the West than it is of people from the Asian (particularly the southern) sub-continent. Whatever else the rejection may entail, it would seem to me that what is essentially being stated is a rejection of the term as a *political* category because this is what black has meant since its construction out of anti-racist struggles from the late 1960s. Black politics have come to have a meaning which some elements now wish to distance themselves from. The essays here, however, use the word unproblematically and this is fully justified because they are concerned almost exclusively with politics.

This leads to a brief mention of what has come to be very loosely called the black political agenda in Britain. The issues on this 'agenda' may be said to include questions relating to the police/community relations and racial attacks;[4] discrimination in immigration and nationality legislation and application of the law; problems of the inner cities including housing, the poll tax, health, etc.; education, employment and so forth. Whilst most black people would agree on the underlying racism which informs these issues, there is no national, non-partisan consensus over means and ends. One of the aims of the conference on black people and politics at Warwick in November, 1987 was precisely to consider the extent to which black politicians from different political parties shared common concerns. The fact that they could discuss a number of these issues together indicate that, irrespective of party membership, black politicians do in fact share common concerns and experiences. This suggests that with time a truly national bi-partisan agenda may emerge in Britain, without necessarily damaging party political loyalty.

The notion of a *black agenda* is, however, highly problematic. In the first place, issues and possible outcomes are not wholly determined by black communities and politicians but, perhaps more importantly, by the white majority and the majority institutions of the land. In this sense such an agenda is necessarily *reactive*[5] and is not the main determinant of outcomes or, put another way, black politics *alone* cannot effect authoritative resolution. What black politicians can do, however, is to convert or develop *problems* into *issues* and to attempt to get these onto the public agenda. The extent to which they are likely to be successful in placing issues onto the agenda turns largely on how these issues are likely or are perceived to be damaging to the interests of politicians who act according to perceived notions of discrete and/or majority interests. The construction of a black political agenda in Britain which may be likely to stand any chance of success hinges upon the ability of politicians being able to articulate black interests in terms which are acceptable to, because complementary with, the interests of sizeable proportions of the majority population. To speak of a black agenda without regard to this overwhelming factor may be tantamount to a wild indulgence in illusions.

This may be variously explained. In the first place, there is the obvious problem of size; the non-white population of Britain amounts to less than five per cent of the nation and whilst its concentration and youth may augur well for the future, these are not likely to be sufficient to make the non-white population a major determinant in the political arena. Additionally, it is too often assumed that black people are not distinguished in any meaningful degree by such factors as class, gender and so on. The potentially different interests these factors may give rise to should suggest that the construction of a unified black agenda may not be possible in Britain. It is more likely that there will be *several* black agendas.

Then, secondly, there are the party political divisions. It is true that the demand for recognition of Black Sections in the Labour party attracts great attention to the presence of black people in that party. But it must not be overlooked that the Conservatives and the Democrats (and in the past, the Liberals and the Alliance) are also concerned to win black support and that their policies and ideologies are preferred by some black people. In one sense, party membership may distract black politicians from unity of purpose and therefore from the construction of a black agenda. In another sense, the distribution of the black vote, membership and support amongst the parties may strengthen the position of black politicians if there is a resolve to ensure that issues which concern them are attended to. Moreover, such a distribution may reflect a growing confidence amongst the non-white population and *class* interests may be slowly taking precedence over other considerations.

The Labour party's Black Sections' statement of what should constitute *the* black agenda must be seen within the context of the party political framework because this statement represents only some members of one party (The Labour Party Black Sections, 1988). A truly national, independent, black agenda could not in fact be constructed within any one of the political parties. In this regard it is instructive to compare the Labour party's Black Sections' demands with the presence and behaviour of black politicians in the Conservative party, particularly as they are represented in the One Nation Forum which succeeded the defunct societies for Afro-Caribbeans and Asians in October 1987. Black Sections' demands within the Labour party are comparatively well known because black politicians in the party are highly vocal and militant (see, for example, Wadsworth, in Ali, 1988, pp.147 ff.); moreover, Kalbir Shukra's piece discusses important aspects of their agenda and need not be repeated here.

In brief, however, whilst she concludes that their main success has been organizational, rather than in successfully placing items on the party agenda, it is fair to say that black politicians in the Labour party have at least been successful in securing selection for 'winnable' seats and have made something of a *breakthrough*[6] in the 1987 general elections (Ali, 1988, pp.137 ff). This is so even if the significance of there being black members at Westminster is only momentary and symbolic. So far, apart from Jonathan Sayeed who was elected in 1983 and who apparently does not regard himself as a black member of the House of Commons, black Tory politicians have not been able to secure seats for themselves. Of course, one important point of distinction between black Tories and black Labourites is that whilst the former's style is low-keyed, quiet and patient, the latter's style of politics has been to express the impatience bred of the long experience of marginality within the party and the anger of black people generally over the racial injustices sanctioned by successive governments. There might also be a class dif ference. The Conservatives do not hide the fact that they are interested in wedding Asian business and professional expertise, notions of discipline and hard work to the party and interested in attracting West Indians who support the party's individualistic ethos and who are willing to display in the interest of the party their distinctive political skills (Conservative Central Office, n.d., but presumably, 1988).

Unlike Black Sections, however, the objectives of the One Nation Forum is not to *demand* a place within the party for itself or even for 'winnable' seats. These politicians have approached the problem of *representation* in a quite different manner from their Labour counterparts. It would appear that, in the time-honoured Tory tradition, the intention is to exercise a degree of *influence* through discrete avenues to ministers and powerful individuals within the government and party. The aim is to attract members from the ethnic minorities and "spread Conservative principles and philosophy throughout the ethnic communities" (Conservative Central Office, n.d., but presumably 1988a). The Forum organizes itself throughout the country and divides into North, Midlands and South groups; there are also national committees dealing with political affairs, the media and special events. The important point to note, however, is that the Forum is nationally organized from central office in Smith Square and is therefore a movement from *above* to the *bottom* as compared to Black Sections which is the opposite. It would seem, then, that

Conservative black politicians such as John Taylor of Solihull or Dr. Raj Chandran (former parliamentary candidate for Preston) in no way wish to replicate Black Sections in their party. Nonetheless, it is possible that the example of Labour in giving the party's support to black candidates could have an impact on the Conservatives and in the next general elections the party may field strong blacks in 'winnable' constituencies, particularly now that the party has black members, such as Shreela Flather, former Mayor of Windsor and Maidenhead and John Taylor, who have served time with the party. If this were to occur at the next general elections, then black voters and politicians would be faced with a new challenge and a new opportunity to serve their communities as well as their wider, more general constituencies. After all, black politicians should not be seeking to serve communal ends. And, notwithstanding much rhetoric in some quarters, these politicians have not seriously sought to do so.

Conclusion

It is, of course, in the nature of politics that alliances are formed, dismembered and reformed around new problems and issues. The unity of black politics is not likely to be an exception. As Afro-Caribbean and Asian politicians win places for themselves in established political institutions such as the parties, town halls and parliament, it is likely that the present prominence of the first generation of active black politicians in post-war Britain, in both town halls and parliament, may become - and correctly so - less noticeable. The outcome is, however, largely dependent on the behaviour of the majority population and the institutions which to one degree or another reflect their interests. This does not, of course, mean that black communities, groups and politicians can afford to be complacent about issues which concern them - especially the issue of representation. The black agenda, therefore, which has still to be fashioned, requires careful thought, a clear political orientation and a vision sufficiently large to encompass the interests of sizeable elements of both the majority and minorities. Nor can politicians afford to forget the fact that so far in Britain black people's effort at mobilization has formed the basis for the black voice to be heard in the nation's politics.

Finally, perhaps for both the present and the immediate future, the central problem on any black agenda must remain the problem of how to transform *formal* rights into *practical* reality for the majority of black people living in Britain. The fact of actual participation and engagement may, in the end, be the only real item we can place on a united non-partisan black political agenda. The following chapters point to some of the ingredients which make this problem a central one for black Britain. The fact, however, that the visible minorities from the former empire have been able to rally under a common banner and effect a common cause - the practical right to participate in the political process - is no mean achievement.

Notes

1. Lewis' argument, with respect to Caribbean scholarship is apposite and is worth quoting here:

   It is this institutionalist bias that accounts for the limited vision of the prevailing scholarship on the New World Antillean experience. We see slavery but not the slave – just as there is a type of scholarship in which we see imperialism but not the imperialist, or trade unionism but not the trade unionist. Ostensibly concerned with the Afro-American experience, it in fact tells us much more about the slaveholders' world than about the world of the slaves. Thereby, we see less than half of the real picture (Lewis, 1983, p.172).

2. A very notable exception, however, is Arif Ali's Third World Impact (1988), which intimates at constructing a *bridge* between media and academic discourses over black politics in Britain.
3. Black students at British institutions of higher learning – universities and polytechnics – frequently express their frustrations in having to discuss 'race relations' matters coolly as if they themselves are not part of the very experience being discussed. Whilst most white academics seem able to abstract themselves from the painfully human aspects of such discussions (of which they too are part and parcel) the black academic or student cannot easily do so due largely to the one-sided emphasis on seeing black people as *passive victims*. On the positive side of this experience, however, is the potential for greater insights and scholarly passion to be brought to the field than are presently been admitted.
4. In the case of Afro-Caribbean people the issue is police brutality and accountability; in the case of the Asian communities the issue is more about the police's failure or refusal to adequately patrol the streets and to take seriously the victimization of Asians by racist thugs.
5. This does not mean, however, that such an agenda is necessarily *reactionary*; the concepts of reaction and being reactive should certainly not be confused, particularly in this context.
6. As both the essays by Fitzgerald and Shukra caution, however, we need to see this *breakthrough* – if such indeed it is – within the context of dependence on one wing of the Labour party, the highly criticized Left.

PART ONE
BLACK VOTERS AND THE ELECTORAL PROCESS

2 The emergence of black councillors and MPs in Britain: some underlying questions

MARIAN FITZGERALD

Introduction

The election of four black MPs in 1987 has been regarded as a major breakthrough in black political development in the UK. The notion that there is now 'a black voice in Parliament' has raised hopes and expectations. And the fact is viewed as a landmark in the process whereby, through involvement with the political parties, the emergence of increasing numbers of black councillors, the steadily growing numbers of black parliamentary candidates [1] and the eventual breaching of the last bastion of white political monopoly, black people might eventually secure proportional political representation in Britain.

Such a scenario is as attractive as it is optimistic and, might be even complacent. It ignores the fact that there were already black MPs long before mass black immigration to this country, (as Anwar's contribution to this volume makes clear). It discounts the little publicised fact that a black MP had already been elected as a Conservative member in 1983.[2] It dismisses the pointers to likely future developments which emerge from a study of black councillors. And it fails to take into account the fact that, by 1987, over 50% of the population (women) were still 'represented' by only 6% of all MPs even though, as a group, they are beset by fewer handicaps than black people in trying to break into the white, male-dominated world of British politics. In short, the notion of 'natural progression' – the idea that black people will achieve 'representation' in proportion to their numbers by a simple process of political evolution – begs a large number of important questions. For the purposes of discussion, these may broadly be categorised as a two-fold problem:

- Do black people face obstacles to achieving elected office which they would not face if they were white?

- Once they have been elected, what can black people be expected to achieve?

This chapter begins by examining a range of factors associated with the first of these questions and then moves on to a discussion of the second.

Obstacles to the Emergence of Black Councillors and MPs

Of all the factors which may have inhibited – and may continue to inhibit – the emergence of black councillors and MPs, racism is the most obvious. As such, however, it has tended to distract attention from other important inhibitors. Moreover, there are particular ways in which racism, in turn, significantly compounds these other factors. For this reason, discussion of the effects of racism will be discussed second. It should also be noted here that the various factors discussed may affect the chances of becoming an MP or a councillor in differing degrees. Where the contrast is pronounced, this is explicitly recognised. For the most part it is simply assumed that their effect tends to be much greater in the case of would-be MPs where competition is very much greater [3] and local standing, influence and own-group support may count for much less.

The first generation of post-war black immigrants were undoubtedly held back from participating in British politics by a variety of factors associated with *newness*. Their energies were consumed by the struggle for economic survival and working long and anti-social hours. Some were handicapped by language difficulties; many were ambivalent about whether they wanted to settle here permanently; and probably many more retained the politics of their countries of origin as their main frame of reference.

With the passage of time, the dissipation of the myth of return and increasing awareness of the need for political influence – not least to secure justice for themselves – it might be assumed that by the second and third generation these brakes on active participation would have been released. Even then, there would have been a time-lag before the emergence of black people into elective office, since the parties expect new entrants first to serve a political apprenticeship, proving their loyalty through routine constituency work as a condition of the dubious honour of flying the party flag in one or more unwinnable seats before getting a real chance of election. But some commentators have pointed also to the likelihood that political involvement is the outcome of a process of socialisation which comes to fruition only over a number of generations. Thus, successful political activists are likely themselves to have a family background of – if not activism – at least political interest. And a further corollary of this which has received less attention but which is of obvious relevance is that, while the Conservative political families are well recognised, many Labour MPs are now the sons and daughters of trade union officials and councillors, or at least the nephews and nieces of Labour politicians. Indeed, it has been argued that there is also now 'a Labour *establishment* based on dynastic and kinship ties' (Kavanagh, 1982, p.104).

Racism apart, then, British party politics is already more difficult to break into than the parties themselves would care to acknowledge. In that sense, 'newness' may continue to be an inhibiting factor well beyond the immigrant generation on whom its effects are relatively obvious.

Moreover, the immigrant generation moved into the socio-economic stratum of British society in which successful, individual, political activism is least likely. And the evidence is that successive generations have begun only marginally to escape from that situation [4] – although it is important to note that the socio-economic distribution of different black groups may vary considerably.[5] Certainly those likely to achieve elective office, even at local level, are rarely drawn from this stratum; and the same is truer still of MPs. A survey of London councillors conducted for the GLC in 1984/5 [6] confirmed how atypical even their local representatives are of the population at large: although there is some variation by party, Table 1 shows that councillors tend to be professional men, with high academic qualifications, aged between 30 and 45.

Table 2.1 Selected Characteristics of London Councillors (per cent)

	All	Lab	Con	Lib
Male	81	78	92	80
Age 30–44	50	54	35	53
Professional occupation	62	65	48	62
Manual worker	9	13	1	2
Possesses degree/ higher ed. qualification	48	48	42	62

Source: Respondents to GLC councillors survey, 1984/5.

At the parliamentary level this situation is more pronounced. Of all new MPs in 1983, less than 15% had not received further or higher education and less than 5% had come from manual jobs.

The extent to which black people are already likely to be disadvantaged in competition with whites as long as this situation obtains is well illustrated by Browns findings (Brown, 1984 p.51). Only 13% of Asian males and 5% of West Indian males were classified as working in professional, employer or management jobs, compared with 19% of whites. Moreover, the GLC councillors' survey confirmed that black councillors in London were at least as well 'qualified' as their white counterparts on these criteria: 63% were in professional occupations and 43% possessed a degree or higher qualification.[7]

Further constraints derive from the intense *geographical concentration* of the black population. As the PSI report points out:

> The British black population is not spread across the country in the same way as the white population; if it were, then each town would have a small black community ... and this is not the case. In other words, a large proportion of the black population lives in a small number of local authority areas, and within these areas the black residents tend to be concentrated in a small number of electoral wards... It.. means that in most areas of the country there are very few black people indeed. Half the white population in Britain lives in towns and rural areas that have less than half of one per cent of their local residents coming from ethnic minorities... Three quarters of the black population lives in a set of enumeration districts in which we find only a tenth of the white population (Brown, 1984, p.20).

Leaving aside whether they have achieved proportional representation in those areas (or whether they are likely to do so), it is certainly the case that by far the majority of black councillors are to be found in that minority of local authorities where there is a concentration of black people. And the fact of restricted opportunities for becoming councillors already has implications for black people's opportunities of becoming MPs. In 1983 it was already obvious that serving on a local authority was becoming an increasingly important route to parliament: nearly 50% of the new intake had been local councillors. By 1987 the overall figure was slightly higher, rising from 52% to 64% for new Labour MPs.

Additionally, the increasing tendency of many local parties to favour local candidates would appear to severely limit the chances of black candidates, particularly so where all local party members have the right to participate in candidate selection (by post if they choose) – as was always the case with the SDP and is about to become the rule for the Labour Party – their chances will be still further reduced. For where people are able to cast their votes without seeing candidates, they have not previously heard of, they will tend to vote for those they have; and these are likely to be either national 'names' or well-known local figures.

Black people are additionally and very seriously constrained in their opportunities for achieving electoral office by their inordinate dependence on a single party. By far the majority of black councillors and all four of the new black MPs elected in 1987 are Labour party members. At the crudest level of statistical calculation, this means that black people have little more than that fraction of the opportunities for elective office which corresponds with the proportion of elective offices held by the Labour Party. Moreover, while this situation obtains, black representatives have access to real political power only in those local authorities where Labour is in control and will only have access to legislative power if the Labour party replaces the Conservatives in government.

Inasmuch as this dependency is a reflection of inordinate black electoral support for Labour, it is worth pointing out here that only a marginal shift was observed in 1987, with the Harris poll for the Asian and West Indian Times showing relatively high levels of Conservative support among that small proportion of the Asian population living in areas of low black concentration.[8] In the main areas of settlement, however, black Labour support was put at 77%, with Afro-Caribbean support as high as 86%. But it is worth noting also that the reasons for this support are complex (Fitzgerald, 1987, pp.12–13) and may well include the fact that their very geographical concentration – in areas which are politically dominated by Labour – has, in turn had an 'environmental effect' on their party affiliation..

Racism as a Compounding Factor

Of all the factors which inhabit black political representation *racism* must be indentified as the most significant, single influence. For, taken in all its forms – direct and indirect, conscious and unconscious, personal and institutional – it is by far the most pervasive. In ways which often overlap, it:

- compounds all of the factors already described
- is manifest in all the political parties and
- influences the behaviour of the electorate.

The problems of 'newness' were compounded by racism at a time when the crudest discrimination in housing and employment, for example, were not yet covered by even the most basic legislation. And, by the time the present level of legal protection was established, much damage had already been done in locking black people into the cycle of social disadvantage where most have remained trapped. Moreover, 'newness' was itself used as a basis for discrimination, for example, in language testing and conditions of eligibility for council housing, thereby adding a further twist to the cycle.

Once the 'new' immigrants were 'old' enough to begin pressing for equal rights or, even, simply making the most modest political demands, such as for planning permission for cultural facilities), institutions were set up – in the form of local CRCs and, nationally, the Community Relations Commission and the Race Relations Board [9] – to channel their concerns (and the political energies of their most active members) through non-party outlets, separate from the mainstream of British politics. Similarly, separate sources of funding were established for meeting needs which in any other sector of the population would have been taken to create special consultative arrangements and enhanced grant-aid. Often from the best of intentions, these have consumed black political energies in intensified inter-group competition for positions and for money which keep them out of the mainstream of political activity, let alone decision-making.

The impact of racism on the original socio-economic position and geographical concentration of black people is obvious. There is evidence that, albeit perhaps not as crudely, discrimination persists to a sufficient degree to inhibit any but the most gradual change, while the disadvantaged position from which black people begin to try to effect such change will additionally handicap them in so doing.[10] Racism has also had an impact inasmuch as while working class individuals may be less than likely to achieve elected office, black people have also been to a large degree shut out of those institutions which campaign on the issues affecting working class people, chief amongst which institutions is the trade union movement. Such has been their exclusion that it has led to intense and often bitter (albeit somewhat theological) academic debate about whether poor black people may properly be considered as part of the working class at all (e.g. Miles and Phizacklea, 1979).

It is worth pointing also to a compounding factor which has hitherto received little or no attention but which runs through the others. Although its precise impact is difficult to quantify, it would appear that a very justifiable *fear of racism* has acted as an inhibitor in its own right and, indeed, that its impact may actually increase as the experience of racism grows and consequent strategies for avoidance are refined.

Arguably, black people are further handicapped in overcoming the disadvantages of their socio-economic situation and their geographical concentration by the fear of racism. Little work, if any, has been done in this area but, if an explanation is to be found for why black people who move into the professions, for example, tend to be concentrated in particular fields, there are two obvious approaches to pursue. One is that they are pushed in that direction - whether by group/family tradition or by outside advice based on stereotyped assumptions. But the other reason is that they know the degree of resistance and hostility they may face if they seek to break in to new areas where black people are not yet accepted and it take an extraordinary degree of determination and courage to choose to face that. The same considerations will apply to moving into areas of low black concentration (or none). It is interesting to note in this context that the PSI report found the process of dispersal by black people has been limited compared with that established by earlier, white immigrant groups. Some movement has, indeed, taken place outwards from the areas of initial settlement, but the main concentrations have remained confined to the same set of local authorities (Brown, 1984 p.58). From informal sources, a pattern is beginning to emerge whereby black people who move into all-white areas and there experience hostility, if not outright harassment, tend to return to 'safer' areas in which other black people, in turn, develop perceptions of the areas from which they have come as 'unsafe' for black people.

How far black people's political affiliations and behaviour are determined by racial considerations is a matter of debate which constraints of space make it necessary to avoid have. It should at least, however, be noted that to ascribe any observed pattern on the part of black people primarily to 'race' is classically to stereotype. There are two important points to be made at this juncture about the reasons for black people's dependence on the Labour Party. One is that, inasmuch as it may reflect their geographical concentration in areas of Labour dominance, by the same token, the other parties have not had the same level of access to black communities because these tend to be in areas where the Conservative and Alliance presence has been lower and their organisation weaker. The second point is that the Labour Party has become 'the Devil they know'. The very fear of racism may again inhibit people in approaching the other parties and it may – however unjustifiably – be reinforced by what they hear of those parties. Thus Conservatives may claim, for example, that the former MP Harvey Proctor and his ilk are unrepresentative of the Conservative Party, but it is their pronouncements on matter of race and immigration which hit the headlines. And it is significant that growing Asian support for the Conservative Party fell back once Mrs. Thatcher made her famous 'swamping' remarks in 1978 (Layton-Henry, 1984, ch.10). Similarly, whatever the old Liberal party's policy was (or the present SLDP's is), black people's perception of them is likely to be determined by publicity about the eviction of homeless Bangladeshis as a matter of policy by the ruling Liberal (now SLDP) group in Tower Hamlets'.[11]

Racism in Politics

On entering the parties, black people are faced with the same range of racist attitudes as are to be found in the majority population at large – from outright hostility to heavy (albeit often quite unconscious) patronization. However self-consciously anti-racist, active party members are probably quite unaware of the reserve they maintain towards newcomers to the groups they have settled into, or of the extent to which those groups are based on social as much as political criteria. Clearing the initial hurdle of getting nominations to positions of trust (even at ward level) within the party may depend significantly on first gaining acceptance within the group; and this is determined by group members deciding that the newcomer is 'one of *us*'. Proving the requisite degree of 'sameness' is arguably always more difficult for black people than for white where (as is most often the case) the group is predominantly or exclusively white. Certainly, it means that the black members with the greatest chance of acceptance are those who can prove they operate according to white norms.

Beyond this, however, there is no doubt that the dispositions of each of the main parties on the basic issue of ensuring equal opportunities for black people varies quite considerably. All, formally, subscribe to that goal. But there is disagreement over the appropriate political measures for its achievement (as reflected in party manifestos) and quite sharply polarised attitudes between members of the Conservative and Labour parties in particular, as illustrated by the tenor of the resolutions these submit to their respective party conferences (Fitzgerald, ch.3 1987). While it has frequently been observed that the activists who go to meetings and pass resolutions tend to represent the more extreme end of the political spectrum covered by party members as a whole and 'core' party supporters, it is on precisely these people that new black members depend for their initial reception and the opportunities they have for rising within the party.

Even among the activists, however, there are important distinctions, with broadly left/right splits in both the Conservative and Labour parties, of which the left has always been the most ready actively to pursue issues of racial equality at a policy level. By the same token, it has also been the most encouraging of black involvement within the parties. Black people's chances, then, are further influenced by which wing of the party is in the ascendancy at any given time and, indeed, as has already been mentioned, the likelihood of their braving the fear of racism and approaching a party at all may be determined by the balance of publicity given to the (supposed) views and activities of either wing. It also means that, for the foreseeable future, while they remain a small minority within the wing which espouses their concerns, those concerns will be subordinate to the over-all concerns of this wing. Thus black councillors promoted by the Left of the Labour party have sometimes found themselves in difficulty for not being prepared to follow the Left 'line'. Nor is it fanciful to argue that the Left's support for Black Sections in the Labour party has as much to do with the fact that the party leadership opposes them as with the argument of principle for autonomous black constitutional recognition. These and related points are, however, fully developed in Kalbir Shukra's contribution later in this volume.

That this dependency on one section of a given party may further reduce the opportunities for black party members is to a degree self-evident. By becoming closely identified with one section, they may prejudice further the support of the opposing section; and yet the promotion of their interests is at the mercy of the changing priorities of their 'patron' group. Recent developments in respect of our final key area – the electorate at large – would appear, however, to have made the situation much more serious.

Whatever their internal wranglings and whatever the personal dispositions of their individual members, the parties' basic *raison d' etre* is securing political power for themselves by winning elections. Nationally, the electorate on which they depend in order to do so is overwhelmingly white. At parliamentary constituency level, it barely reaches 50% black electors in at most three of the 523 English seats.[12] It is only at ward level within a minority of local authorities where black electors are in a minority of wards within those authorities. Black candidates are, therefore, for the most part dependent on white voters' willingness to support them.

Inevitably the white electorate reflects (if it is not the actual embodiment of) the racial attitudes of the white population at large. There has, therefore, always been a significant seam of racism to be tapped for electoral gain and, at various times, various parties or their individual candidates have chosen to do so. Black candidates have, of course, been particularly vulnerable, as was classically illustrated in Labour's loss of Clapham in 1970 when Dr. David (now Lord) Pitt was defeated in a bye-election where his opponents openly canvassed Labour supporters saying 'You're not going to vote for a black man, are you?'

However, it is broadly true to say that since the early 1970s until 1987, there was an unspoken agreement between the parties that 'the race card' was not to be played in national elections. Generally speaking, the results of black candidates for the Conservative and Labour parties [13] have been comparable with those of their white colleagues. This has been particularly true of general elections and of full local elections where they have stood as part of a 'slate' and where voters have made their choice primarily on party lines rather than by reference to the personal characteristics of the candidates.

But, by 1987, 'the race card' had come to be played again - albeit in a more coded and sophisticated form. Essentially, the parties realised that there was little scope for making significant in-roads into 'the black vote' and little to be gained from doing so anyway. The votes they were competing for in the 'key' seats were white; and white Labour support looked most fragile when the Liberal party had already discovered in 1986 when it wrested control from Labour in Tower Hamlets, one of the most deprived of inner city areas). Black interests, however, were identified most closely with the Left (by now popularly dubbed the 'Loony Left') of the Labour party - as were Labour's black parliamentary candidates; and, as the polls agreed, the electorate's two main reservations about returning to government were the party's defence policy and the influence of its 'extremists'.[14]

Undoubtedly the explicit tag of 'extremism', with its potent but rather less explicit racial connotations was damaging to the Labour party. But, ironically, the racist backlash on which this depended seems to have resulted also in something of an 'own goal' for the Conservative and Alliance parties, since their black candidates suffered differential swings which were more marked than those for Labour Black candidates as Table 2 shows.

Table 2.2 Regional Swings : Black Candidates in the 1987 General Election

	Difference from projected wing for party
Seats fought by 5 black Tory candidates	−2.54
Seats fought by 14 black Labour candidates	−1.94
Seats fought by 7 black Alliance candidates	−5.23

Source: British Public Opinion. MORI. August 1987

The broader irony, however, is that with the election of four black MPs, the chances of black political representation may have been reduced further. If the other main political parties abandon identification with black political interests not only to the Labour party but to the far Left of that party; if they thereby become less prepared actively to encourage and welcome black members; and if they revert to viewing black candidates as an electoral liability, there will be little prospect of all-party black representation drawn from a cross-section of constituencies.

Expectations of Black Councillors and MPS

> Every movement and every vote of theirs will be identified with the community and the latter held morally responsible for their public act...
>
> What if it should be our misfortune to be represented by men only nominally Jews....Would it not be better for the Jewish community not to have any of its members in Parliament than to be represented by men of this kind?

(Jewish Chronicle. 8 February 1861, quoted in Adeeman 1983, p.30)

Written over a hundred years ago, the above passage well illustrates the hopes and fears of oppressed minority communities on first achieving parliamentary representation.

The symbolic importance of 1987 was reflected even in the run-up to the campaign when the black press - which, in 1983, had concentrated on the main political issues and questions about black turnout and influence on the result - devoted massive space over a number of months to profiling black voters in its finding that 32% of its total sample (see Table 3) said they would be more likely to vote for an ethnic minority candidate.[15]

Table 2.3 **Likelihood of Voting for Ethnic Minority Candidate (per cent)**

	All	Asian	Afro-Caribbean
More likely	32	30	38
Less likely	7	8	6
No difference	51	55	42

Source: Harris Political Attitudes Survey for Caribbean/Asian Times, 1987

However, other evidence suggests that ethnic loyalty does not override party loyalty. Moreover, there is some question over how far black voters identify with black candidates standing for the party they usually support but who are not of their particular ethnic group. Certain Asian groups in local authorities with Asian councillors but who were not of their faith have complained of neglect because their interests were not being 'represented'. Indeed, despite the usual preeminence of party loyalty, it is not unknown for Asian voters to prefer a white candidate of the 'wrong' party to an Asian candidate of the 'right' party but the 'wrong' origins (LeLohe, 1975).

But where the elected member is of the 'right' party and the 'right' origins, expectations – in terms of what they have in their power to achieve and the priority they will give to their 'own' group's demands and interests – may be enormously high. They may, in fact, be so high that members are bound to fail. And, additionally, the group's fear of them so doing may exert additional pressure. Their every move may be watched in anticipation of betrayal. And one councillor I interviewed summed up the pressures thus:

> Black people are so used to failure, if you're a success they can't believe you're one of them any more. They so desperately want to trust you to stand up for them, they end up distrusting you for fear of being disappointed.

Against these impossible expectations, black elected members face countervailing pressures from the parties and from their wider electorate.

The parties expect loyalty to the party line to prevail over all else. And the Labour party seems to place a particularly high premium on this to a degree which, at local government level, marked it off very sharply from the Conservative and Alliance Parties.[16] Moreover, it is important to note that – *by contrast with the U.S.A.* with which facile parallels are often drawn – Britain has no real tradition of ethnic politics. The parties accept caucusing by political factions (up to a point); they accept lobbying by groups of members on behalf of particular causes; and they accept that individual members may have particular interests such that they act and speak on behalf of outside pressure groups. But such activities are supposed to be subordinate to accepting the party 'whip' and, although religious affiliation may often be the basis for organisation on certain moral issues (where free votes are usually allowed), up to the present, race as such has never been.

So the parties might not be prepared to countenance black members organising and voting on an exclusively racial basis and would decry any notion that they were representative of and accountable to anyone but the party and their constituents. Yet they have often recruited these people in the first place on the basis of their community activism (or, more cynically, the votes they are assumed to be able to deliver to the party as a consequence). They then tend automatically to expect black members to take the main responsibility for issues connected with 'race'. And the corollary of this is that black members may not be asked or expected to speak on other issues. If, however, they fail (albeit through lack of opportunity) to develop wider areas of expertise, they are likely to be labelled 'single-issue politicians', their career prospects constrained and their arguments regarded as predictable. Meanwhile, white party members may be exempted (by choice, by default or because they fear being cast as 'trying to speak for black people') from involving themselves centrally in 'race' issues. Thus they leave an exclusively black minority with the sole responsibility in this area, thereby compounding black politicians' ghettoisation.

Similar pressures are exerted, in turn, by the electorate at large, not least as a consequence of the publicity generated around black politicians. Some have complained that they only receive publicity in respect of 'race' issues; and certainly the media routinely seem to refer to the origins of nationally known black politicians, whatever the subject of the news item. But, while the stereotyping within the parties may constrain their career prospects, stereotyping by the media and, in turn, the electorate may cost them their seats. There are, of course, a number of wards in which black councillors may be elected primarily or even exclusively on black votes but (as has already been noted) this is true in only a small minority of cases. For the most part, black councillors and, certainly, black MPs will depend on white votes if they are to be returned when they come up for re-election. If, in the interim, white voters have come to conceive of them as 'only' interested in their black constituents, they run the risk of losing their seats. For many, as well as defending themselves against the suspicions of black communities and copying with the ambivalent expectations of their parties, there is the additional burden of having to *prove* to white people that a black person can adequately represent them.

Thirdly in the set of potentially conflicting expectations of black politicians are the perceptions they have of themselves. The view they take of their role may vary widely from individual to individual, from party to party and from one ward or constituency to another, depending on the ethnic make-up of the electorate. Many of those currently holding elected office came into party politics via community group activism; and a number of black councillors also hold professional positions associated with the development of race equality policies. It would, of course, be natural if the main political concerns of such individuals were also in this field. (Although even here it may be necessary to distinguish between those with a broad commitment on race equality issues and those whose interest is more narrowly ethnic-specific). Even so, most of those interviewed in the course of the GLC councillors' survey laid great emphasis on the multi-racial nature of their electorate and set considerable store by the fact that white constituents as well as black came to them with their problems. Beyond these, however is another group who appear positively irked to have any racial label put on them. They are at great pains to insist that they are simply the representative of their political party or aspirations. Such is Jonathan Sayeed, the Conservative MP for Bristol East who is, in fact, half Indian.[17]

Finally, these three sets of expectations of black politicians need to be tested against the basic, obvious but largely unasked question: what can black politicians *realistically* be expected to achieve? Any attempt at an answer needs to be made at two levels: first, what can black politicians be expected to achieve in terms of policy delivery? Secondly, what can black politicians be expected to achieve in personal career terms?

At the level of policy delivery a black politician – as any other – will only achieve his/her goals under certain conditions. These are: a favourable political climate; sufficient support from parliamentary or council colleagues; and that the issues in question have all–party backing or that the politician be a member of the ruling political party. Currently it is arguable that the political climate has become even less hospitable to the promotion of race equality policies. Even if they were represented in proportion to their numbers, black councillors would remain dependent on the support of white colleagues in all local authorities; and in parliament this would be overwhelmingly the case. And, as has already been remarked, black politicians are members of ruling political parties only in a small number of local authorities.

Even if they work closely as a group around an agreed set of race–specific goals, then, black politicians *on their own* cannot (and, perhaps, should not) be expected to achieve significant changes in policy delivery. In personal career terms, there are, of course, successes to point to, with black council leaders, black mayors and committee chairs. But many still have enormous suspicion to contend with and feel the onus doubly on them to prove themselves deserving of positions of trust. Even then, the positions they are given may prove marginalising by confirming their stereotype as single–issue politicians.

Yet the prospect for black politicians need not be as bleak as the above might suggest. Geoffrey Alderman has traced the political development of a small ethnic minority community (the Jews) who have themselves suffered severe racism in politics as elsewhere, and the majority of whom also arrived in Britain as poor immigrants. They have achieved parliamentary representation which is more than proportionate to their numbers in the population and which has included Cabinet ministers.

Alderman's account of how this has been achieved, however, must give further pause for thought. Reduced to its essentials (and thereby, necessarily, simplified), he describes a process which began over one hundred years ago with the election of a number of wealthy Jews to parliament once Jews were no longer constitutionally debarred from such office. This was at a time when the Jewish population was still very small and predominantly middle class and well before the main migration of refugees from Europe in the early part of the twentieth century. Before this migration, however, there was already an active interest in certain quarters of the British Jewish population in the nascent political philosophy of socialism (born, crudely, one would suggest from the combined influences of an intellectual tradition, the experience of discrimination and an international perspective). Over the main period of migration, the new settlers became concentrated in the poorest sections of the working class in many of the areas where the socialists first began to build a practical, electoral base for their philosophy and here, inevitably, began what was to be, in Alderman's words, a long 'love affair with the Left' (Alderman, 1984, p.180).

Over time, though, and most noticeably after the Second World War (that is, more than half a century after the story begins) increasing affluence and the attendant dispersal from the areas of initial settlement significantly weakened the links with the Left although, for practical, electoral purposes the impact of this was delayed by perceptions of a strong tradition of anti-semitism in the Conservative Party. By the 1980s, however, while a strong Jewish socialist tradition (deriving from the same, original roots) persists, Jewish voters at large had swung decisively to the Right in a move which reflected as much as anything their new 'class interest' and their political environment.

The parallels with the black groups whose origins derive primarily from a generation of immigrants some 50 years younger than the Jews, are immediately but sometimes deceptively obvious. For, in any attempt at extrapolation, important differences would also need to be taken into account. There is, for example, no obvious parallel to the issues surrounding the state of Israel, which has been such an important political litmus test for Jewish voters and such a source of political tension in their relations with the main political parties. The role of the Jewish Board of Deputies – however contentious – is also not matched by any such embodiment of a black 'Establishment' and this, in turn, is a reminder of the very much wider diversity of black British groups. But the most important difference of all may yet prove to be the contrast in the pattern of dispersal from the areas of initial immigrant settlement.

Conclusion

Full discussion of these issues merit a study in their own right. But Alderman makes at least one further observation which is of particular and sobering relevance to the immediate concerns of this chapter. He argues that:

> ...although the community is justifiably proud of Jewish MPs, Jewish representation in Parliament is of strictly limited benefit. Only a handful of Jewish MPs can be persuaded to act for the community; most regard themselves simply as MPs who happen to be Jewish. (Ibid).

Notes

1. In 1979, the main parties fielded five black candidates; in 1983, the figure rose to eighteen; and by 1987 there were twenty seven.
2. See reference to Jonathan Sayeed, Bristol South-East, below, footnote 17.

3. Thus, in England and Wales, there are around 560 parliamentary seats to compete for while, in Greater London alone, there are 1,914 council seats. Of these parliamentary seats, moreover, only a minority at any given election will truly be 'up for grabs'. Most will have an incumbent MP who will either be unchallenged or well placed to fight off any challenge to their claim to contest the seat again. In local government, however, the turnover rate is much higher.
4. The PSI report of 1984 (see footnote 9) noted:

   For the most part .. Britain's well-established black population is still occupying the precarious and unattractive position of the earlier immigrants. We have moved, over a period of 18 years, from studying the circumstances of immigrants to studying the black population of Britain only to find that we are still looking at the same thing. (p.323)
5. Thus, the PSI report found 22% of African Asian men in the 'Professional, Employer, Management' category, compared with 10% of Pakistanis and only 4% of Sikhs. (The figure for whites was 19%). p.197
6. The survey, which was based on a questionnaire sent to all London councillors, achieved a response rate of 25% but replies were not proportionately representative of the relative strengths of the political parties. 42% of London Labour councillors replied, but only 9% of Conservatives. A full report was prepared for the last meeting of the Ethnic Minorities Committee before the abolition of the GLC but, in the event, this was cancelled.
7. Also, 52% of black councillors had been 20 or over on leaving full-time education, compared with an average of 48%. None possessed no academic qualifications, although this was the case for 11% of the sample as a whole.
8. The poll, undertaken between 25 and 29 May, 1987, sampled 1006 black adults, of whom 707 were Asian and 299 Afro-Caribbean. Of the 136 who lived in areas of low black concentration, all but three were Asian.
9. These two bodies were merged under the 1976 Race Relations Act to become the Commission for Racial Equality.
10. Thus, below average living conditions, above average unemployment and the social, psychological and physical consequences of these are of themselves debilitating and, thereby, calculated from the outset to inhibit attempts to transcend them.
11. In 1987, the Council began to evict numbers of Bangladeshi households from the temporary accommodation it had given them, on the grounds that it had no statutory responsibility towards them under the 1985 Housing Act as they were 'intentionally homeless' because they had chosen to leave permanent accommodation in Bangladesh.
12. According to the 1981 Census, the constituencies with the largest NCWP populations were Brent South, Ealing Southall and Birmingham Ladywood, figures at that time being respectively 46%, 44% and 42%.
13. The former Liberal Party, however, (and, by extension the SDP, Alliance and now SDLP) relied less on a hard core of traditional support and stood to gain more than the two main parties from 'floating' voters and those wanting to register a protest. As such, its black candidates appear to have been more vulnerable to racial prejudice than candidates for the two main parties where traditional loyalty may have overridden racial prejudice.
14. According to the BBC/Gallup general election survey, references to Labour Party 'extremism' rose from 19% to 27% in the public at large between 1983 and 1987; but

for Labour defectors the figures were 25% and 42% respectively. And among the 35% of the public who believed defence was one of the most important issues in the campaign, the Conservatives had a 63% lead over Labour.

15. A GLC political attitudes survey of Londoners in 1984 had found 22% of both Afro-Caribbean and Asian respondents saying they would be more likely to vote if they had a black candidate to vote for.

16. The GLC London councillors' survey confirmed other findings in the place accorded to party loyalty among the loyalties ranked as 'very important' by respondents, as follows:

	All %	Lab %	Con %	Lib %
Loyalty to National Party	42	54	17	9
Loyalty to Local Party	67	78	44	39
Loyalty to Party Group	65	68	61	52

17. Interviewed in 'Race to Power' (BBC Radio 4, 2 May 1985 and the subject of an article by Nakib Narat in 'The Listener' of the same date), Jonathan Sayeed was adamant that his ethnic origin was totally irrelevant to his role as a Conservative MP.

3 Ethnic minorities and the electoral process: some recent developments

MUHAMMAD ANWAR

Introduction

The estimated present day number of non-white ethnic minorities in Britain is 2.6 million or about 5 per cent of the total population of the UK. They can no longer be considered 'immigrants' since almost half of them are now British-born. Of the others, some came as children and have spent almost all their formative years in this country. Most of the other ethnic minorities have British nationality. They are here to stay. Therefore, Britain is now permanently a multi-racial and multi-cultural society. However, because of differences in colour and cultural backgrounds ethnic minorities face racial prejudices and racial discrimination. There are facts of daily life for most members of ethnic minority communities. But despite these difficulties, as the papers in this volume show, ethnic minorities are playing an important role in British life, including the British political system (Anwar, 1979).

Ethnic minorities are not evenly distributed throughout the country. They are mainly concentrated in inner-city and industrial areas, because most of them came to Britain as economic migrants. For example, in 1981, 56 per cent of ethnic minorities were found in London and the South-East, 23 per cent in the Midlands, 16 per cent in the North and North-West, 4 per cent in the South-West and Wales, with relatively few (2 per cent) in Scotland.[1] The contrast between the general population in Greater London and the South-East (31 per cent) and the ethnic minority population (56 per cent) is particularly marked. Moreover, they are heavily concentrated within these regions in certain local wards and parliamentary constituencies, which makes them statistically significant in the political process.

Importance of the Ethnic Minorities' Vote

The participation of ethnic minorities in the British political process is an important indication of their involvement in the society. Because of the historical links of ethnic minorities with Britain they, as British and

Commonwealth citizens living in this country, have a legal right to participate fully in politic. This includes the right to vote and to be a candidate in elections. However, such participation is not new. Three MPs from the Indian subcontinent were elected to the House of Commons before the Second World War. The first, Dadabhai Naoroji, was elected as long ago as 1892 as a Liberal with a bare majority of five at Finsbury Central. The second, Sir Mancherjee Bhownagree, was twice elected as a Conservative for Bethnal Green North East in 1895 and 1900. The third, Shapurji Saklatvala, was twice elected for Battersea North as a Labour candidate in 1922 and as a Communist in 1924. In the House of Lords, there was one member from the Indian sub-continent, Lord Sinha of Raipur (1863-1928). However, since the Second World War there has been no MP from the ethnic minorities until 1987. There have been three members of the House of Lords, Lords Constantine, Pitt and Chitnis (Anwar, 1986).

Since ethnic minorities are not randomly distributed throughout the country, their concentration in particular conurbations means that, at least in statistical terms, they are in a position to influence voting strength in those areas. Within these conurbations, they are even further concentrated in some parliamentary constituencies and local election wards and are therefore in a position to make an impact on the overall voting turnout in those inner-city constituencies and wards. For example, according to the 1981 census, there were 58 constituencies with more than 15 per cent of the total population living in households with heads born in the New Commonwealth and Pakistan. Nineteen of them had more than 25 per cent and seven had over 33 per cent, with three approaching almost half: Birmingham Ladywood, Brent South and Ealing Southall. There are many others with an ethnic minority population, of between 10 and 15 per cent. These figures do not take into account ethnic minorities where the head of household was born in this country. But, it is estimated that in 1987 there are about one hundred parliamentary constituencies in England with an ethnic minority population of over 10 per cent.

As far as the local election wards are concerned, there are now several hundred with more than 15 per cent ethnic minority population, and several with almost 50 per cent. The highest ethnic minority population of 85.4 per cent was in Northolt Ward in the Borough of Ealing, where it was estimated that almost 76 per cent of electors in 1981 were Asians out of a total of 8,148 electors on the register. Glebe ward in the same borough had almost 60 per cent Asian electors. It must be pointed out, however, that counting Asian names on the register is an under-estimation of their actual numbers in the population as some Asians have anglicized names. There is also under-registration among Asians compared with whites. This means that the real number of eligible Asians in the register will be greater than estimated.[2] This applies to other ethnic minorities as well.

The level of political awareness among ethnic minorities has also increased over the past two decades. This is partly because they have recognised that their sense of security in this country can be buttressed by such an awareness, and partly because an increasing number of ethnic minority organisations are articulating issues which impinge on their sense of security. The ethnic press has played an important role in the creation of this awareness. In this regard, these communities are responding to speeches and comments that are widely disseminated by the mass media, including the ethnic press, particularly during election campaigns. These communities are, therefore, in a position to take such action individually or through the organisations to which they belong to guarantee their own future in this country.

The response of the major political parties in this context is obviously important. These parties have not only felt the need to take steps to involve ethnic minorities in their activities and campaigns but also openly sought their votes in various elections between 1974 and the general election in 1987. This pattern also applies to local elections. But the participation of ethnic minorities in the political process depends on several factors. These include whether they are entered on the Electoral Register; if they are on the register, whether they turn out to vote; and how they compare with white people in these respects.

Registration and Turn-out

To what extent do ethnic minorities register to vote? We look at this phenomenon since 1974 (Anwar & Kohler, 1974; Community Relations Council 1975; Anwar, 1980; Anwar, 1984; Anwar, 1974; Anwar, 1975). In 1974 a sample survey showed that 27 per cent of Asians, compared with 37 per cent of Afro-Caribbeans and 6 per cent of whites from the same areas, were not registered. In 1976 checks in two areas where field work had taken place in 1974, showed a great improvement in the registration level of ethnic minorities. In Birmingham it was found that 5 per cent of Asians and 13 per cent of Afro-Caribbeans were not on the register compared with 4 per cent of whites. In Bradford, 9 per cent of Asians were not registered as against 5 per cent of whites from the same areas.

At the 1979 general election a survey in 24 constituencies spread throughout the country showed that 23 per cent of Asians, 19 per cent of Afro-Caribbeans and 7 per cent of whites were not registered. Compared with the 1974 survey referred to above, the level of registration among Afro-Caribbeans rose by 18 per cent (from 63 per cent in 1974 to 81 per cent in 1979), while among Asians it increased marginally from 73 per cent in 1974 to 77 per cent. Among the white population it remained virtually constant (94 per cent in 1974 and 93 per cent in 1979). However, it is relevant to point out that the results showed wide variations from area to area. Part of such variation was linked with the policies of local electoral registration offices and with the interest taken by the political parties and ethnic minorities' organisations in persuading and helping ethnic minorities to register.

The results of the 1979 survey were confirmed by an OPCS study undertaken in 1981 at the time of the census (Todd & Butcher, 1982). The study showed that in Inner London both the Asian and Afro-

Caribbean people had about double the non-registration rate of white people (27 and 24 per cent as opposed to 12 per cent). We again monitored registration in 1983 in the same areas as in 1979. This survey showed that among those qualified to be registered, the Asians' level of registration had increased from 77 per cent to 79 per cent. But the level of registration among Afro-Caribbean had fallen in 1983 from 81 per cent in 1979 to 76 per cent, as Table 3.1 shows. The fieldwork for the survey was undertaken in inner city wards where registration levels are generally low.

When we looked at the 1893 survey results at constituency level, it showed that there was a variation in registration levels as far as ethnic minorities were concerned. For example, particularly low levels of registration (60 per cent or less) were recorded among ethnic minorities in Ealing Southall, Croydon North-East, Hackney North and Stoke Newington, Norwood, and Walsall South constituencies. On the other hand, Wolverhampton South-West, Preston, Rochdale, Sheffield Heeley, Leicester South, Manchester Gorton, Birmingham Sparkbrook, and Battersea constituencies had over 80 per cent registration among ethnic minorities.

During 1986, in a CRE funded research project in five areas in the North of England, Michel Le Lohe found that 18.2 per cent of Asians and 14.6 per cent of Afro-Caribbeans were registered compared with 18.1 per cent whites from the same areas. However, after taking out those who had a good reason for non-registration (moving house, not eligible because of nationality or not sure of the reason etc) 4.7 per cent Asians, 8.4 per cent Afro-Caribbeans and 3.9 per cent of whites were not registered because they had some cause for concern. In his chapter in this volume Le Lohe draws upon this work but the details of this category is to be found in his report (Le Lohe, 1987).

Although steady improvement has taken place in the registration levels of ethnic minorities in the last 13 years, the high level of non-registration amongst ethnic minorities and also now among whites in the inner cities calls for some action. Reasons for non-registration include the newness, the language difficulty that Asians and some other ethnic groups face, the general alienation of some groups, and feared harassment and racial attacks from the National Front and other such organisations, who could identify Asians from their names on the register. There is also the fear of 'fishing expeditions' by immigration authorities. Finally, low registration could be due to the administrative inefficiency of the registration offices.

At the same time steps are being taken to improve the higher level of non-registration among ethnic minorities. Several areas now use either special leaflets designed for ethnic minorities in several languages which go with Form A or a translation of Form A into different languages. Some registration offices - Ealing, for example - now employ full time, year round, field-workers who visit homes from which no Form A has been received during the previous year. Among others, Lambeth and Haringey in London, Birmingham, and Bradford have made special efforts. Hackney in London started a special registration campaign. The Home

Table 3.1 Registration by Racial Groups: Comparison of Recent General Elections

	White			Total ethnic minority			Afro-Caribbean			Asian			Other ethnic minority		
	1983	1979	1974	1983	1979	1974	1983	1979	1974	1983	1979	1974	1983	1979	1974
	994	1041	150	1020	774	183	152	145	41	822	570	142	46	59	-
	%	%	%	%	%	%	%	%	%	%	%	%	%	%	%
Registered	81	93	94	78	77	70	76	81	63	79	77	73	78	73	-
Not Registered	19	7	6	22	23	30	24	19	27	21	23	27	22	27	-

Office has issued a Code of Practice for EROs, electoral registration officers, which is also relevant in this context. The ethnic minority press has been used and ethnic programmes on radio and television have also helped to make people aware of the importance and the timing of registration. Political parties in some local areas, some ethnic minority organisations, and some local Community Relations Councils have also made special efforts to increase registration among ethnic minorities.

It is due to such efforts, and an increasing awareness among ethnic minorities of the political process, that their registration level is edging nearer that of white people. But do those who register come out to vote at elections?

Over the last two decades surveys at the time of various local and general elections have shown that on average Asian turnout is always higher than non-Asians from the same areas, for example, at the October 1974 general election a survey in Bradford and Rochdale showed that the turnout rate among Asians was 57.7 per cent compared with 54.6 per cent for non-Asians (Anwar, 1980), and this trend for Bradford is borne out by Le Lohe's contribution to this volume.

At the 1979 general election turnout rates at certain polling stations in 19 constituencies were calculated for Asians and non-Asian voters. In 18 of the 19 areas the Asian turnout was higher compared with that of non-Asians. On average it was 65 per cent for Asians and 61 per cent for non-Asians. Eight selected polling stations in the three constituencies of Bradford West, Burnley and Rochdale were also covered at the same election. Once again, it was confirmed by the findings that the level of turnout among Asians was higher than that of non-Asian voters (73.1 per cent compared with 56.5 per cent), as shown in Table 3.2.

To look at this trend for Asians' higher rates of turnout than non-Asians we monitored another type of election, the European Parliamentary election in June 1979. Again it was discovered that the Asian turnout in Bradford and Burnley (for four polling stations monitored) was higher than non-Asians - 38.5 per cent compared with 21.3 per cent. It is indeed significant that, while the turnout rate among all electors nationally for the European Parliament election was lower than their turnout rate for the general election a month earlier, the turnout rate among Asians was not only higher than that of their non-Asian neighbours who voted at the same polling stations, but also higher than the national turnout rate of 32.1 per cent. Asians turnout rate of 38.5 per cent was almost twice that of their non-Asian neighbours and this rate was achieved at an election which the general electorate clearly did not consider to be as important as the general election a month previously (Anwar, 1980; Le Lohe, 1984).

Although there are methodological difficulties of calculating the rates of turnout for Afro-Caribbeans and other ethnic groups who have anglicized names which are not easily identifiable from the Electoral Register, however, some studies have shown that Afro-Caribbean turnout was also higher than whites from the same area.

Some further work at the 1980-82 local elections also confirmed the trend of high minority, particularly Asian participation. For example, in

Table 3.2 Asian and Non-Asian Turnout in Bradford West, Burnley and Rochdale – 1979 General Election

Polling station	Asian electors	Non-Asian electors	Asian proportion %	Asian voters	Asian turnout %	Non-Asian voters	Non-Asian turnout %
Bradford Drummond	773	398	66.0	531	68.9	206	51.8
Bradford Grange	1692	1894	47.2	1333	78.8	998	52.7
Bradford St Andrews	332	253	56.7	185	55.7	162	64.0
Bradford Southbrook	1093	2006	35.3	821	75.1	905	45.1
Bradford (4) AV Totals	3890	4551	46.1	2870	73.8	2271	49.9
Burnley Stoneyholme	472	1038	31.2	355	75.2	729	70.2
Rochdale West St	326	285	53.4	199	61.0	187	65.6
Rochdale Silver St	137	1135	10.8	112	81.8	735	61.8
Rochdale Shepherd	581	477	54.9	415	71.4	308	61.6

Ealing in one ward at the 1981 local election turnout rate among Asians was 59.1 per cent compared with 32.8 per cent for non-Asians. In 1982 in Bradford, results for one ward showed that the Asian turnout was 58.4 per cent compared with 23.1 per cent for non-Asians.

Twenty constituencies were monitored at the 1983 general election as part of a Commission for Racial Equality (CRE) survey to look at the turnout of different ethnic groups. Some of these constituencies were those that were covered in the 1979 survey referred to above. Interviewers recorded the total number of voters leaving the polling stations, as well as their ethnic group. At this election, 81 per cent of Asian voters turned out to vote compared to 60 per cent of non-Asian voters. In 18 of the 20 constituencies covered, turnout among Asian voters was higher than among non-Asians. Almost a quarter of the electors on the register in the areas surveyed were Asian, and the greater likelihood of their turning out to vote suggests that they had a significant impact on the final outcome in each constituency (Anwar, 1980).

These results suggests that Asians and other ethnic minorities could be more reliable voters and are consequently in a better position to influence the outcome of elections where they vote.

Voting Patterns

Let us now look at who the various ethnic groups, including whites voted, for in the last three general elections, 1979, 1983 and 1987. It must be pointed out that the CRE surveys in 1979 and 1983 were mainly undertaken in inner city areas where support for the Labour party is usually higher.

At the 1979 general election a sample of voters from 24 constituencies was asked to record (on duplicate 'ballot' papers) the way they voted in the polling stations. The 'ballot' papers were similar to those used in the real election, except that they were marked by the interviewers to record the voter's ethnic group. The 'ballot' papers were placed in a box by the voters as they left the polling booth. The results show that the majority of ethnic minority voters actually voted for the Labour party as against other parties. While 50 per cent of whites voted Labour, 90 per cent of Afro-Caribbeans and 86 per cent of Asians in the sample voted Labour.

Among whites in the sample, Labour had an 11 per cent lead over the Conservatives compared with a 78 per cent lead among Asians and 85 per cent among Afro-Caribbeans. When we compare the 1979 survey results with another undertaking in 1974, we find that in the wards in seven constituencies where comparisons of voting were possible, it appeared that the Conservative vote among ethnic minorities, particularly Asians, had increased in 1979 when compared with 1974. It was found that ethnic minority 'swings' to the Conservative party were largely accounted for by the voting pattern of Asian voters as against Afro-Caribbean voters. Whereas Afro-Caribbean voters solidly backed the Labour party, Asian voters spread their votes between the Labour and Conservative parties in such a way that higher proportions voted for the Conservative party in some constituencies than in others. In seven constituencies out of the 24 we surveyed, over 15 per cent of Asian voters cast their votes for the Conservative party.

The CRE's exit poll of the 1983 general election on election day based on 4,240 voters in 25 constituencies showed that 71 per cent Asians voted Labour, 5 per cent Conservatives and 11 per cent for the Alliance candidates, as shown in Table 3.3.

As a group, 70 per cent ethnic minorities voted Labour. It must be pointed out that most of the 25 constituencies covered in this survey were Labour-held at the time of the 1983 general election and this had some bearing on these results. However, a national exit poll which was conducted by the Harris Research Centre for ITN also confirmed this trend. It showed that the majority of ethnic minorities had voted Labour (57 per cent) but 24 per cent and 16 per cent of them had voted Conservative and Alliance respectively.

The Gallup polls at the 1983 general election also showed 21 per cent of ethnic minorities supporting the Conservative party compared with 64 per cent and 15 per cent supporting Labour and the Alliance respectively.

The comparison of the two CRE surveys showed that the Asian support for Labour had decreased from 86 per cent in 1979 to 71 per cent in 1983. Another survey showed that 21 per cent of ethnic minority voters who had voted for the Labour party in 1979 switched from Labour to other parties at the 1983 election (The Guardian, 13 June, 1983). But, in comparison, the Labour vote had remained strongest among Afro-Caribbeans. Only the Liberal/SDP Alliance had substantially increased its share of the vote in these constituencies among both white and ethnic minority voters. The highest recorded ethnic minority vote for the Labour party was in Bristol East (93 per cent), for the Conservatives in Croydon North-East (27 per cent), and for the Alliance in Rochdale (54 per cent), the last two with predominantly Asian electorate. This pattern was consistent with the CRE survey of the 1979 General Election referred to above. Monitoring of these three constituencies had shown that the personal popularity of the respective candidates for these parties was one of the key factors in attracting the ethnic minority vote.

A survey for the Hansib group of papers conducted by the Harris Research Centre during the 1987 general election campaign (25-29 May) about the voting intentions of Afro-Caribbeans and Asians showed that 86.8 per cent of Afro-Caribbeans and 66.8 per cent Asians intended to vote for the Labour party compared with 5.7 per cent and 22.7 per cent respectively for the Conservative party. Ten per cent Asians and 7 per cent Afro-Caribbeans intended to vote for the Alliance. No white electors were included in the survey. As these were only intentions we do not know how these ethnic minorities actually voted on the polling day (Asian Times, 5-11 June, 1987).

Another poll conducted by the Harris Research Centre in London between 8-9 June, 1987, however, showed that 64 per cent ethnic minorities intended to vote Labour, 23 per cent for Conservative and 11

Table 3.3 Voting Patterns by Ethnic Group: 1983 General Election

	Ethnic Group (per cent)					
	Total (4240)	White (2190)	All ethnic minority (2050)	Afro-Car (603)	Asian (1375)	Other E.M. (72)
Labour	48	35	70	72	71	49
Conservative	20	29	6	6	5	22
Alliance	14	17	9	4	11	9
Others	1	1	1	1	1	-
Refused	16	18	13	17	12	19

per cent for the Alliance. On the other hand 32 per cent whites intended to vote Labour, 45 per cent Conservative and 23 per cent for the Alliance.

The indication of ethnic minority voting patterns at the 1987 general election came from an ITN exit poll also conducted by the Harris Research Centre. It showed that 61 per cent Asians and 92 per cent Afro-Caribbeans had voted for Labour compared with 31 per cent whites. On the other hand 20 per cent Asians, 6 per cent Afro-Caribbeans and 43 per cent whites had voted for the Conservative party. The Alliance received 17 per cent votes from Asians, and 24 per cent from whites and none from Afro-Caribbeans in the sample. It must be pointed out that these results are based on a small sample of ethnic minorities.

The voting patterns of ethnic minorities depend on may factors. However, it appears that regular contacts between political parties and ethnic minorities, their organisation and mobilisation at elections, the candidates personal familiarity with the ethnic minority electors, and their party policies generally and about race and immigration issues in particular are important factors in attracting ethnic minority votes. Also recent research shows that the ethnic minorities now vote on party lines and not on ethnic lines (Anwar, 1980).

Political Parties' Response

To encourage ethnic minorities to participate in the political process the policies and initiatives taken by the political parties are very important. The major political party leaders have openly sought ethnic minority voters support in recent years without the fear of losing white voters. Some political parties have special arrangements to attract the support of the ethnic minorities. For example, the Conservative party has had an ethnic minority unit in their Central Office's Department of Community Affairs since 1976. Its objective has been to make party members aware of the growing electoral importance of Asian and Afro-Caribbean electors and to influence party policy to improve the image of the party among ethnic minorities and, thus, attract their support. The unit had help from the now defunct Anglo-Asian Conservative Society which tries to recruit Asians directly into the party. This was followed by the formation of Anglo-West Indian Conservative Society with the same objective. However, at national level the Anglo-Asian and Anglo-West Indian Societies have been replaced by another organisation called One Nation Forum with roughly the same objectives. It appears that the societies at the local level will continue as before.

These societies had representation on the area and national committees of the National Union of Conservative and Unionist Associations. Until recently there were 27 local Anglo-Asian Conservative societies throughout the country. Among their other activities they arrange meetings between Conservative candidates and Asian and Afro-Caribbean groups at election times. The Labour Party Race and Action Group (LPRAG) was set up in 1975 as a pressure group to educate and advise the party on relevant issues. More recently Labour's NEC has set up a Black and Asian Advisory Committee similar to the party's women's and local government committees, to attract ethnic minorities support for the party. The old Liberal party did not have special arrangements for ethnic minorities within its constituentional framework but it had a Community Relations Panel which had ethnic minority members. It met regularly to discuss issues relevant to the ethnic minorities and also formulated policies which the party implemented to attract ethnic minority members, as well as campaign strategies at elections specially directed at them.

Like the Liberal party, the old SDP did not have any special arrangements for ethnic minorities within the party's constitution. However, it encouraged ethnic minority candidates for its National Council. There were two directly elected ethnic minority members on the council. The SDP had started a Campaign for Racial Justice and the Committee had been asked to nominate two members from the ethnic minorities to the council to make it more broad based and more reflective of the composition of its membership. However, with the merger of the Liberal and SDP parties there is likely to be new arrangements to attract ethnic minority support in the future.

Another way to examine the response of the political parties to the question of ethnic minority participation is to look at the number of candidates adopted by the main political parties in the last few years. What sort of constituencies had they contested? What support did these candidates receive from the party machinery? What success rate did the ethnic minority candidates achieve? Why did a number of 'independent' and 'fringe' party ethnic minority candidates stand at elections? Do they succeed and how does their success rate compare with that of ethnic minority candidates who stand for the main political parties?

The first ethnic minority candidate since the Second World War put forward by a major political party for a general election was Sardar KSN Ahluwala who contested Willesden West for the Liberal party in 1950. Dr David Pitt (now Lord) contested Hampstead in 1959 and Clapham in 1970 for the Labour party. In 1970, there were also three ethnic minority candidates who stood for the Liberal party. In February 1974 the Labour party put forward a Pakistani, Councillor Bashir Man, from Glasgow to contest East Fife. Dhani Prem (Coventry South East) stood for the Liberals. None of them had any chance of winning. In the October 1974 General Election there was only one ethnic minority candidate, Cecil Williams who stood for the Liberal party. In the 1979 General Election there were five ethnic minority candidates put forward by the three main political parties. These included, one Labour, two Liberals and two Conservatives. This was the first time since 1945 that the Conservative party had nominated ethnic minority candidates. In the event, none of the candidates was elected because they contested seats where they had no chance of winning.

At the 1983 general election there were 18 ethnic minority candidates who stood for the major (four) parties. Most of the ethnic minority candidates in 1983 who stood for the main political parties performed like any other candidate for their respective parties. For example in 17 of the 18 constituencies contested, where comparison with the notional party position in 1979 was possible, the parties' position was unchanged (Anwar, 1974). However, like 1979 no ethnic minority candidate contested a winnable or 'safe' seat (except Paul Boateng who fought Hemel Hempstead, a notionally winnable seat on redrawn boundaries).

The analysis of the independent or fringe party ethnic minority candidates who stood in general elections between 1950 and 1983 shows that their performance, on the whole, had been 'poor' compared with those who stood for the main political parties. But why did these candidates stand in those elections? A close examination of their campaigns shows that some, like other fringe or independent candidates in elections, stood because they wanted to protest against the lack of ethnic minority representation in the House of Commons.

At the 1987 general election out of the 27 ethnic minority candidates for the four main political parties, four were elected. The four, all Labour, were Keith Vaz (Leicester East), Diane Abbot (Hackney North and Stoke Newington), Paul Boateng (Brent South) and Bernie Grant (Tottenham). The three London MPs were all elected in 'safe' Labour seats. However, Keith Vaz won with a swing of over 9 per cent from the Conservative candidate Peter Bruinvels, compared with a swing of just over 2.2 per cent for Labour candidates in other seats in the East Midlands. The performance of other ethnic minority candidates was, in general terms, like other party candidates in the same regions.

However, it must be pointed out that the phenomenon of the performance of an ethnic minority candidate is complex. There could be many factors and these could vary according to party label, characteristics of the area of contest, personal popularity of a candidate, rejection by some white voters on grounds of colour, and whether the seat is 'safe' or 'winnable'. Some of these reasons could equally apply to a white candidate. However, there is enough evidence to indicate that in the late 1980s, generally ethnic minority candidates are being accepted as 'party' candidates. In local elections many ethnic minority candidates have succeeded in the last few years and more recently in the 1987 general election. For example, in Greater London boroughs elections in May 1986, over 130 ethnic minority councillors were elected members. Outside London others were elected in Leicester, Bradford, Birmingham, to mention a few areas. Altogether it is estimated that there are over 200 ethnic minority councillors throughout the country.

The main political parties have continued their efforts to attract ethnic minority electoral support. Some of these efforts were reflected in the selection of several ethnic minority candidates for the last general election and the recent local elections.

Conclusions

The participation of ethnic minorities in the political process must be seen in the wider context of British society in which racial discrimination is a daily reality for far too many ethnic minorities. Similarly, political parties as part of the society are not free of prejudice and discrimination on the part of their members against the ethnic minorities. These could be conscious or unconscious acts. Therefore, the political parties need to educate their own members and try to stamp out any racial prejudice and racial discrimination which exist within the parties. They also ought to set an example for others of promoting racial equality and good relations. It is by doing this that ethnic minorities would be encouraged to join the political parties and become integrated into the political process without any fear of harassment, or less favourable treatment. The importance of ethnic minorities in the political process is unquestionable. However, the integration of ethnic minorities into the political process requires their 'effective' representation and involvement and not 'tokenism' as has happened so far. They need to feel equal and to participate fully in the decision-making process. This will, in turn, make them feel that they are accepted as full citizens of this country, rather than a 'problem' and one which is to be 'deplored'. The question arises, how can this be achieved?

This is a two way process: the political parties need to open their doors to ethnic minorities and welcome them as members by removing all the obstacles; and the ethnic minorities to feel free to join the political parties and take initiatives without any fear of rejection or prejudice. The political parties need to make sure that their ethnic minority members also get an equal chance to represent the party at all levels to make their representation effective. We can learn from the United States, where concerted efforts in the 1970s both by the political parties and the blacks helped to achieve a breakthrough in the political process for blacks. As a result, the representation of blacks increased dramatically (Cavanagh, 1984). And in Britain, Jews, not more than half a million in number, are a good example of success in the political process (Alderman, 1983).

To increase ethnic minority representation in the political process, and looking at the Jewish experience in this respect, ethnic minorities need to join the political parties in greater numbers, seek office and work hard through the political parties' hierarchy to become candidates and get elected. They also need to get involved actively in trade unions, as many MPs for the Labour party are sponsored by the unions. The process of political party membership among ethnic minorities has actively started in several areas, for example, Bradford, Leicester, Birmingham and several areas of London.

The research evidence presented have shows that ethnic minorities are getting increasingly involved as electors and voters and that racial prejudice against ethnic minority candidates is diminishing. Since ethnic minorities are concentrated, their votes count. Political parties cannot afford to ignore this fact in the future.

Notes

1. The 1981 census did not provide us with the complete picture of the ethnic minority population in Britain since an 'ethnic' question was not asked in the census. Because the information collected was based on birthplace and was asked without a question on parents' birthplace, those UK born ethnic minorities who have established separate households from their overseas - born parents were not identified in the 1981 census. This means that, for areas like Cardiff, Bristol and Liverpool with long established ethnic minority communities, the 1981 census information about ethnic minority groups in meaningless. There fore, 1981 census information used in this paper should be treated as an under-estimate. Furthermore, we are already in 1987 and thus the size of the ethnic minority population has gone up since the 1981 census.

2. It was estimated that in 1983 almost one fifth of the Asians in some areas were not on the register.

4 Black electoral participation: an analysis of recent trends

ZIG LAYTON-HENRY

Introduction

It is clear from the preceding chapters that considerable interest and research has been devoted to the electoral participation and voting behaviour of the black [2] electorate, despite its relatively small size and the host of methodological problems involved in obtaining representative samples and accurate data (Studlar, 1983, pp.92–100). This interest is partly because political scientists and the media are as obsessed with elections, whether local or parliamentary, as are politicians; and also because the British electoral system in the post–war period has facilitated both close results and governmental change. The parliamentary ascendancy of the Conservative party in the 1980s is exceptional, even compared with the 1950s when the Conservatives also won three successive general elections. This ascendancy is, of course, much more marked in parliament than it is among the electorate and cannot therefore be taken too much for granted, even though the Conservatives now appear in a very strong electoral position. The entry of new, distinctive and rapidly expanding groups in the electorate is naturally of considerable interest to both politicians and political scientists in such an electoral system and it is thus not surprising that the electoral behaviour of black voters has attracted widespread attention.

Importance and Growth of the Black Vote

Concern about racism in British society and the impact of racial discrimination upon the ethnic minorities has led to anxiety that the political response of the black communities may be political apathy, alienation and even rebellion. Participation inelections, in contrast, is often seen as a hallmark of political integration and support for democratic politics. The registration, turnout, distribution of political opinions, the salience of issues and the levels of party support can all be used to assess the similarity or distinctiveness of groups in the electorate and their involvement in the mainstream of politics. Electoral behaviour may thus throw some light on the degree of political efficacy or feelings of powerlessness and even on the alienation of groups of electors (Layton-Henry & Studlar, 1985, pp.307–318).

In the 1960s there was little interest in the voting behaviour of black Britons. The numbers of black voters were relatively small and, though residentially concentrated, they were scattered over many urban centres in different parts of the country. It was widely believed that many black voters were not registered and also that most lived in safe labour seats where, even if they voted, the result was a foregone conclusion. It was the impact of the immigration issue on the white electorate that was the centre of attention, especially after the Smethwick result in the general election of 1964 (Foot, 1965; Studlar, 1978). This was also true in the 1970 general election, although the Nuffield election study noted a considerable rise in the registration and turnout of black voters as compared with the 1966 general election. This increased participation in the election was, the authors felt, due to the impact of Enoch Powell's anti-immigrant campaign which, they argued, mobilized immigrant voters against the Conservatives (Butler & Pinto, 1971, pp.406–7). Nationally, Powell's campaign is thought to have contributed significantly to the Conservatives' unexpected victory in the 1970 general election (Miller, n.d.; Schoen, 1964; Studlar, 1978). The defeat of Dr. David Pitt (now Lord Pitt) at Clapham, normally a secure Labour seat, was also thought to have been partly due to anti-immigrant voting by voters who usually supported the Labour party candidate.

It was the two general elections of 1974 which stimulated interest in the electoral importance of black voters. These hard fought and close run elections created a situation where the major parties were anxious to attract every vote and were willing to appeal to even small, distinctive groups in the electorate. This opportunity was brilliantly exploited by the Community Relations Commission in their publication, The Participation of Ethnic Minorities in the General Election, October 1974 (Community Relations Council, 1975). The main conclusions of the report were that:

(1) The ethnic minorities played a significant part in determining the outcome of the election;
(2) The minorities swung more to Labour than the electorate as a whole, partly at least in response to the Labour government's action to benefit the minorities;
(3) Members of minority groups were five times as likely not to be registered to vote as whites in the same areas;
(4) Although most members of the minorities conformed with their socio-economic group in voting Labour, other parties were able to attract support among the minorities when they made the effort;
(5) Anti-immigrant candidates made little or no progress at the election.

The report argued that there were 76 constituencies in the February 1974 election and 85 constituencies in the October election where ethnic minority voters could have made a significant impact on the outcome as the size of the black population was larger than the majority of the winning candidate. It emphasized that 13 of the 17 seats won by Labour from the Conservatives in the General Election of October 1974 were seats where the black population was larger than the majority of the winning candidates in both these elections.

The assumptions and conclusions of the report were controversial and were hotly disputed. It now seems clear that the report exaggerated the significance of black voters in marginal constituencies and their willingness to switch votes between the major parties (Crewe, 1978; Layton-Henry, 1978). However, the report was a political success. It alerted the parties, especially the Conservatives, to the fact that many black voters resided in marginal constituencies and that they were a fast expanding part of the electorate that should not be ignored (Layton-Henry, 1978).

The growth in the black electorate has been dramatic in the last twenty years and this has had an important impact on parliamentary candidates and parliamentarians sitting for urban constituencies in England. Since the late 1960s immigration difficulties have been a major source of problems raised in MPs' surgeries in inner city areas. Many MPs have seen their constituencies transformed and have had to adjust their priorities to keep in touch with their new electors.[3] Also, as the Labour party's support has declined among the white working class in the 1980s so the importance of black voters for Labour party MPs has risen. This growing displacement of black voters for Labour MPs is reflected in the campaign for Black Sections in the Labour party and is one of the reasons why the parliamentary leadership wishes to reach an accommodation with black activists.

An indication of the expansion of the black electorate can be given if we compare the constituency census data for 1971 and 1981. In 1971 there were 18 constituencies where the black population (defined as those born, or with one parent born, in the New Commonwealth or Pakistan) made up 15 per cent or more of the population. They ranged from 29.6 per cent in Birmingham Ladywood to 15.3 per cent in Newham North-West. In 1981 there were 51 such seats, ranging from 45.7 per cent in Brent South, to 15 per cent in Westminster North. In the general election of 1987 thirty-three of these seats were held by the Labour party and eighteen by the Conservatives. There is no doubt that the next census in 1991 will also show a considerable increase in the number of such seats, given the youthfulness of the black population.[4] Thus, despite the qualifications that need to be made about 'ethnic marginals' and the electoral significance of black voters, they have become a very important part of the electorate in specific areas, especially in cities such as London, Birmingham and Leicester and in northern towns such as Bradford (as the chapter by Lelohe in this volume shows), Blackburn and Huddersfield.

The Community Relations Commission (CRC) and the Commission for Racial Equality (CRE) have been concerned to investigate levels of electoral registration among the adult black population and to encourage increased registration so that members of the ethnic minority communities take part in electing the decision-makers in society, and are thus in a position to exert some influence on them. The CRC report found substantial levels of non-registration among members of the ethnic minorities in October 1974. Only 6 per cent of whites were not registered as compared with 24 per cent of non-whites. If new voters and recent movers were excluded, 94 per cent of whites, 73 per cent of Asians and 63 per cent of Afro-Caribbeans were registered (Community Relations Commission, 1975, pp.13-14). In 1970 the CRE carried out a survey of 24 constituencies with a sample of 1,927 to establish the proportions of people from different groups who were registered to vote. Most of the constituencies surveyed included significant proportions of ethnic minority voters and so were not representative of the population as a whole. This survey found higher levels of registration among black voters. The results revealed that 93 per cent of whites were registered, compared with 81 per cent of Afro-Caribbeans, and 77 per cent of Asians (Anwar, 1980). In 1983 the CRE found 79 per cent of Asians and 76 per cent of Afro-Caribbeans registered, but only 81 per cent of whites (Commission for Racial Equality, 1984) - a dramatic fall in white registration which does not accord with other studies even of inner city constituencies. It seems probable that this is a maverick result which is partly due to the inner city nature of the constituencies in the sample. The Harris poll in 1983 found 82 per cent of Afro-Caribbeans and 94 per cent of Asians to be registered.

An OPCS study in inner London in 1981 found 25 per cent of ethnic minorities and 12 per cent of whites to be unregistered. The national figures for non-registration in England and Wales were 14 per cent for those born in the New Commonwealth, compared with 3 per cent of those born in the U.K., Ireland or the Old Commonwealth (Fitzgerald, 1987, p.8).

The diversity of these results suggests that registration varies significantly in inner city areas where such factors as poverty, population mobility and residence in multi-occupied buildings, for example hotels specialising in bed and breakfast accommodation for people on benefit, combine to reduce electoral registration. If it is widely believed that the electoral register will be used as the basis for collecting poll tax, the effect on registration in inner-city areas could be dramatic.

The turnout of Afro-Caribbean and Asian voters is likely to vary considerably depending on such factors as period and length of settlement, education, occupation, residence, membership of associations and feelings or political confidence and integration. Generally, research suggests that Asian voters participate at higher levels than their white neighbours, which is perhaps not too surprising, given that white voters in inner city constituencies have below-average rates of turnout.[5] However, in some polling districts monitored by the CRE in 1979, Asians had exceptionally high rates of turnout - for example 95 per cent in Nuneaton and Brent East, and 91 per cent in Leicester South. The lowest turnout rates were 72 per cent in Hackney and Stoke Newington and 69 per cent in Wandsworth and Battersea (Anwar, 1980, p.38). In contrast to Asians, lower rates, though in the by-election in Lambeth Central in April 1978, Afro-Caribbean turnout was recorded as being very similar to that of Whites (Crewe, 1983). In a local by-election again in Lambeth Central, monitored by the CRE, it was found that Afro-Caribbean turnout was higher than that of their white neighbours, confirming the trend, according to Anwar of increasing levels of turnout of ethnic minority voters (Anwar, 1980).

The data from national samples suggests that Asian and white voters have rather similar rates of turnout, significantly above those of Afro-Caribbeans. The 1979 pooled Gallup surveys found that between 76-80 per cent of Asians and whites claimed to be certain to vote compared with 66 per cent of Afro-Caribbeans (Layton-Henry & Studlar, 1985, p.310). In 1983 the Harris poll found the voting intentions of Afro-Caribbeans and Asians in 1983 were as follows:

Table 4.1 Voting Intention Among Non-Whites 1983 (%)

	Afro Caribbean (649)	Asian (527)
Absolutely certain	33	61
Certain	18	23
Probably will	21	10
Probably won't	9	1
Certainly won't	13	2
Don't know	6	3

Source: Harris Poll, 1983.

Interestingly, the analysis of the pooled Gallup surveys taken in the run up to the general election of 1979 found that Afro-Caribbean voters were more interested in who would win the general election, felt the election result mattered more, and discussed politics more than Asian voters (Ibid). The paradox of a relatively apolitical but voting Asian electorate and a more politically interested but non-voting Afro-Caribbean electorate has been confirmed by the Greater London survey of the political attitudes of white, Afro-Caribbean and Asian Londoners carried out in 1984 (Fitzgerald, 1987, p.17) Possible explanations for the high turnout of Asians probably relate to membership of associations and groups with positive attitudes to voting. The Greater London survey found very strong endorsement by Asians to the question, 'Does voting at general elections give people a say in how the country is run?' In response 70 per cent of Asians agreed compared with 65 per cent of Whites and 55 per cent of Afro-Caribbeans. Only 17 per cent of Asians disagreed compared with 32 per cent of Whites and 40 per cent of Afro-Caribbeans (Ibid., p.18). Surveys suggest that while Afro-Caribbeans have resided in Britain longer than Asians, they are more disenchanted with life in Britain. Thus their relative unwillingness to vote may include a degree of political alienation, particularly among young people who may reject voting as a pointless activity (LeLohe, 1987).

particularly among young people who may reject voting as a pointless activity (LeLohe, 1987).

Political Attitudes and Preferences

Surveys of public opinion and the preferences of black voters have been plagued by problems of inadequate sampling procedure and the possibility of environmental effects due to the geographical distribution and residential concentration of ethnic minority populations. However, these surveys suggest an overwhelming concern among black voters with economic issues – a concern that is, of course, equally shared by the white electorate. Unemployment and the cost of living have been the two most important issues for both black and white electors over the last ten years. International affairs and defence have seemed much less important issues to black voters than to whites in British general elections. This does not mean, however, that particular aspects of international relations are not tremendously important for groups among the ethnic minorities. The crisis over Khalistan which erupted in the Anglo–Asian Conservative Society in 1984 and caused the disbandment of the national association shows how 'homeland' politics can intrude into party politics in Britain. Some ethnic minority groups may have an intense interest in the politics of their country of origin and also in relations between Britain and their 'homeland'.

Immigration and nationality issues appear to be a low priority for Afro–Caribbeans and a declining issue among Asians, particularly the young, but it remains important for about a third of the Asian electorate. The actions of the present government to phase out the right of Commonwealth citizens to registration rather than naturalisation and the continuing efforts to increase immigration controls by the introduction of visas, 'carrier' liability and restrictions on dependants may increase the salience of these issues. Education and relations with the police are continuing to grow in importance for black voters but remain far behind economic issues in their importance. There thus appears to be no distinctive set of political priorities which divide black and white electors (Studlar, 1986).

However, responses to general questions in surveys may fail to elicit the distinctive concerns of black people such as might become apparent if questions were asked on how best to resolve such issues as unemployment, the educational problems that face their children and relations with the police. When offered three alternative ways of reducing unemployment significant minorities of Afro–Caribbeans and Asians felt there should be stronger action to stop employers discriminating against ethnic minorities in the allocation of jobs. The preferred solution was the creation of new jobs through increased government spending (Fitzgerald, 1987, p.17). On education, pluralities of Afro–Caribbeans and Asians felt there should be more attention to the specific needs of their children and more ethnic minority teachers. As far as relations with the police were concerned, the to local people and saw little need to give the police more powers to catch criminals. Asians wished the police to devote greater efforts and resources into preventing racial attacks and were more likely to endorse the proposition that the police should have more powers to catch criminals (Ibid.).

It has long been clear that support for the labour party is very high among Afro-Caribbean and Asian voters. The level of this support may have been exaggerated in the past by quota sampling in areas of ethnic minority concentration where class, housing and environmental factors all contribute to high levels of labour party support. In some cases the timing of the polls may also have had this result.[6] The pooled Gallup pre-election surveys in 1979 gave the distribution of party support within ethnic groups as represented on Table 4.2.

One of the striking features of this table is that Labour voting was higher in 1979 among professional and non-manual black voters than it was among the white working class. Overall 28% of black voters intended to vote Conservative, 66% Labour and only 6% Liberal. Surveys carried out by the Commission for Racial Equality in inner city areas found, not surprisingly, much higher levels of support for the Labour party (Anwar, 1986, p.80).

Table 4.2 Voting by Social Class Within Ethnic Groups, 1979 (%)

	Con	Lab	Lib	Non-Voter	(N)
White					
A,B,C1	57	20	9	15	(3588)
C2	40	35	5	20	(3290)
D,E	32	38	5	25	(3145)
Afro-Caribbean					
A,B,C1	17	41	7	35	(29)
C2	11	49	8	32	(37)
D,E	15	48	3	35	(40)
Asian					
A,B,C1	25	42	6	28	(36)
C2	28	50	3	19	(32)
D,E	25	50	0	25	(40)

Source: Gallup Pre-Election Surveys, 1979.

Similarly analyses of black voting in the general election of 1983 also provide contrasting results, while confirming the high levels of support for the Labour party. A large quota sample of black voters in inner city areas carried out by the Harris Research Centre for the television programmes *Black on Black* and *Eastern Eye* found that 86% of Afro-Caribbeans and 80% of Asians intended to vote Labour, 8% of Afro-Caribbeans and 6% of Asians intended to vote Conservative and 5% of Afro-Caribbeans and 12% of Asians intended to vote Alliance. In contrast the Gallup-BBC exit poll found that 21% of black voters claimed to have supported the Conservatives, 64% Labour and 15% the Alliance. The Harris-ITN exit

exit poll found that 21% of black voters claimed to have supported the Conservatives, 64% Labour and 15% the Alliance. The Harris–ITN exit poll found that 24% of black voters said they had voted Conservative, 57% Labour, 16% Alliance, while 3% refused to say how they had voted. Although the exit poll results are based on relatively small numbers of black respondents, it seems clear that inner city polls significantly exaggerate black support for the Labour party, particularly among Asian voters.

The Harris Poll in 1983 found that 76 per cent of Labour voters among Afro–Caribbeans and 64 per cent of Labour voting Asians gave their reasons for Labour support as being because Labour supports the working class. Only 7 per cent of Afro–Caribbeans and 31 per cent of Asians said it was because Labour supported Afro–Caribbeans and Asians. Interestingly, the GLC survey of 1983 found white respondents more likely to assign themselves to a class and to the working class in particular than either Afro–Caribbeans or Asians. The willingness to assign themselves to a class was particularly low among Asian respondents.

Black Voters and the General Election, 1987

The data on which this analysis is based consists of two polls carried out by the Harris Research Centre. The first is a poll of 871 black people interviewed face to face at 40 sampling points in areas of high ethnic concentration. In addition, 136 black people in areas of low ethnic concentration were interviewed by telephone. The areas of low ethnic concentration chosen included Dorking, Edinburgh and Ipswich. The poll was carried out for the Asian and African Times and was published in June just before the general election. The interviews were carried out between 25th and 29th May 1987. The second poll is a national poll of 1072 electors carried out by the Harris Research Centre for the Observer at the same time as the poll for the Asian Times. This poll will be used for purposes of comparison.[7]

The Harris Poll indicates that the Labour party remained the overwhelmingly popular choice among black voters. Taking the ethnic minorities as a whole, 72 per cent intended to vote Labour, 18 per cent Conservative, and 10 per cent Alliance. Women were slightly less likely to support the Conservatives (15 per cent) than men (20 per cent), and were more likely to support Labour (75 per cent to 70 per cent). Labour support was highest among the older age groups and lowest in the 25–44 range. There were significant differences in the distribution of support between Asians and Afro–Caribbeans, as Table 4.3 shows:

Table 4.3 Voting Intentions of Asians and Afro-Caribbeans May 1987 (%)

	Asians (592)	Afro-Caribbeans (228)
Conservative	23	6
Labour	67	86
Alliance	10	7
Other party	–	–

Source: The Harris Poll, May 1987

The comparable figures from the poll of the national electorate for May 1987 were Conservative 41.2 per cent, Labour 36.8 per cent, Alliance 20.5 per cent and other party 1.5 per cent. Support for the Labour party among black voters is thus almost double that among the national electorate.

The Harris poll for the Asian Times was the first poll which attempted to survey ethnic minority voters in areas of low ethnic concentration. As a telephone poll it may be biased towards more prosperous ethnic minority voters in these areas and also by the fact that almost all those in the sample are Asian. Nevertheless, if we compare ethnic minority support for the parties in areas of high and low ethnic concentration, then we find a considerable rise in Conservative support in areas of low ethnic concentration. It is also significant that support for the Alliance more than doubled.

Table 4.4 Party Support of Ethnic Minority Voters in Areas of High and Low Ethnic Concentration (%)

	High (709)	Low (111)
Conservative	15	39
Labour	77	43
Alliance	8	17
Other party	–	1

Source: The Harris Poll, May 1987

It seems clear that as members of the ethnic minority communities become more prosperous and move out into suburban areas, there will be some attrition in support for the Labour party. This may not be as dramatic as the above table suggests as the most prosperous groups may be over-represented among the ethnic minority sample in areas of low ethnic concentration in Table 4.4. Support for the Conservative party and the Democrats will be influenced by the salience of race and immigration issues, the willingness of local constituency parties to mobilize ethnic minority support and welcome them as members and also on the scale of suburbanisation and whether it occurs close to or far from existing areas of ethnic minority concentration. One can speculate that the attrition in the

Labour vote will proceed relatively slowly and much faster among Asian than Afro-Caribbean voters. This is suggested by the distribution of party support by class among ethnic minority voters in Table 4.5. This confirms that while class differences in party support are significant among black voters, a majority of all class groups continue to support the Labour party.

Table 4.5 **Party Support by Class Among Ethnic Minority Voters (%)**

	A,B (48)	C1 (206)	C2 (241)	DE (290)
Conservative	33	30	14	10
Labour	54	52	78	84
Alliance	13	17	9	5

Source: The Harris Poll, May 1987

The groups of Asians and Afro-Caribbeans most likely to vote were Conservative supporters, professional and managerial groups and those over 65 years of age. Those least likely to vote were Afro-Caribbeans, skilled workers, and those between 18 and 24 years. Women were less certain about going to vote than were men, and Alliance supporters were less sure than either Conservative or Labour supporters. The most significant differences were between Asians and Afro-Caribbeans, and by age, as Table 4.6 shows.

Table 4.6 **Certainty to Vote of Ethnic Minority Voters in the General Election, 1987 (%)**

	Asian (707)	Afro-Caribbean (299)	18-24 (200)	25-44 (519)	45-64 (257)	65+ (30)
Absolutely	74	51	58	69	70	77
Fairly	13	18	16	14	15	13
Not very	7	14	14	8	6	10
Not at all	2	2	2	3	1	-
Don't know	4	15	11	7	7	-

Source: The Harris Poll, May 1987

However, if we compare Table 1 and Table 4.6, we find a remarkable rise in the proportions of both Asian and Afro-Caribbean voters who report that they are absolutely certain to vote in the general elections of 1983 and 1987. (The absolutely certain category is the one pollsters find is the best indicator of actual turnout.) One can speculate that the much larger number of black candidates selected by the major parties, the fact that a number of these were in safe Labour seats and stood an excellent chance of being elected, combined with the publicity these candidates received, may have increased black voters' commitment to voting in the election. In the national poll carried out by the Harris Research Centre 72 per cent of electors said they were absolutely certain to vote, a further 20 per cent said they were fairly certain, 4 per cent not very certain, and 2 per cent not at all certain. Only 1 per cent said they did not know (The Harris Research Centre, 1987).

The Most Important Issues

When ethnic minority electors were asked what issues would be the most important in determining how they would vote, unemployment was by far the most often mentioned issue. It was equally important for Asians and Afro-Caribbeans, and most important for the young and for those in the lowest occupational categories. Law and Order was the issue most often mentioned second, and was most important for the professional and managerial groups, those over 65 years of age, and Conservative supporters. It was mentioned equally often by Afro-Caribbeans and Asians. Housing was next in order of priority being mentioned almost as often as law and order. In fact for Afro-Caribbeans housing was the second most important issue, significantly above law and order, but for Asians the reverse was true. Housing was a particularly important issue for semi-skilled and unskilled workers, the very young, the very old and women. Racial discrimination was the fourth most important issue for ethnic minority voters and was particularly so for Afro-Caribbean respondents.

Conservative supporters emphasized unemployment, law and order and economic policy most often. Labour supporters emphasized unemployment, housing and law and order, and Alliance supporters emphasized unemployment, economic policy and racial discrimination. The major contrast between ethnic minority voters and the electorate as a whole is the low priority given to defence and foreign policy issues including nuclear disarmament. The trade unions were also not seen as an important electoral issue. Afro-Caribbeans were overwhelmingly concerned with standard of living issues being most anxious about unemployment, housing, racial discrimination, law and order and poverty. One quarter of Afro-Caribbeans mentioned poverty as an important issue which would influence how they decided to vote. Asian voters had similar concerns, listing unemployment, law and order, housing, economic policy and racial discrimination as their five most important issues.

A majority of ethnic minority respondents were satisfied with Labour's policies on race and immigration issues (54 per cent), and dissatisfied with the government's record on these issues (55 per cent). Most did not know whether they were satisfied or not with the Alliance's policies (59 per cent), but more said they were dissatisfied (25 per cent) than satisfied (16 per cent), which confirms that the Alliance failed to make the impact they hoped on ethnic minority voters. When asked whether the parties stand on race and immigration issues would affect their vote in the general election, black voters were equally divided, with 38 per cent responding 'Yes' and 40 per cent saying 'No', and 23 per cent indicating that they did not know. Alliance supporters were the most likely to reply positively, and Conservative supporters negatively.

Most respondents reported that it would make no difference to their vote whether there was an ethnic minority candidate or not (51 per cent), but older voters (63 per cent) and a significant minority of Afro-Caribbeans (38 per cent) said that they would be more likely to vote for an ethnic minority candidate. There was more support for the view that ethnic minority candidates would represent respondents' interests better than another member of parliament (37 per cent), but again more said it would make no difference (43 per cent).

Finally, a question was asked about whether respondents approved or disapproved of the setting up of black sections in the Labour party. More disapproved (45 per cent) than approved (33 per cent) and 21 per cent did not know. Disapproval was highest among those groups least likely to be sympathetic to the Labour party such as professional and managerial people (63 per cent), those in areas of low ethnic concentration (58 per cent), Alliance supporters (58 per cent) and Conservative supporters (57 per cent). Older respondents (43 per cent), Afro-Caribbeans (39 per cent) and Labour supporters (39 per cent) were the most approving, but only among older respondents was there a plurality in favour.

Conclusion

The Harris poll data indicates that the black electorate continues to remain a bulwark of Labour party support, with 72 per cent of black voters intending to vote Labour in the general election of 1987, compared with a national result for Labour of only 31.6 per cent. Only 18 per cent of black voters intended to vote Conservative, compared with 43.3 per cent of the electorate as a whole, and only 10 per cent intended to vote Alliance, compared with 23.1 per cent of the electorate. Even middle class black voters were more likely to vote Labour than Conservative although a significant minority of Asians in areas of low ethnic concentration supported the Conservatives (39 per cent). However, more Asians in these areas preferred the Labour party (43 per cent).

Support for the Labour party is high for a number of reasons. The black electorate is more working class than the electorate as a whole. In the Harris samples 68 per cent of the black sample was manual working class compared to 60 per cent of the national sample, only 6.1 per cent of the black sample was professional and managerial compared to 16.4 per cent of the national sample. In addition black voters give a higher priority to issues where the Labour party is seen as more worthy of the electorate's trust such as unemployment, housing and racial discrimination. They give a low priority to issues where the Conservatives are more highly ranked such as defence and foreign affairs. The exception is law and order which is a major concern for both Asians and Afro-Caribbeans but, although the national electorate trust the Conservatives more than Labour on law and order (Ibid.),[8] this may not be the case among the ethnic minorities. Afro-Caribbeans in particular prefer Labour's proposals to make the police accountable to local communities. On racial discrimination Labour's policies are endorsed much more strongly than those of the Conservatives. Satisfaction with Labour's policies on race and immigration is particularly high among Asians (60 per cent satisfied to 13 per cent dissatisfied) and dissatisfaction with the government's record is very high among Afro-Caribbeans (76 per cent dissatisfied to 8 per cent satisfied).

It is widely believed that there is a trend towards the Conservatives among Asian voters compared with previous elections. This may be true among particular groups such as Asians from East Africa but this is speculation as there is little evidence available on particular Asian communities. Among the Asian electorate as a whole no such trend can be clearly established. This is because most surveys before 1987, with the exception of the pre-election Gallup surveys in 1979, were carried out in inner city areas and thus exaggerate Labour party support among Asian voters. The Harris poll in 1987 shows that there is significant support for the Conservatives among Asians in areas of low ethnic concentration which is to be expected and is likely to have always been the case. Among Asians as a whole the pooled Gallup surveys in 1979 found support for the Labour party to be 57 per cent. The Gallup and Harris exit polls in 1983 found total ethnic minority support for Labour to be 64 per cent and 57 per cent respectively. The 1987 Harris poll finding that 67 per cent of Asian voters intended to support the Labour party suggests that Asian support for Labour has been consolidated rather than eroded in the last four years. The continuing concern of the government to tighten immigration controls by new legislation and tough administrative action is likely to be a major factor contributing to the reluctance of middle class Asians to support the Conservatives. Similarly, the willingness of Labour members of parliament to take up immigration problems and oppose Conservative legislation consolidates support for the Labour party. The impact of the poll tax on ethnic minority families, especially Asian families, is likely to be particularly severe. This could be a major factor inhibiting any swing to the Conservatives among Asian voters. The publicity given to the much increased number of Labour parliamentary candidates from the ethnic minorities and the selection of several of these in 'safe' Labour seats must also have consolidated and increased black support for Labour in the general election.

Are black voters becoming more or less integrated into electoral politics? The evidence from the general election of 1987 suggests that they are becoming more integrated even though their distribution of party support is very different from that of the rest of the electorate and acknowledging that significant levels of political alienation may exist among young Afro-Caribbeans. One striking feature of the evidence from the Harris poll in 1987 is the considerable rise among both Asians and Afro-Caribbeans in the proportion saying they were absolutely certain to vote in the general election compared with 1983. The number of Asians saying they were absolutely certain to vote rose from 61 per cent to 74 per cent, a figure very close to the national turnout of 75.5 per cent. Afro-Caribbeans intentions to vote rose even more strongly albeit from a lower base, those saying they were absolutely certain to vote rose from 33 per cent in 1983 to 51 per cent in 1987, a rise of 18 per cent.

The nomination of more black candidates in 1987 by the major parties (28 compared with 18 in 1983) must have raised black interest in the campaign and the election. The success of four of these candidates in becoming the first black members of parliament since the war is of tremendous symbolic importance for the ethnic minority communities. Moreover they have greatly reduced the fears that black candidates will cause prejudiced voting by white electors or abstentions. In Leicester East, Keith Vaz achieved a remarkable swing to Labour of 9.42 per cent from the Social Democratic Party and an above average rise in turnout of 5.4 per cent to 78.6 per cent. There was also an above average rise in turnout at Hackney North and Stoke Newington where Diane Abbott was elected. The election results generally suggested that voters were more willing to support black candidates than in the past.

In the future, one would expect that class voting will increase among members of the black electorate but there are a number of reasons why this is likely to be rather slow. These include Mrs Thatcher's continuing determination to bring New Commonwealth immigration to an end, her lack of sympathy for anti-discrimination measures and her willingness to allow the Labour party to be identified with what she regards as unpopular minorities. Finally, at least in the short term, the impact of the poll tax on black families is likely to be a major factor consolidating opposition to the Conservatives among both Asian and Afro-Caribbean voters.

Notes

1. I am grateful to the Economic and Social Research Council for a personal research grant which assisted the research for this chapter.
2. The term 'black' will be used to refer to people of Afro-Caribbean or Asian ethnic origin, except where it is felt necessary to distinguish between these communities. The data does not enable distinctions to be made between the various Asian and Afro-Caribbean communities.
3. A good example of an MP who now devotes much more attention to the concerns of his Asian electors than in the past is Mr. Roy Hattersley in Sparkbrook.
4. The 1981 Census shows that while 22 per cent of the general population is under 16 years of age, the proportion of Asian is 40 per cent and of Afro-Caribbean 30 per cent.
5. The most careful monitoring of Asian turnout has been done by Dr. M. Le Lohé in Bradford.
6. The Survey on attitudes to race and immigration published by National Opinion Polls in February 1978 gave the following distribution of support for the Labour party among West Indians and Asians. This poll was conducted shortly after Mrs.

Thatcher's 'swamping' interview on Granada Television which greatly raised the salience of the immigration issue:

Support for the Labour Party Among West Indian and Asians by Social Class (%)

Social Class	West Indian	Asian
A, B, C	90	86
C2	94	93
D, E	99	97

Source: N.O.P. February 1978.

7. I am grateful to Mr. Robert Waller of the Harris Research Centre for making this data available and for permission to re-analyse the data.
8. The Harris poll found that 42 per cent of the electorate trusted the Conservatives most on Law and Order, 28 per cent Labour, 12 per cent Alliance and 18 per cent did not know.

5 The Asian vote in a northern city

MICHEL LE LOHÉ

Introduction

Within the United Kingdom Bradford has the highest percentage of the population in which the head of the household was born in Pakistan. The percentage, according to the Census of 1981, is actually not very high since the 29,423 individuals enumerated amounted to only 6.5 per cent of the total population. A more recent estimate of 62,000 (The Guardian, 19 November, 1988) would double the percentage of Pakistani origin and would probably raise Bradford higher on the table of places with substantial ethnic minorities for there were, in 1981, eight London Boroughs and seven District Councils shown as having a higher percentage (than Bradford's 11.2 per cent) of persons with origins in the New Commonwealth or Pakistan. The unusual feature of Bradford's ethnic minority population, even in 1981, was the proportion originating in Pakistan, for amongst the five principal sources, 3.0 per cent came from East Africa, 3.7 per cent from Bangladesh, 7.6 per cent from the Caribbean, 25.5 per cent from India and 60.3 per cent from Pakistan (Ibid).

Thus, although the Indian community, largely Sikh, is certainly not insignificant it is the community which has origins in Pakistan which is by far the most significant in Bradford and this community also has significance nationally. Benazir Bhutto came to Bradford and photographs of her at the party rally appeared in the local newspaper. The Pakistan People's Party was quick to be first to invite the new Prime Minister to visit Britain, or to be more precise, their British headquarters in Bradford. The party claims that they have in Bradford four Labour councillors and a score or more jostling to become the city's first Conservative councillor (Ibid). There is also a group within the city which favours the Islamic Democratic Alliance and there was, of course, enormous interest in the outcome of the elections 'back home' in Pakistan. In April 1986 the Pakistan Ambassador Ali Arshad came to Bradford and made a headline in the local newspaper with his advice to 'Vote here, not in Pakistan' (Bradford Telegraph & Argus, 17 April, 1986).

His advice was no doubt sincere. But it was also superfluous for in recent years the citizens of Bradford with origins in Pakistan have voted in Bradford in impressive numbers and their votes have consequently gained considerable significance in the local political system. Their significance is occasionally exaggerated because the community is concentrated in relatively few localities, yet the potential is considerable. On the occasion of the Ambassador's visit almost three years ago, the Lord Mayor, Councillor Ajeeb, a first-generation Pakistani, took the opportunity to point to this potential by mentioning that 'Bradford had 50,000 people who had a special relationship with Pakistan and that this figure was expected to grow by the end of the century to almost 20 per cent of the city's population' (ibid.) The extent to which the younger generations either could, or would be inclined to, be associated with the internal politics of Pakistan is debatable. The manner in which these citizens have organised themselves to participate in Bradford's politics is not debatable, for they have shown a willingness to register as electors and to turn out to vote in great numbers.

Electoral Registration

In 1987 a survey was undertaken in a part of Bradford to determine the extent to which citizens were omitted from the electoral register and to attempt to discover the reasons for non-registration (LeLohé, 1987). The desire to interview as many Afro-Caribbeans as possible led to the selection of the particular part of the inner city where there was some concentration of that ethnic group as opposed to a solidly Asian area. Of the 547 residents interviewed, 323 were of Asian origin as against 108 who were of Afro-Caribbean options and 116 who were of native white origins.

This research was concerned with the reasons why residents were not listed in the electoral register at that address. Where the respondent was omitted two broad categories of explanation were identified. One of these categories was described as 'cause for concern', indicating that respondents were alienated from the political system and were expressing that position by refusing to have their names entered on the register. The other category was described as 'good cause' indicating that, most commonly, a recent change of address or, less commonly, personal need for anonymity or religious beliefs had led to absence from that register. Citizens of Asian origin had, apparently, a high level of non-registration but this was largely a matter of good cause since they had changed address but were registered elsewhere. Only 0.9 per cent of all Asian respondents were missing from the register on the grounds that they did not want to be involved in the political process. The numbers involved in Bradford are too small to be statistically significant, but the two other groups, native white and Afro-Caribbean, had much higher levels of alienation and the pattern was the same in the other four towns surveyed. People of Asian origin have the greatest desire of any ethnic group to be registered as electors, they have the greatest desire to cast their vote, and they reside in an area which is essentially marginal.

The Marginality of Bradford

Bradford is marginal where all three levels of government are concerned. At the European Assembly level Bradford is the principal component of the highly marginal seat of Yorkshire West. For the elections of June 1984, when new boundaries became effective, the seat was classified as a Conservative marginal and thus the election of a Labour MEP was reported as a Labour gain. (The Times, 19 June 1984). At the Westminster level there are five constituencies within the city and three of these are marginal. Bradford North was won by the Conservatives in 1983 with a small majority of 3.4 per cent but became a Labour gain in 1987 with a majority of 3.3 per cent. The situation was unchanged but was actually closer at Bradford South which had Labour's second smallest majority 0.2 per cent in 1983 and kept that position with 0.6 per cent in 1987. The third seat classified as marginal in 1983 (The Times, Guide to the House of Commons, 1983, p.282) was Keighley which then had a majority of 2,774 and was listed as the 35th seat which Labour would gain if there was a uniform swing in their direction.

At the third level, that of the City Council, the situation could hardly be more marginal. Basically the core of the city, the old County Borough before the reform, has continued to elect a majority of Labour councillors in most years but the extension of the boundaries when it became the new Bradford Metropolitan District in 1974 added an area which elects a majority of Conservative councillors and the city's two Conservative Members of Parliament. The Metropolitan District retained the old name and title as a city but it included the neighbouring areas of Baildon, Bingley, Ilkely, Keighley, Queensbury and Shipley which are now.[1] represented by 39 councillors. In the last six elections this new area's results have been in the proportions Conservative 69 per cent, Labour 26 per cent and the Democrats 5 per cent. The old city returns 51 councillors and they have been, over the same six elections, in the proportions of Labour 65 per cent, Conservative 31 per cent and Democrats 4 per cent. The balance for the whole area is actually perfect for there have been 86 Conservative victories, 86 Labour victories and 8 by those we now call the Democrats.

This fine balance of seats on the council fairly represents the distribution of votes between the two principal parties which, again for the last six elections, divides as 49.4 per cent Conservative and 50.6 per cent Labour. Furthermore the balance is also found in most of the 30 wards for 16 of them have changed hands at least once in that same period. Consequently there has been no consistent party control of the council, the Conservatives have been in power for six years, Labour for four years and there have been four years in which neither party had an overall majority. In September 1988, following a by-election gain, the Conservatives had 45 councillors opposed by 43 Labour and two Democrats. The Lord Mayor used his second, or casting, vote to give his own party control and thus the council swung back to the Conservatives.

To have a council which swings between the two major parties and which has most of its seats classified as marginal is unusual. It is also a situation in which the votes of particular groups, if organised and located in the marginal wards, could be so crucial as to give such groups considerable power. The Asian communities are certainly well organised to exercise their voting power. Indeed the Conservative Leader in the Council stated that they were well aware that research showed Asians were twice as likely to turn out to vote in council elections as white voters. As he put it, 'One Asian vote is worth two white votes'.[2]

The Conservative and Labour organisations have both been concerned to check these rates and this author has observed them over the years (LeLohé, 1984). Originally, counts of Asian votes were made by observers at polling stations and these were then compared with the Asian names on the electoral registers. In recent years observing polling stations has not been necessary for local elections since it is now possible to purchase the marked electoral registers showing those who voted and those who abstained. Turnout figures for the Asian community show how that community has awakened to its potential power. Going back to the 1966 records 1 found five polling stations, BH, GF, KB, KD and LA, where the average Asian turnout, with 114 voters out of 2,512 electors, was only 4.5 per cent. Polling district boundaries have changed since that time but in much the same area in the local elections 20 years later the situation was very different indeed. In an Asian electorate of 2,608 no less than 1,546 (59.3 per cent) turned out to vote in the local elections of May 1986.

Perhaps the most remarkable piece of evidence concerning the mobilisation of the Asian electorate is the turnout level in the elections for the European Assembly at Strasbourg. In June 1984 a careful count at the most interesting polling station, 27H University Ward, was made (marked registers are not available for these elections). There were 3,603 electors on roll of whom 2,140 had Asian names. Of these, 905 came out to vote giving a turnout rate of 42.3 per cent, whereas the 'other' 295 voters achieved a level of only 20.2 per cent. This Asian turnout rate of 42.3 per cent does not appear impressive until one is reminded of the very low level of turnout in these elections in England. No English Assembly constituency achieved so high a figure, the highest being 38.0 per cent for Cornwall and Plymouth (European Parliamentary News, June 1984). In England Asians appear to hold the record as the most diligent Europeans as far as turns out at elections are concerned.

This outstanding performance was actually expected, for a similar result had been achieved in the Assembly elections of 1979. Three polling stations were observed on that occasion in Bradford with Asian turnout at 44.4 per cent, 40.9 per cent and 27.9 per cent, which was far ahead of the comparable turnout of the white European electorate. The overall Asian average in 1979, with 1,372 voters from an electorate of 3,558, was 38.6 per cent which was well ahead of the national average turnout of 32.1 per cent. If being a good European was to be measured by voting in that election the best Europeans in Britain were Bradford's Asians.

Relative Turnout Rates: Asians, Blacks and Whites

Between 25 and 29 May 1987 the Harris Research Centre conducted a survey for the Asian Times. They interviewed 707 Asians of whom 74 per cent stated they were absolutely certain to vote and 299 Afro-Caribbeans of whom 51 per cent said that they were certain to vote. That research clearly suggests that Afro-Caribbean electors are less interested in turning out to vote than Asian electors. There is, however, a special problem in determining Afro-Caribbean turnout because many Afro-Caribbean persons cannot be distinguished from white persons on the electoral register by their names. Thus since we, normally, do not know the size of the black electorates, we have a problem in that we cannot calculate the turnout level.

In the registration survey sponsored by the Commission for Racial Equality I had an opportunity to avoid this problem. By visiting every house listed in the register it was possible to determine whether, for example, a person named Green was actually black or white. It was then possible to annotate the marked register with symbols indicating black, white or Asian electors. Since only those still resident and present at home answered the knock on the door the researchers missed those who had moved to a new address. Those who had moved would have had difficulty in voting at their registered polling station and their turnout rate would have been very low. Those who were resident and were able to responded to our interviewers were the disproportionately active section of the total electorate and therefore their turnout rates exaggerate the performance of all persons on the register.

In Bradford 60.2 per cent of the Asians still resident had voted; for the whites the figure was 39.8 per cent and for the Afro-Caribbeans 26.3 per cent. Taking the results of the surveys in all five towns the pattern was the same, with 63.8 per cent of Asian, 45.2 per cent of white and 36.3 per cent of Afro-Caribbean respondents being shown as having voted. Whilst these figures, since they take no account of electors who had moved, exaggerate the turnout levels they clearly suggest that the Afro-Caribbean communities in these places have not achieved the same level of organisation as the Asian communities. There is clearly a potential here which could be developed in the interests of that community.

A factor crucial to the influence of the Asian and Afro-Caribbean communities is their location within the wards which elect the city councillors. There are two sources of evidence about this distribution: one being definitive in the form of the electoral register; the other, since it does not define electors, is the Census. The difficulty with the electoral register is that although electors with Asian names can be identified, and there can even be refinements about Sikh, Hindu or Muslim names, there can be, as already indicated, formidable problems of identifying Afro-

Caribbean electors. The advantage of the Census of 1981, though it has many disadvantages, is that specific groups of, for example, Afro-Caribbeans, Bangladeshis or East Africans can be identified and one can thus be more specific about the origins of the population. The population is not, of course, the same as the electorate, since young persons under eighteen years of age are not registered.

Table 5.1 **Numbers and Percentage of the Population Living in Households in Which the Head was Norn in the New Commonwealth or Pakistan: Census of 1981, Small Area Statistics for Eight Wards**

University	7,576	67.6%
Bradford Moor	3,511	37.8%
Toller	2,777	31.3%
Little Horton	2,843	28.1%
Heaton	1,773	20.2%
Bowling	2,029	19.7%
Undercliffe	1,566	17.9%
Keighley North	1,467	15.4%

Table 5.2 **Relative Percentages of the Five Principal Ethnic Groups in Eight Bradford Wards: Census of Birthplaces 1981**

	Afro-Caribbean	Bang-ladeshi	East African	Indian	Paki-stani
University	3.4	1.8	6.8	20.5	67.5
Bradford Moor	2.2	1.9	4.0	33.5	58.4
Toller	5.7	1.2	3.0	12.6	77.4
Little Horton	13.5	4.9	5.4	21.4	54.8
Heaton	4.3	0.5	5.0	9.9	80.3
Bowling	6.0	4.7	7.5	20.7	61.0
Undercliffe	4.3	25.0	2.7	16.5	51.6
Keighley North	1.2	14.4	0.2	2.0	82.2

The Census has already been used to indicate the balance of the electorate between the principal ethnic groups, and the point about the predominance of those originating from Pakistan has been made. The overall position in the city, however, needs refining by reference to the eight wards in which the Census indicated that more than 15 per cent of the population resided in households where the head was born in the New population in several other wards but Table 1 indicates the percentages in those where it is substantial. Table 2 then breaks down each of these populations in terms of the five principal locations from which they originated.

Party Preferences of the Asian and Afro-Caribbean Voters

In a survey of voting in 24 constituencies in 1979 an overwhelming degree of support for Labour amongst Asians and Afro-Caribbean was identified (Anwar, 1984). In this survey 871 Asians and 285 Afro-Caribbeans indicated their party preferences: the former indicated 86 per cent support for Labour and 8 per cent for the Conservative Party, the latter 90 per cent Labour and 5 per cent Conservative. Many Conservatives have argued that this overwhelming preference for the Labour Party may not be sustained in the long term. The argument runs that a substantial proportion of the Asian community, in particular, has values and interests which make the Conservative Party their natural home. The development of Anglo-Asian Conservative Associations was seen as part of a strategy which would hasten a movement of Asian voters from Labour to the Conservative Party.

The Harris Research Centre survey for the Asian Times in late May 1987 produced figures which clearly suggest that some movement amongst Asian voters has taken place. Whereas 66.8 per cent of the 707 Asians stating a preference named the Labour Party, the support for the Conservative Party had grown to 22.7 per cent. Amongst the Afro-Caribbeans the predilection to vote Labour appears unchanged, for 86.8 per cent of the 299 respondents were for Labour as against 5.7 per cent for the Conservatives.

These, however, are national figures and are not necessarily true for Bradford. The Conservative MP for Bradford North, Geoff Lawler, elected in 1983, had made considerable efforts to attract Asian support and had a good record as a constituency MP. This constituency, however, did not have as many (15.0 per cent) residents of ethnic minority origin as Bradford West where Max Madden, the Labour MP, had an equally good record of constituency care and the support of Asian Labour councillors. Conservatives in Bradford have adopted Asians as council candidates though none have been elected. Although the national organisation of Anglo-Asian Conservative Associations was abolished, an East-West Conservative Association continues to flourish in Bradford. At the count in June 1987 the Conservative agent for Geoff Lawler paid particular attention to the opening of ballot boxes from the areas with Asian voters, and his estimate was that between one fifth and one quarter of these votes were for Mr Lawler. Conservative observers in Bradford West also believed that they had gained ground amongst the Asian community. Asian people and Labour voters in Bradford West ridiculed this view and there is really no evidence one way or the other.

The strength of Labour support within the Asian community was tested on 14 June 1984 in the elections for the European Parliament at Strasbourg. This election was fought on redrawn boundaries which, hypothetically, would mean the Labour MEP, Dr Seal, should lose his seat to a Conservative. The Alliance candidate was Edward Lyons who had been a Member of the House of Commons for Bradford between 1966 and 1983. Mr Lyons was recognised as a good constituency MP who had worked hard for the Asian community and was well-known in the particular area, University Ward, which we surveyed. The survey area was a small fraction of the European constituency of Yorkshire West which had a total electorate of 560,190.

The Conservatives looked outside the survey area for their votes, and that was just as well, for our Asian interviewers did not find one respondent who had voted Conservative until late afternoon. In his fight to keep the seat Dr Seal had the support of the local Asian Labour councillors, and, once again, their organisation, which had given Councillor Ajeeb his massive victory the previous month, was truly impressive. Faithful supporters of Mr Lyons and the SDP councillor Iftikhar Qureshi were also well-organised, though clearly fewer in number, providing the only real challenge to Labour in University Ward which was chosen for this survey.

Asian interviewers at four different polling stations in the ward were given responses indicating party preferences by 219 Asian voters. Of these 195 (89 per cent) said that they had voted Labour, 22 (10 per cent) had voted SDP but only two (1 per cent) had voted Conservative. On this evidence the Asian community is far more solidly Labour than the mining communities of South Yorkshire ill so far voting goes.

The Power of the Asian Vote

The Asian communities in Bradford, then, have excellent records of electoral registration, an excellent polling-day organisation with very high turnout levels and a remarkable degree of support for the Labour Party. But the question is, do these votes count? Or, to put it another way, are they located in wards where they can influence the results? The answer is that they could certainly be better distributed if their power was to be maximised, for, of the eight wards listed in Table 5.1, five are normally very safe Labour seats. Yet the vote does appear to have been critical in the three which are marginal and these will be examined more carefully along with the ward where the Asian community has its greatest strength.

The greatest strength is in University Ward. Table 5.1 indicates that 67.6 per cent of the population is of New Commonwealth or Pakistan origin. Yet there are so many young people in this population that, despite the good registration record, only half the electors (49.4 per cent) are of Asian origin. An outstanding result was achieved in this ward in May 1984. The best performance by any candidate in the whole of the North of England was that of Mohammed Ajeeb in University Ward. He attracted 4.321

votes, producing a majority of 3,601. This majority was unequalled by any candidate, irrespective of party, across the region. The two nearest challenges came from Conservative candidates who had a larger number of votes but smaller majorities, these being at Wetherby (4,624 votes, majority 3,495) and at Woolton, Liverpool (4,696 votes, majority 3,488). Enormous majorities may be good for the morale of the winner but from the Labour Party point of view it would have been better if they could have been located in either of the two neighbouring marginal wards of Heaton and Toller.

Heaton Ward had long been regarded as an unassailable Conservative stronghold. Today this is no longer true since the Metropolitan District incorporated middle class areas including Ilkley, but, prior to the reorganisation of 1972, Heaton Ward was always regarded as the weakest Labour seat, one which had always been handsomely won by the Conservatives. It has retained this cachet as the 'best address' in Bradford and as a good, safe, though no longer the safest, Conservative seat. In the 1986 elections the biggest shock was Labour's gain at Heaton.

The local newspaper made reference to the nail-biting recount and stated that the beaming victor had, ' ... revealed that the secret weapon which won voters over was his father, a Durham County Councillor who had brought his electioneering loudspeakers down to Bradford' (Bradford Telegraphs Argus, 9 May 1986). No student of elections would be convinced by that explanation though it is noted that the message was broadcast in Urdu. A better hint of the true explanation came not from newspaper text but from the photograph of the victor surrounded by six cheering supporters, two of whom were young whites, one a young Afro-Caribbean University student and three rather more elderly Asian men. The photograph led to a check of the Asian vote through the purchase of marked registers, conversations with local activists and a careful assessment of the extent to which this victory had been exceptional.

The previous election for Bradford City Council had been in 1984, for there were no elections in 1985 following the abolition of the Metropolitan Counties. In 1984 Labour had won 16 seats in Bradford, the Alliance two and the Conservatives 12, and of these Heaton had been the seventh safest for the Conservatives. The result was:

Conservative	2,930	60.0%
Labour	1,398	28.6%
Alliance	555	11.4%
(Conservative majority:	*1,532*	*31.4%)*

The result in 1986 was:

Conservative	2,317	40.8%
Labour	2,400	42.2%
Alliance	931	16.4%
Revolutionary Communist Party	35	0.6%
(Labour majority	*83*	*1.4%)*

The swing to Labour would be conventionally calculated as an impressive 17.5 per cent. This was by far the largest swing to Labour, for the mean swing for the remainder of the city was only 2.8 per cent. Heaton moved down from seventh to eleventh position in the league table of Conservative support and out of their list of winners. It was indeed an impressive Labour victory and conversations with activists confirmed that there had been a very impressive organisation of the Asian vote.

The Asian community is actually concentrated in one of the seven polling districts. This is the one nearest the town centre with a total of 2,601 electors, of whom 1,297, almost exactly half, have Asian names. A careful inspection of the electoral register reveals two interesting attributes of this Asian community. One is that 19 of them showed birth dates which meant that they were just under 18 years of age and therefore could not vote which, compared with just one white person under age, suggests a significant difference between the age ranges of the two groups. The Census in 1981 actually showed that in Heaton no less than 47.0 per cent of the Asian and Afro-Caribbean residents were under fifteen years of age. This age difference is also suggested by the 75 persons, none of whom were Asian and most of whom were in rest homes, who were registered to vote by post. The second attribute is that the Asian names included only 14 which were Hindu and 25 which were Sikh; the remaining 1,258 were Muslim.

Those with non-Asian names were overwhelmingly white, for there were only three with African names and, so far as was known, only 14 other black people. The remaining 1,287 or so Europeans included 64 who originated in Eastern Europe. The balance between Asians and others in the electorate may have been even, but their willingness to turn out and vote was not. No less than 763 of the 1,278 Asians (59.7 per cent) who were entitled to vote did so, but only 346 of the 1,227 others (28.2 per cent) entitled to vote in person came out. This solid block of 763 voters was clearly a crucial factor in Labour's success for it was the Labour Party which mobilised this vote. Asian Labour Party workers achieved a remarkable level of organisation without which the Conservative stronghold would not have fallen.

In the redrawing of boundaries prior to the elections of 1980 a new ward named Toller was carved out of parts of the old Allerton, Heaton and Manningham Wards. The former two old wards were leafy suburbs but the Manningham part housed a substantial Asian community and the percentage of the population which was Asian or black, 31.3 per cent, is the third highest in the city. However, as at Heaton, a large proportion is under voting age. The age pattern of the total population is typical of the inner city with 27.8 per cent under fifteen years of age and 27.5 per cent of households occupied by pensioners. The ward has always been marginal, in recent years moving steadily towards Labour. The first election held in the new ward was to elect three councillors and the Conservative and Labour Parties each had three candidates. The combined votes of the Labour candidates amounted to 6,793 (50.03 per cent) against 6,965 (49.97 per cent) for the Conservatives. Split votes allowed one Conservative in to join the two successful Labour candidates. The ward was a super-marginal.

In the euphoria of the Falklands War the Conservatives won at the next election with a majority of 4.3 per cent and also in 1983 but with an even narrower 1.2 per cent. Since that occasion Labour has won every time with steadily growing majorities and by 1987 Toller had become the eighth safest Labour seat. There is no doubt that Asian voters are an essential element in Labour's strength and the Labour councillor who broke through in 1984 readily acknowledges its importance.

The third marginal ward is Keighley North, the fifth largest ward in the city covering over five square miles in contrast to the one square mile of Toller. Most of the area is moorland and farmland with a picturesque village, some highly desirable residences and a seventeenth-century manor house owned by the National Trust. It also includes the part of the town of Keighley with poor housing in which there is a concentration of Asian people, almost all of whom are of Pakistani origin. In the first election in 1980 the three Conservative candidates, two of whom were elected, won 6,159 votes and the Labour candidates, with one success, won 5,835. The relative percentages were 51.4 per cent and 48.6 per cent, again a highly marginal seat. In subsequent elections the Conservatives won on four occasions but, on average, a swing of 2.0 per cent would have dislodged them. In 1984 they were dislodged.

This Conservative defeat was attributed in the local newspaper to white backlash against the Conservative Education Chairman who had defended the availability of halal meat for school dinners. The front page of that newspaper had his photograph with the word 'Backlash' in inch-high letters below it and the words 'Tory Race Policy Chief Out' (Bradford Telegraphs and Argus, 4 May, 1984) above it. The newspaper was clearly regretting the defeat of an able Chairman who was anti-racist, but it was nonsense to suggest his defeat was remarkable. In fact, in terms of loss of support, that Conservative had done better than 12 of his colleagues but worse than 13 of them; he was the most typical Conservative. There was nothing remarkable about his defeat, and on the 'swing' of 1984 it was entirely predictable.

A further gain at the next election in 1986 was therefore predicted and marked registers were obtained following that election for the two polling districts in which the Asians are concentrated. At polling district 14G no less than 338 of the 448 (75.4 per cent) of the Asian electors turned out. At 14H 641 out of 925 Asians (69.6 per cent) went out to vote. Clearly the Asian community had achieved a quite astonishing level of mobilisation in this marginal seat. It might be anticipated that their votes would again bring Labour victory but despite these Asian turnout rates the Labour candidate lost. Some white Labour supporters stayed at home and more white Conservatives came out, for the Labour candidate was a local man named Liaqat Ali. The 'swing' against this Labour candidate was 6.6 per cent but the average in Bradford, excluding for the moment Heaton, was 2.8 per cent in favour of Labour. If the gigantic swing of 16.5 per cent to Labour in Heaton is included, the city average becomes 3.4 per cent.

Compared with 1984 Heaton was by far Labour's best performance; Keighley North was by far Labour's worst.

The Asian communities at both Heaton and Keighley were consistent, just as diligent in voting in 1983, 1984, 1986 and 1987. The problem was not the Asian voters, it was the whites and their prejudices about Asian candidates. The Labour candidates in Heaton in 1982 and 1983 were Asians and they had helped build up the Asian vote. When they stood down for a white candidate the Asians still voted Labour and their votes elected the winner. The reverse situation sadly does not apply for, in non-central Bradford white voters display a prejudice against Asian candidates. In addition to Liaquat Ali's misfortune in 1986 Labour lost Odsal in 1987, which has an overwhelmingly white electorate, in 1987 with Shah Khokhar as the candidate and in 1988, despite the support of the sizeable Asian community (see Table 5.1) Shaukat Ahmed lost the supposedly safe Labour seat of Undercliffe.

Conclusions

The political agents' slogan 'horses for courses' then sadly applies and Bradford had a remarkable example of this with a Conservative candidate in 1987 and 1988. When Dr Skinner fought University ward with its large Asian population in 1987 he used his Muslim name of Abdul Rashid but the following year when he came to fight Toller ward which has a majority of white electors he used his Christian name of Edward George. His Labour opponent commented that 'He seems to be Edward one year and Abdul the next depending on the ethnic complexion of the ward'(Bradford Telegraphs and Argus, 25 April, 1988). This variation of name was explained as a legal problem by the Conservatives but it could also be regarded as a recognition of the significance of the Asian vote. Clearly the votes of the Asian community are critical in these three marginal wards and the party organisers know it. Other things being equal, these votes, except in a poor year for Labour nationally, can bring Labour victory. Labour knows this and aspires to keep this support; the Conservatives know it and aspire to gain some of that support for themselves.

This Asian willingness to go out and vote does appear to have brought benefits to the community in terms of Council policy. It is not to be asserted that electoral calculus is the only factor in determining the Council's relatively helpful attitude to the Asian communities, but one can assert that it is influential.

Notes

1. There were 31 Metropolitan District wards between 1973 and 1980, but boundaries were redrawn with effect from 1980 to produce 30 wards and 90 councillors.
2. Conversation reported by T Humphreys.

6 Some aspects of black electoral participation and representation in the West Midlands

MARK R. D. JOHNSON

Introduction

As the chapters in this first part of the volume amply demonstrate, there has been in recent years an increasing interest in the 'ethnic vote' among analysts of British politics, and in the significance of ethnic or racial minorities in the British political process (see Layton-Henry & Rich, 1986). The most significant issue in this chapter, is not the attention paid to 'race' issues in electoral manifestoes (however important this may be), or the circumlocutions employed by politicians faced with a question which might expose their thinking on race and racism. Nor do I here intend to go over the ground covered by Le Lohe (1983, 1984) or Fitzgerald (1983) and in this volume regarding ethnic minority candidates. Rather, I set out to ask the same set of questions of the political or 'representational' structures of this country that we seek to ask of the educational, health or other services: this is toi say are black citizens, or ethnic minority settlers and their descendants of Asian and Afro-Caribbean origin, receiving an equal share of whatever passes for the 'benefits' of that 'service', and do they participate in the use of that activity in the same fashion as white citizens? The answers to these questions should then better enable us sensibly to 'account for the behaviour' of black voters, by knowing whether similar behaviour on the part of black citizens brings the same 'rewards' as it does for white participants.

As Studlar has indicated, 'the views of non-whites on policy issues have been only rarely analysed' (Studlar 1986, p.165) , but when examined they do demonstrate a similar type of shopping-list, with the crucial addition of the need to pay attention to issues of racial discrimination, racist attacks, and nationality status. In other words, there does exist a black policy agenda (see for example Labour Party Black Section's, Agenda, 1988), which those who vote will expect to see addressed. The question remains, however, as to whether the votes of black citizens are regarded as meriting attention to those demands - although that itself may depend upon the politicians perceptions of the value to them of those 'black votes'. This chapter cannot hope to explore such a territory, but by use of survey material will attempt at least to illustrate some of the views of black constituents in the West Midlands.

Voting Behaviour

Some writers investigating the 'ethnic vote' have sought explanations for the failure of various models to predict the eventual voting outcomes in so-called 'ethnic marginals' (Studlar 1983; Layton-Henry 1983) but the majority of such studies have relied on projections of national or general data without the benefit of in-depth local survey information. Indeed, a large number of the references to the 'ethnic vote' appear to be journalistic analyses of local situations dependent upon a few key informants (usually local politician) and some census data (Phillips, 1981, Travis, 1983). A typical comment in these would be that cited from Cllr. James Hunte; 'I depend on black votes in Handsworth ... Any candidate who wants to stand here has to satisfy black people, and there are more than a dozen constituencies in this country where that is true' (Phillips, 1981). The problem arises in knowing how far this is in fact true, and to what extent 'race', social class, or religion (Johnson 1985), or indeed some combination of these, is the dominant factor affecting turnout and voting.

A household survey in the West Midlands, conducted in five wards representing five different constituencies, three in Birmingham and one in each of Coventry and Wolverhampton, allows us to examine with hindsight some of the dynamics of the 'ethnic vote'. The survey itself was intended to inform an enquiry into delivery and receipt of public services (Johnson & Cross 1984) but collected at the same time, in early 1981, information on voting behaviour and intentions or beliefs along with allied data. Thus we are able to compare behaviour in the 1979 General election and the 1980 District elections with responses to questions on party and trade-union membership and a more general one on 'the party that most closely represents (your) interests', and of course the normal kinds of data ordinarily expected about social class, income, etc. One caveat should be entered here [1] - the SDP did not announce its formation until we had begun our survey and so may be under-represented in the replies we received. However, in none of the constituencies surveyed did the SDP or the Liberal party make a substantial showing in subsequent elections, so this may not be too significant at a local level, albeit having its implications for the (new) SLD and indeed the 'Owenite' SDP at a national level. These implications were indeed followed up in 1986 by a Liberal Party enquiry, which called for a higher profile to be taken by Alliance politicians in talking about racism, and insisted that this was unlikely to lose the party votes (Liberal Party, 1986).

Table 6.1 gives the results in various elections covering the survey wards and, incidentally, demonstrates (as did the Liberal Party analysis referred to above) how little impact on voting share an ethnic minority candidate appears to have when standing for a minority party.

Table 6.1 Results of Elections in the Survey Areas

Ward Constituency)	1979 General*				1980 District			1982 District		
	Con.	Lab.	Oth.	T%	Con.	Lab.	Oth.	Con.	Lab.	Oth
Deritend (B) (Edgbaston)+	54	34	12	68	12	78	10	14	76	10
					&					&
Perry Barr (B) (Perry Barr)	46	48	6	75	51	37	12	50	36	13
Selly Oak (B) (Selly Oak)	49	39	13	74	47	41	12	48	36	16
Graiseley (Wolv'ton SW)	53	31	16	77	35	55	10	44	31	25
							&	&	&	&
Foleshill (Coventry NE)	57	35	8	73	17	82	1	15	70	15
			&							

T% = Turnout & = Ethnic Minority candidate stood

* General Election includes other wards in the same Constituency

\+ Revised boundaries 1982, into Sparkbrook

Source: Johnson & Cross, 1984

Overall, our survey data do not appear to show great divergence from what we have learned to expect on the national pattern - given the kind of urban constituency they represent.[2] Very few people are members of any political party, and men are slightly more likely to join than women, while Asian women were found to be least likely of all (1.5%) to hold any party membership. Variations between wards eclipsed those between ethnic groups, and we are not led to believe that there is an 'ethnic component' in propensity to support political parties in this way, although as the stereotype might have led one to expect we found rather few Asian and no Afro-Caribbean members of the Conservative Party in our sample. Just over half our white sample, and 95% of black respondents said that they believed the Labour party best represented their interests, and to a very close extent this distribution was reflected in voting behaviour in the two previous elections (see Table 6.2). While a very small group, whose responses may be atypical, those Tories of Afro-Caribbean origin who we did locate appeared to be significantly more likely to vote than those whose political affiliation was Labour-inclined. What is more significant is confirmation of Le Lohe's find ups reported in this volume, and Anwar (1980), regarding the relatively high turnout of Asian voters. Additionally, and contrary to some authors' beliefs, we found that Afro-Caribbean participation (at least in the Midlands, and despite a clearly stated belief by many that no political party represented them) was not significantly lower than that of white voters in the same areas.

Whatever their beliefs about the quality of the candidates or policies on offer, the responsibility of citizens to participate in communal decision making was evidently taken as seriously by the black voters as it was by their white neighbours. Further, contrary to the findings of Todd and Butcher (1982), our survey (which was designed to alleviate the expected problems of non-registration) did not find that black households were significantly under-represented in the electoral register: there were as many 'unregistered' white households located as those with an Asian or Afro-Caribbean head. This finding may assume even more significance when the present system of local government finance is replaced by the 'Poll Tax' or community charge, when it is assumed that the propensity to register and vote will be affected by strategies to evade or at least minimize liability for the new system of local taxation (CARF, 1988 p.17; Oppenheim, 1988).

Analysis of these results by gender indicated that while female electors of ethnic minority origin were considerably more likely to support Labour, among both Asian and white groups they were significantly less likely to vote. Among whites, the distribution of votes actually cast by women - although not their expressed preference - was virtually identical to that for males. Even so, Asian women were more likely to vote than white men.

Table 6.2 Political Allegiances by Ethnic Group (1981)

	M'ship	1979 General				1980 District				'Interests'			
		Con	Lab	Oth	%	Con	Lab	Oth	T%	Con	Lab	Oth	None
Whites (917)	5.6%	41	52	7	76	38	53	9	56	32	55	14	23
Asians (878)	3.8%	6	92	2	85	4	94	1	76	3	94	3	20
Afro Caribbean (366)	3.7%	8	90	1	72	8	91	(-)	54	4	95	(--)	31

Note: Party shares after excluding Dont Know/Did Not Vote/None.

Source: Johnson & Cross, 1984.

Table 6.3 Voting in General and District Elections Compared (per cent)

	White	Asian	Afro-Caribbean
Voted in Neither	22	13	25
Voted in General only	22	10	20
Voted in Local only	3	2	4%
Voted in Both <u>of which</u>	53	75	51
Changed vote	8	4	5
(N)	(877)	(801)	(341)

Source: Johnson & Cross, 1984

It is apparent (and well known) that voting participation in local elections is less than in general elections. It is therefore of interest to observe, as Table 6.3 shows, how voting behaviour varied between the two elections. There does not appear to be any significant difference between ethnic groups in the proportions voting only in local elections or in the degree to which voters changed allegiance between elections. On the other hand, it is apparent that while white and Afro-Caribbean electors' attitudes towards participation are remarkably similar, Asian electors are significantly more likely to vote, and to vote at all opportunities, as suggested by Anwar (1980) in Bradford/Burnley. This raises the interesting question of the relationship between attitude (or 'preferred party') and voting. Unfortunately, without a *prospective* (as opposed to <u>retrospective</u>) study we cannot be definite about such links since attitudes may alter or may be used to justify behaviour, but we did ask about party preference before asking about voting in order to minimise the latter problem. The results of this exercise are rather complex, but are laid out in Table 6.4.

The first observation which may be made from this table is the consistency of partisanship – that is, the degree to which electors had voted for a particular party and continued to believe that it was their best representative. Of those who had voted (in either election) three quarters of whites, slightly more Afro-Caribbeans, and 84% of Asians still considered the same party 'best to serve their interests'. Perhaps these figures could be reversed in interpretation, to say that only 16% of Asian voters but 26% of whites had voted for a party which they (now) did not believe served their best interests. Either way it suggests a high degree of partisanship on the part of Asian electors, and an interestingly intermediate position among Afro-Caribbeans. The lack of aggregate change, or the stability of the outcome over time (illustrated by the similarity of figures for the 1979 General and 1980 District Elections) is also striking.

Table 6.4 **(Previous) Voting Behaviour Compared with Party Preference, by Ethnic Group (per cent)**

	White	Asian	Afro-Caribbean
General Election			
Partisan (of voters)	74	83	78
Alienated Abstainers	51	40	58
Agnostic voted Labour	19	51	36
Agnostic voted Conservative	21	8	5
Labour Abstainers	19	8	17
Conservative Abstainers	9	8	(10)
District Election			
Partisan	74	84	79
Alienated Abstainers	68	49	66
Agnostic voted Labour	14	46	30
Agnostic voted Conservative	12	4	4
Labour abstainers	38	17	36
Conservative abstainers	33	24	(40)

Source: Johnson & Cross, 1984

Conversely, those whom I have characterised as 'alienated abstainers', that is, who believed that no party represented them and had not voted, are again even rarer among Asian electors. Table 6.2 showed the proportion believing no party represented them, which was highest among Afro-Caribbeans and lowest among Asians; the line representing Afro Caribbeans on Table 6.4 represents the probability of acting on that belief (or at least of having acted on it) by not voting. While only a third of the disaffected white and Afro-Caribbean electors had voted in the local election (and not quite half in the General Election), very substantially higher proportions of uncommitted Asians had done so. It will not come as any surprise, perhaps, to note that these 'agnostics' (next two lines of Table 6.4: Agnostic voted Labour, Agnostic voted Conservative) voted for parties in proportions very close to the overall distribution of votes for their ethnic group – 43% of whites for Labour, 90% of Asians and 88% of Afro–Caribbeans in the local elections while 44% of white, 86% of Asian and 85% of Afro–Caribbean 'agnostics' had voted Labour in the General Election.[3]

Consideration of those who did express a party preference, however, gives a further twist to our understanding of levels of party support. It is a 'well–known fact' among political activists that there are differences in propensity (or possibly genuine physical ability or capacity) to go along and vote between supporters of parties. This trend is evident in the final two lines of each section of Table 6.4, where Afro–Caribbean and white supporters of the Labour party are seen to have an almost identical rate of not having voted, considerably higher than that for Conservative supporters. Failure to vote among Asian 'party supporters' is half as likely in the case of the Labour party – but for the smaller number identifying with the Conservatives we found that, while still more likely to vote than other groups, there was an attenuation of this difference. Contrary to expectations, support for a minority party (in this community) does not lead to a higher degree of commitment but instead perhaps a feeling of isolation or of internal conflict leading to a lower turnout than might have been expected.

If, however, we regard the 'present' attitude to party as predominant, which may be a reasonable assumption, then we find that a clear 'ethnic' distinction in attitude towards party appears. Using the same base figures as for 'agnostic voters', nearly 30% of those Asians and Afro–Caribbeans who had voted Conservative in the General Election believed at the time of our survey that *no* party represented them, compared to only 15% of whites. Further, while 17% of Afro–Caribbeans who had voted Labour now believed in 'no party', only just over 10% of Asian and white Labour voters were so disenchanted. For the (probably more committed) voters in the local elections, the proportions are virtually identical. In other words, there is some evidence of growing disillusion with what the Conservatives had so far delivered to their Asian supporters, mirrored by a perceived failure of the Labour group to reward Afro–Caribbean supporters. Clearly, at the time of our survey the ground was ready for the 'Black sections' movement. On the other hand, we observe that the 'other party' category (which largely represents what was then the Alliance group) had made substantial gains from both Conservative (9%) and Labour (7%) *white* voters but only slight inroads on black voters: in fact a mere four of the Asian General Election Conservatives, one *per cent* of the Asian Labour voters, and only one Afro–Caribbean. Interpretation of these figures depends very heavily on one's own party affiliation, but it would seem that the Alliance parties had failed to make much impression on the ethnic minority electorate and/or that black Labour party solidarity was unshaken despite the even then growing dispute over 'Black Sections', which is discussed in a leter chapter of this book, by Kalbir Shukra. On all accounts, white voters appear more volatile than black ones.

Class and Voting Behaviour

Of course, voting behaviour is generally regarded as being related to the individual's social class, as reflecting in a sense 'class identity'. Certainly when one analyses the white voters' perception of the party best representing their interests by their occupational status (Table 6.5) a clear gradient can be seen, with the self-employed being twice as likely to name the Conservative party and 'other parties' (substantially, the Alliance) being most frequently mentioned by the managerial group. Something similar can be observed also among our Asian respondents, where the self-employed record much higher levels of support for the Conservative party - but in nothing like the proportions demonstrated by the white respondents. Furthermore, these are a very small proportion (10%) of the Asian community. Among our Afro-Caribbean sample the occupational distribution is so skewed as to make such an analysis virtually meaningless.

Table 6.5 Employment Status (for those in employment) by Party Identification (per cent)

	White				Asian	
	SE	M	F	EM	SE/M	EM
Cons.	66	42	34	32	14	2
Labour	17	24	46	56	77	94
Other	17	24	20	12	6	4
No Party	28	16	19	22	15	20
(N)	40	37	43	414	41	348

SE Selp Employed
M Managers
F Foremen
EM Employee
Afro-Caribbean, and Asian Foreman omitted: Numbers too small to show differences.
Source: Johnson & Cross, 1984

Naturally, the very fact of inequalities of socio-economic distribution in itself affects voter preference - if there is little evidence of social mobility or successful entre-preneurship among a community then a party offering that ethic is unlikely to gain much support there. Given the concentrated residential location (since 'segregation' is not a good description of the process) of the ethnic minority communities, it is perhaps not surprising that the 'party of solidarity' has held on to its support - and it is noticeable that most of the few black Conservative/Alliance supporters in our survey did live in the 'outer areas' of our sample – that is, not in the truly inner-city locations. However, by this stage we are reduced to talking in terms of individuals rather than groups, and statistical presentation or analysis ceases to be sensible.

Indeed, given the present state of the labour market, both in respect of ethnic minorities generally and their location within the West Midlands (where in Birmingham alone over 40% of jobs in manufacturing and construction disappeared in the ten years following 1971 and were not replaced in other sectors) the key difference to look at may rather be not the status of those in employment but whether or not the individual actually has a job. Table 6.6 presents the answer to our question of 'party identification' in terms of this variable. Since our sample largely excluded pensioners by its construction, it will be appreciated that the majority of those 'not in the labour market' in this study will be women – there were few full-time students in these areas.

The differential rates of unemployment between ethnic groups can also be seen, and obviously enough such variations as they occur between areas will affect the final distribution of political preference. However, for black voters, it does not appear that this significantly affected party support, except insofar as those not in the labour market seem to be the keenest supporters of the Labour movement. Among white voters there is a clear effect on support for Conservative policies, with a distinct fall among those unemployed. Equally, it seems that position in the labour market does not affect the probability of white electors dismissing the relevance of political parties, nearly a quarter of all three categories believing *no* party reflected their interests. Such alienation (or anomie) is more marked among non-employed black voters, especially the Afro-Caribbeans. I am at a loss to explain the slightly higher enthusiasm for party identification demonstrated among Asian unemployed. I would, however suggest that the higher rate of 'no-party' responses from Asians 'not in the labour market' can, *in this instance*, probably be attributed to the gender question alluded to above. For Afro-Caribbean voters, I am reluctant to advance such a hypothesis because of the extensive need to rely upon female employment to maintain family incomes, and in any case apathy or alienation among these unemployed is close to that of those not seeking employment (NILM). Explanations for apparent low political participation among Afro-Caribbean voters could do worse than to consider these data and consider whether the long-term unemployed have any reason to believe in party politics. Those who *have* a job seem as likely to involve themselves in party identification as do white electors.

Using the Political System as a Consumer

So far in this chapter I have concentrated on the traditional aspects of 'participation': voting behaviour, party identification, and 'turnout'. These are not the only dimensions of political participation in our society. I should therefore like to refer briefly to our data on some other aspects of

Table 6.6 Labour Market status by Party Identification (per cent)

	White			Asian			Afro-Caribbean		
	Empl	Unemp	NILM	Empl	Unemp	NILM	Empl	Unemp	NILM
Con.	34	20	30	3	4	2	5	5	3
Lab	51	70	58	92	91	97	95	95	97
Other	15	11	11	4	6	1	--	--	--
None	24	24	21	17	14	25	25	37	42
(N)	551	87	232	401	117	293	198	63	66

NILM - Not in Labour Market - Student/Retired or Sick/Housewife

Source: Johnson & Cross, 1984

political behaviour – what I have characterised as the 'consumption' of politics. It is illuminating to observe to what extent, having cast or not cast a vote, people then use or appreciate the institutions which those votes are supposed to affect. The results of this exercise may then be used to draw some conclusions about the relationship between voting and other forms of participation.

Table 6.7 Knowledge and Use of Elected Representatives (per cent)

	White	Asian	Afro-Caribbean
M.P.			
Known	38	13	19
Inaccurate*	5	8	7
Not Known	61	79	74
Ever Contacted	11	4	3
Councillor(s)			
Ever Contacted	11	4	4
Knowledge of how to contact			
– 'Direct'	19	15	11
– via LA/Party/RA+	44	23	35
– Other (Indirect)	6	2	7
– Don't Know	31	59	47

* including 'Party' given but name unknown.
\+ including 'Surgeries' and Residents Association.
Source: Johnson & Cross, 1984

Testing a person's knowledge of the name of their M.P. is perhaps a very marginal way of measuring the degree to which people are involved with the political process, but it does provide an indication of their level of 'current awareness'. Table 6.7 indicates the results we obtained in our survey, which are likely to be very disappointing to those MPs who might have thought themselves well-known and liked. Asian and Afro-Caribbean respondents had significantly lower levels of 'knowledge', although we noted that a substantial proportion mentioned the names of the M.P. for an adjoining constituency who was (in most cases) more sympathetic to ethnic minority issues. Some also mentioned the party holding that seat rather than the name of the incumbent but since we did not specifically ask for that (and therefore did not record it systematically) we cannot imply that 'knowledge' at that level is necessarily as low as our data might appear to imply. Even so, the level of knowledge among white respondents leaves quite a lot to be desired (especially no doubt by M.Ps. who see themselves as having some standing in their constituencies). Only in the 'outer Birmingham' wards could more than half the white respondents name their M.P. as compared to over 70% of Afro-Caribbeans). In Coventry virtually 80% of white respondents could not even attempt a guess at the names of their M.P.s, while the Afro-Caribbean electorate in Wolverhampton (23% correct) was not substantially worse informed than the white electors of Graiseley (27% correct).

Evidently 'class' or some such measure of community type, and the individual activity of M.Ps. (perhaps to a lesser extent) have a substantial impact upon the electorate's awareness of their representatives. As to the 'usefulness' of elected representatives, it is perhaps sufficient to note that only around 10% of white and 3–4% of black people appeared to have ever contacted their M.P. or Councillor. In our constituencies this was lowest, again, in Coventry, as one might anticipate given the low levels of 'knowledge' displayed there. Such lack of contact cannot be directly ascribed to a lack of knowledge of *how* to contact a councillor. Substantial numbers of respondents claimed to be able to do so 'directly' (at home or through work or other contacts) and the periodic 'surgeries' held in community centres were a frequently mentioned phenomenon. There were high numbers of those saying 'Don't Know', but many of these may simply never have felt the *need* to know. Nonetheless, we were perhaps a little surprised at the lower figures (for both *use* and *knowledge*) elicited from Asian respondents, especially given the significance of involvement by MPs in immigration matters, and the particular needs of Asian communities in Local Authority provision. It is, of course, possible that (since we were not surveying in wards with ethnic minority councillors) minority electors may contact a black councillor by choice. I do not have any evidence to justify this suggestion but would observe that it was not until 1988 that Asians in Coventry had that opportunity, despite their long history of settlement and political activity in that city.

What then are the alternatives? The black vote has long been taken for granted or ignored, and no party has gone out of its way to 'select' either Afro-Caribbean or Asian candidates for winnable seats, although the Black Sections have more recently had some impact upopn the activity of the Labour Party as Kalbir Shukra shows in her contribution to this volume). In the circumstances, with neither representation nor representatives, it is more to be wondered that black voters have remained so faithful to parties and voting, than that some of them have become disillusioned. Can it be, perhaps, that other channels of influence and consultation exist, which have served to divert anger and ensure some inputs to political and policy debates? Obviously there will be individuals who perform such a role, but for significant impact we should also look at (Table 6.8) an institutional channel of 'representation' only effectively available to ethnic minorities (although not exclusively to black people).

Table 6.8 Relationship with Community Relations Council (CRO)

	Asians	Afro–Caribbeans
Active Contact	10	7
Deliberate Avoidance	5	5
Passive Knowledge	85	87
(N)	(436)	(214)
'Not heard'	49	38
(N)	(854)	(344)

Source: Johnson & Cross, 1984

Because of problems in identifying white minorities, we only asked Asian and Afro–Caribbean respondents about their relationship with the (local) Council for Community Relations (CRC). These clearly play a significant role in the eyes of some local government agencies, being (at least partially) funded and also heavily criticised by such bodies. However, in our study we did not gather much support for the notion that the CRC had provided an 'alternative' to democratic representation. Remarkably large numbers claimed never to have heard of the organisation, and a substantial number avoided it completely or expressed their opposition to it. This is not to discount the work done by the CRCs and their CROs – we do not *generally* discount the representative function of local authorities (or Parish Councils) because of low turnouts in elections and so we cannot write off the work of the CRC. Further, those who are involved in the work of CRCs would argue that a large part of their work consists of providing a channel for other ethnic minority organisations to speak with Local Authorities and other agencies. It is possible that members of those organisations give them primacy and may be unaware of the 'umbrella' function of the CRC. The recent study by Gay and Young (1988) has certainly indicated that there remains a continuing need for the *advocative* functions of these agencies. In another recent study we also observed with interest the ways in which Local Authorities manipulated the consultative arrangements available to them in pursuit of the funding and provision of 'ethnic minority specialists' in social services (Johnson, Cox & Cross, 1989). As Gay and Young observe 'The establishment of a 'buffer' relationship depends as much on the local authority's stance as on the CRC's own aspirations' (1988, p.30). Certainly the issue of 'representation' is complex, and while existing institutions remain as impervious to 'black need' as they seem to be, use of all possible channels will be required to ensure that some form of consultation does take place within the framework of local and national government, and indeed in other arenas of life.

One such arena, of course, is the workplace, and the accepted forum for consultation therein remains for most purposes the Trade Union (or Unions), even if the power of these has been attenuated of recent years. It is now well established as a matter of historical fact that black workers of Caribbean and Asian origin have consistently been 'good unionists', in the sense that they have been likely to join a trades union than their white co-workers. Indeed when no union existed, they acted to create such associations and in due course to affiliate or amalgamate with established unions (see Jouhl, in Rice & Patel 1988, p.34). Brown in his national study (1984) ascribes the high membership rates he observed to the industrial or occupational location of black workers, while conceding that they were also very likely to participate in union meetings. The data from our study (Table 6.9) reiterate the evidence of high membership rates, notably amongst both Asian and Afro-Caribbean males, and Afro-Caribbean females, and examination of the types of union to which these respondents belonged gives some support to Brown's hypothesis.Black males are much more likely to be found in general manual unions, as are Asian women, while Afro-Caribbean women were more likely to be members of health service and similar 'non-manual' unions. Clearly these data show a similar pattern to that demonstrated in data regarding the occupational or industrial location of black workers more generally. The second part of the table shows the response to a question asking whether or not the respondent believed that 'all workers should belong to a Trade Union': black workers (and especially Asian males) were very definite in their belief that this was true, very few saying it was not so. The numbers thinking that this was a personal decision were remarkably similar across the groups, with the slight exception of Asian males whose support was rather more definite.

In his study of 'Black and White Britain', Brown was able to draw upon comparable data collected in 1974. He found from this that since the earlier data the gap between black and white propensity to join unions had narrowed. He does not speculate on the reasons behind this, but as he and others have also observed (notably Wrench, 1986), black workers are heavily under-represented in union officership. Further, as Wrench states, 'it is a fact that even at the best of times Trade Unions have traditionally put a rather low priority on equal opportunity and anti-racist action...'(Wrench, 1986). It may well be that perception of the low priority placed upon black workers' needs has hindered their continued enthusiasm for participation. Certainly, as data from the 'Urban Institutions' survey utilised in Rice & Patel's study of low pay in the West Midlands illustrate, the gains to be expected from union membership are less for black workers. In that analysis (Rice & Patel, 1988 p.34) it was shown that although non-unionised workers were strikingly more likely to be working for 'low pay', being a member of a trade union did not eradicate the 'ethnic differential' in wages, Afro-Caribbean males in unions being more than twice as likely as white male union members to earn less than £60 per week. Once again, despite the enthusiastic participation of, and support given by, black workers, it appears that the benefits to be gained from involvement in the democratic institutions of our society are vitiated by racism.

Table 6.9 Trade Union Membership (per cent)

	White		Asian		AfroC	
	Men	Women	Men	Women	Men	Women
Member *	68	45	83	39	86	66
Non-Member	32	55	17	61	14	34
(N)	(393)	(381)	(419)	(188)	(140)	(172)
Of members:						
General Unions (TGWU, etc.)	35	23	63	39	56	24
Skilled Unions (AUEW, etc.)	29	8	20	18	24	12
Non-Manual (COHSE,NALGO)	21	41	5	17	3	50
Others	14	28	12	27	13	16
Belief in Membership						
All workers should	38	28	66	44	55	45
Up to individual	38	47	29	46	38	47
No, not necessary	25	25	4	10	7	8

* The question on Trade Union membership was asked of all who were employed or had been in the previous 5 years; for those not currently in employment membership may have lapsed.

Source: Johnson & Cross, 1984

Conclusion

Throughout this volume, we have seen that ethnic minority or black citizens have demonstrated their commitment to participation in the institutions of British society. As Studlar (1986) and Fitzgerald (1984) have stated, black voters are not significantly different from whites in the way that they behave, although their structural position leads them to be concentrated in certain sectors, as they are geographically also concentrated. Given that their interests are consistently and unreasonably ignored, and their support frequently taken for granted, it is time that attention was focussed upon the rule makers, the white majority, and some credit given for that consistent support of democratic means of reform, rather than seeking to 'blame the victim' for not 'playing the game'. If following the rules and joining unions or voting for parties have produced no improvement in the overall representation of black peoples' needs, then nobody should be surprised if future generations are less inclined to believe in the value of such participation.

Notes

1. That is, the original Social Democratic Party which was later to merge with the Liberal Party and form thereby the present SLD, out of the Alliance. Reference here to SDP and Liberal parties reflects those historical facts and not the groups now constituted independently of the 'new' Democrats.
2. These data represent the views of heads of households or their spouses, obtained from a stratified random sample of households structured in order to achieve roughly equivalent numbers of male and female respondents. 'Elderly' white households, consisting only of pensioners, were excluded, and various sampling fractions employed, so that results in tables cannot be grossed up to form population estimates.
3. Readers will appreciate that I use the term in its dictionary sense of uncertainty and disbelief, rather than seeking to inpugn electors religious convictions.

PART TWO
SOME GROUPS AND ISSUES

7 The contribution of West Indian groups to British politics

HARRY GOULBOURNE

Introduction

Much work remains to be done on the political behaviour of Britain's ethnic minorities *outside* the mainstream of the country's political institutions. As I indicated in the Introduction to the present volume, this is as true of West Indians as of other non-white groups who have settled in Britain after World War Two. Whilst it is the case, however, that these groups were too preoccupied with the day to day difficulties of life to be able to actively engage in either national or local politics in the 1950s–60s (Fitzgerald, 1988) they were nonetheless quick to form organizations espousing a wide range of issues. By and large, the formation of these groups was determined by a two-fold concern. First, there was, and remains, a natural enough desire to keep in touch with events and developments 'back home'. Secondly, and in the main, there has long been the commitment to defend common interests and promote working and amicable relations with the institutions of the host or majority community with whom West Indians share a wide range of socio-cultural and political assumptions.

This chapter is, however, only a preliminary comment on some aspects of the politics of these groups from such a broad perspective. In particular, some questions are raised around the central proposition that the basis for the active participation of younger West Indians in mainstream party politics in the 1980s was laid during the periods of entry and settlement, but especially the late 1960s and the early 1970s. It is important to bear in mind that the discussion is necessarily bald because it is, in part, an outline for further work on this much neglected, and where not neglected frequently misunderstood, area of West Indian life in post-World War Two Britain.

Towards a Typology of West Indian Groups

Generally speaking, it is possible to classify West Indian organizations, which sprang up in communities throughout Britain, into welfare/cultural, broker and political groups. These categories are not, of course, mutually exclusive. Expectedly, there is a great deal of overlapping between them, but the demarcations do help to point to major tendencies. There is a rough correspondence between these groups and the periods which may be crudely marked-off by the experiences of a jolting entry, a reluctant settlement and a kind of schizophrenic consolidation of West Indian communities in post-World War Two Britain. These groups also correspond to the kinds of issues which have concerned people of West Indians backgrounds during the period as a whole.

Nor is the attempt to classify these groups entirely new. One notable, and perhaps the most important, effort has been made by Rex and Tomlinson (Rex & Tomlinson, 1979, ch. 8). The effort here, however, to sketch a general typology of these groups differs in several important ways from their own. In my view it is necessary to construct a general history of West Indian communities in Britain, placing their entry, settlement and consolidation in a proper and balanced context. These must then be placed alongside an assessment of whether West Indians, like other groups of highly visible non-white complexion, are becoming more or less acceptable as part of the national British community. The purpose of Rex & Tomlinson's typology is no doubt much the same. Whereas, however, their model reduces, perhaps understandably, for the purposes of analysis, the complex social life of West Indians to a rather static four-cornered situation for all West Indians, there is a need to develop a more appropriate model to accommodate the complex life of this highly visible but really quite small group which has emerged to become the litmus test of British liberalism.

Rex & Tomlinson's four-cornered universe of West Indian politics in Birmingham depicts the behaviour of Rastafarians and pentecostals as a condition which typifies a situation in which people have withdrawn from society; secondly, there are those, such as political groups of the 1970s, which seek to confront society and exhibit aggression towards it; thirdly, there are those groups which actively pursue integration and/or peaceful co-existence and accommodation with the majority white society; fourthly, there are those groups which seek to ally themselves with radical white groups. The model is initially presented as one applicable to both Asians and West Indians within Birmingham, but the writers confess that it applies less to the former than to the latter 'because it is designed to draw parallels between white and black groups, and the Asians share less with the whites than do the West Indians' (Ibid., p.245).

It is usual to treat seriously an argument which is presented seriously by its proponent. And it is in this light that my criticisms of aspects of this model must be taken. After all, the book in which the argument appears has been one of the most widely read texts in recent race relations literature and no doubt it has had a profound impact on a generation concerned about the conditions of the two major non-white groups in Britain. The presentation, therefore, of West Indians as almost pathological in their propensity to raise the voice of protest must be seen as either a serious weakness in the overall analysis or as the representation of a most unusual moment in the life of West Indians in Britain.[1] In specific terms, the Rex/Tomlinson model is now inadequate for understanding West Indian groups in Britain for at least the following reasons. First, the model is frozen within a specific moment of the overall experience of a people engaged with the multiple problems of entry, settlement and consolidation. To freeze a moment of this highly complex experience and analyse it as if it were typical of the whole can be misleading. Obviously, this is a problem social analysts have to confront when we attempt to understand complex social reality by abstracting salient aspects which are themselves arrested in time and physical space. One way of overcoming this is usually to present the moment as part of a greater whole or totality. And one conclusion which may be drawn from this is closely related to a second main point.

This is the fact that the groups analysed are physically located in Britain's second city, which is of course important in itself, but ignores the far more representative situation of London where the majority of West Indians in the UK have settled and where their political behaviour has been significantly different from that depicted for groups in Birmingham. It goes without saying that the experience of one set of black people in one part of a highly unified country and homogeneous society as Britain is more than likely to be much the same as in other parts of the country. But, without a general historical account to provide necessary background, it may be misleading to assume that particular patterns found in one part of the country may be applicable, irrespective of time and physical space.

Thirdly, there is much in the presentation of the analysis to suggest that West Indians in Birmingham may be responsible for their conditions by their disposition to be *confrontational* and *aggressive* towards the majority *white-society*, particularly the well-intentioned white researcher. This leads to a fourth point: the vocabulary of the analyst and the activists stand in sharp opposition. This in itself should not be unexpected because the analyst ought not to feel that he or she is responsible or accountable to any segment of society, but to his or her own conscience and to the intellectual integrity shared by the majority of the necessarily alienated community of scholars/intellectuals. Nonetheless, the grounds for describing what activists and many others take to be *resistance* to blatant racism as *confrontation* and *aggression* are not clear. Unfortunately, however, these adjectives are becoming the standard words with which many academics, journalists and others describe West Indian protests (eg. Dench, 1986).

In short, suggestive as the model undoubtedly is, it fails to account for what I see as the *cycle* of West Indian experience, a cycle to which West Indian organizations and modes of participation in British politics generally corresponds: entry/expectation, settlement/frustration, consolidation/engagement/participation within the mainstream political institutions. An account of these groups, constructed along these broadly drawn lines, is likely to yield helpful insights into the dynamic life of a community still very much in formation. This, of course, is an additional reason for seeking to situate that community's overall political behaviour within a general historical perspective.

Cultural/Welfare Groups

Expectedly, the cultural/welfare type of group has been by far the largest and most mixed of the three categories I have suggested. These include the churches, sports and leisure clubs, centres for the elderly, groups concerned with education, prisoners, probation, the mentally ill, the cultural roots of West Indians, and so forth. Some of these groups have long existed in the communities whilst others have sprung up more recently. Some of them, like the churches, were partly taken on the passage from the West Indies. In the main, however, these groups originated as a response to conditions found here. Some, again like the churches, have found Britain to be fertile ground whilst others, such as the Rastafarians, have had a mixed experience of popularity and indifference.

The groups which drew most directly upon the West Indian experience 'back home' have most probably been the Christian denominations. Perhaps because they are more accessible than most other groups to researchers these groups have also been among those elements most commented upon.[2] Most of the denominations established themselves under very austere conditions, (Afro-West Indian United Council of Churches, 1984, pp. 1–19). Several factors contributed to the growth of these churches in a period when the churches of the white majority population were declining. These, Howard suggests, included rejection both by the majority white society as well as by the congregations of white churches; the class differences between white English Christians and the majority of West Indian practising Christians; and the evangelicism of West Indian Christians (Howard, 1987, pp.11–12). To these may also be added the strong feeling amongst many West Indian Christians that they take their faith more seriously than do their white brethren and sisters.

These factors combined to force practising Christians to be amongst the first West Indians to think of alternative organizations to those they found here. In the early years, therefore, they had to establish for themselves places of worship. Thus, the single rooms or front rooms of the 'saved' became in those years temples of God where small groups would meet for devotion and refuge. Some have maintained links with their congregations 'back home' or in the USA from where many of these denominations originated (Howard,1987, ch. 2). Others were able to establish contacts with white pentecostals, members of the elim or assemblies of God churches and so forth. In general terms, therefore, pentecostalism is far from being an expression of withdrawal from the majority white religious Christian community as has been suggested (Rex & Tomlinson, 1979, p. 247). In the main, however, because the devout Christian from the West Indies was amongst those who most considered themselves members of a universal community – in this case the Christian church – their actual as well as perceived rejection resulted in a two-fold response. One of these was the emergence and growth of what is being called the 'black-led' churches [3] in Britain. The second response has been the political quietism which their theology implies.

The contribution of the churches to the political awareness of West Indians is, therefore, problematic because at least two fairly clear lines of departure may be picked up from their activities and predispositions. First, it may be argued that the churches have demonstrated a decidedly firm position to adhere to Jesus' injunction to pay unto Caesar the things that are Caesar's and unto God the things that are God's. It should, however, be recognized that in so doing the churches played an important part in maintaining that spirit of respect (some would probably say fear) for the laws of the land which was a major characteristic of the first generation of post-World War Two West Indians who came to Britain. This may have been of crucial importance in keeping young West Indian males out of the books of the law at a time when, it seems,[4] the state was keeping a keen eye on the new arrivants to determine whether they were criminals. This kind of avoidance may not have contributed directly to any discernible active or participatory political orientation but at least it was helpful during the period of settlement if only by delaying the process whereby the West Indian population would become a criminalized segment of the population. It may be suggested, therefore, that the churches were a net contributor, or an indispensable resource to West Indians in the process of settlement during their post-World War Two sojourn to the centre of the empire.

Moreover, the Christian denominations provided an avenue or forum for many young men and women with musical ability to express themselves and for those with leadership qualities to display them. Today when there are comparatively more avenues for modest upward social mobility, admittedly if only for the few, it is perhaps too easily forgotten that for West Indians of all social backgrounds in the first two or so decades of entry and settlement British society offered no alternative to the doldrum of the meanest unskilled work available. In the Caribbean the churches of the middle-classes - the Anglican, Baptist, Catholic, etc. denominations - offered a respectable avenue of upward social mobility for ambitious young men of talent who wanted to serve their communities (Goulbourne, 1988, ch. 3). An intending clergyman in the churches of the subordinate classes; did not however, need to attend college before being called of God to serve His people. This suggested a kind of laissez-faire principle which operated within the churches of the working people - the evangelical/pentecostal denominations - and enhanced certain functions of the religious life in a new environment. In Britain, the young man or woman of tolerable fundamentalist principles could, during the early days of settlement, devout himself or herself to the service of a people still groping to make ends meet and thereby gain the respect of his or her community-in-formation. A few were even able to devote their full time to such service instead of reporting at the factory gate.[5]

Similarly, from an early stage of settlement, Rastafarianism reinforced aspects of the evangelical Christian's political quietism. Since the pioneering study by Nettleford, Smith and Augier almost thirty years ago in Kingston, Jamaica, Rastafarianism both in the UK and Jamaica has attracted a good deal of attention (Nettleford et al, 1960; also, for example, Nettleford, 1978; Barrett, 1977; Constant, 1982). This is no doubt largely due to the fact that in cultural terms, Rastafarianism has been a protest movement against the cultural arrogance of a dominant and hegemonic culture. On the other hand, Rastafarianism appears to be an incipient religion which emphasizes the estrangement of the *exile* with the hope of redemption in an eventual *return*. On the other hand, like most religions in their infancy (for example, Christianity or sikhism) rastafarianism can embrace aspects of a broad social protest movement against injustice.

Its contribution to the development of West Indian political consciousness in Britain at first was concerned, as in Jamaica, with distancing believers from the day to day problems of Babylon with the messianic hope of a return to Ethiopia. By the 1980s the movement appears to have moved to the stage of active and therefore political protest against social injustice. In general terms, however, the major contribution of Rastafarianism must undoubtedly be its influence on popular black culture, particularly music (reggae), poetry (dub), cuisine, hairstyle and general (counter) deportment. It is therefore perhaps unfortunate that it is the negative aspects of Rastafarianism, such as the smoking of marijuana and the subordinate position of women, which are generally perceived to be and, indeed, sometimes defended, as being reflective of its most fundamental principles.

If Rastafarianism bridges the truly religious and the broadly cultural, then we must not forget the more clearly defined cultural groups in the West Indian communities. Although drawing upon traditions carried from the West Indies some of which are derived ultimately from Africa and Europe itself, these groups are distinctly (black) British in expression. The variety of such groups is immense. It is easier, therefore, to speak of the kinds of work they have engaged themselves in than to attempt to focus on any one sub-type or the other.[6]

The concerns and activities of these groups fall into three broad categories. First, there have been and are those groups whose principal concern has been to educate West Indians about their past. This involves learning and imparting knowledge about Africa and the diaspora. The popular history which emerges from this runs the danger of being highly selective partly because its purpose is conceived in terms which are perhaps too simplistic to do justice to the complexity of the heritage of black people in the West. Inevitably, therefore, not all the new myths which are being built out of the past are necessarily clearing the way forward. In general terms, however, the work of such groups must be welcomed because they are building people's confidence in a heritage too long denigrated both in the Caribbean and in Britain (Nettleford, 1978, ch. 1; also, King & Morrisey, 1988).[7]

Secondly, many of these groups have sought to re-establish links with Africa as well as to initiate a new triangular link between people of African descent in Britain, the Caribbean and the USA. It is, of course, historically proper that Britain should become the meeting point for Africans and Afro-Caribbean people as well as a location from which a new kind of link between black people in the diaspora is being forged. After all, British ports and cities such as Liverpool and Cardiff were the points at which slaves from Africa were separated and sent to different destinations throughout the Americas and the Caribbean. The attempt to forge new links, therefore, may be seen as part of the general background to the growing confidence of West Indians in British politics and society after the experience of swallowing the bitterness of unexpected rejection.

Third, welfare and cultural groups provide much valuable and needed advice to people as well as take up the day to day tasks of bringing to realization, however imperfectly, some of the issues more politically-orientated groups highlighted in the 1970s. In the 1980s there are plenty of examples to be found in education, health, housing, the law, child-care, youth work and care of the elderly and so forth. These groups are largely *occupationally-based* thereby reflecting in much finer detail the problems black people face during this period of quasi-consolidation.

Expectedly, different issues and problems receive more or less attention depending on their recency or urgency. In the late 1960s and the early 1970s the education of black children was introduced on the agenda as an issue by political groups but as the seventies wore on it was left to these largely cultural/welfare groups to pick up the pieces and form new discernible patterns out of the puzzles. In doing so, I suggest that these groups contributed to the existence of an environment in which problems faced by West Indian communities could be aired even if such voices stood little chance of being heard and even less of being listened to. They neither determined nor controlled the agenda for the 1980s, contrary to Carter's optimism (Carter, 1986, p. 14). But these groups reminded individuals and collectivities that they have a legitimate voice in articulating what goes towards constructing the public agenda.

Brokerage

In sharp contrast to the multiplicity of welfare/cultural groups there has been only one West Indian broker group at national level to speak of, the West Indian Standing Conference (WISC). This must seem a little unexpected to those who have promoted the view, both within and without the West Indian communities, that West Indians are a highly fragmented people. Before looking briefly at the work of WISC it may be useful, therefore, to consider some of the possible reasons for this kind of homogeneity amongst a people given to debate. Additionally, it is important to do so not only because WISC is an umbrella organization, but also because much the same degree of cross-island membership of groups (quite apart from the specifically island associations) are to be found throughout the West Indian communities in the country. In this regard I would suggest that there are at least three main reasons for this situation to obtain.

First, the extent of island divisions amongst West Indians are sometimes exaggerated. In general and comparative terms West Indians are not as divided a people as is often made out. Even the exceptions, such as Trinidad and Guyana, prove the rule. After all, the Commonwealth Caribbean has been one of the least newsworthy parts of the world in recent times (apart from natural disasters such as hurricanes and the invasion of Grenada in 1983 by the Americans). Indeed, the stability of the region sometimes borders on what the St. Lucian poet, Derek Walcott, called 'malarial enervation' Quoted in Sherlock 1980, p.64. But what this indicates is that although the region suffers from some of the usual conditions of underdevelopment, there are no large questions concerning, for example, the ethnic or racial composition of the nation which people in most other regions of the contemporary world are having to confront.[8] Thus, whilst being a highly democratic people West Indians are not necessarily a divided people, notwithstanding the number of politically sovereign states the region boasts and the mixed racial composition of the region.

Secondly, the reception-experience of West Indians in Britain has helped to foster a spirit of mutual need and assistance. After all, Afro-Caribbean people are treated in a common manner by the majority white population irrespective of whether they may be from Barbados, Jamaica, Guyana, Antigua, etc. Even if in the West Indies groups of people knew of themselves in communities distinguished by islands and territories, the uniformity of treatment and overall experience in the United Kingdom was bound to effect a degree of unity of response. Moreover, the 'ethnicization' of West Indians in Britain has isolated non-Afro-Caribbean people in a way quite unknown in the post-colonial West Indies. For example, people of Chinese, East Indian or European backgrounds from the West Indies are generally not included in this new ethnic definition of West Indian as being exclusively Afro-Caribbean (Goulbourne, 1988a). On the other hand, the new definition is such that some small groups which have quite distinct identities of their own are commonly included in 'Afro-Caribbean'. An example of this is the Afro-British who are generally regarded as Afro-Caribbean. Thus, even well informed commentators will sometimes refer to there being three members of parliament who are of Afro-Caribbean background when in fact there are only two.

Third, these experiences had largely preconditioned individual West Indians (who were to act as brokers) to see themselves not so much as Barbadian, St.Lucian, Jamaican and so forth but as West Indian. In addition, the early years of sizeable proportions of West Indian entry to Britain also coincided with the process of constitutional decolonization in the region, partly as a result of a new West Indian awareness. In short, the times were auspicious for the then less than four million people occupying a territory smaller than Wales (not including Guyana which is roughly the same size as Britain, although having one of the smallest populations in the region, less than half of a million souls) to be both treated, and to perceive themselves, as having a common heritage and destiny. With the abolition of the slave trade at the beginning of the eighteenth century, and at the end of the American Civil War in the 1860s, many black people in the diaspora felt that these were appropriate moments to consider a return to mother Africa. Many did so both before and after these dates. The formation of Sierra Leone by the British towards the end of the eighteenth century and Liberia by the Americans during the first two decades of the nineteenth century are perhaps the most obvious cases of realization of the *return*. With decolonization from 1944 onwards the movement of people of African descent was to take place within the large enclosure of the diaspora itself. One major feature, however, of this wave of migration was that its destination was the very centre of the albeit decaying empire – England, France and Holland.

It is hardly surprising, therefore, that the single outstanding organization which sought to act as broker for the growing, then settling population of West Indians in Britain should reflect aspects of a pan–West Indian mood. The example the West Indian Standing Conference (WISC) and pre–World War Two groups (such as Dr. Harold Moody's League of Coloured Peoples founded in 1931 in Peckham, South London) has had a profound effect on subsequent groups. They have generally tended to be cross–island and inter–regional in character. In this respect at least, the specifically island/national associations which sprung up in the 1950s–1960s seem doomed to extinction with the passing of the first generation of West Indians. At the very least, these groups will become more restricted to broadly defined cultural activities.

WISC was founded in response to felt needs of West Indians in 1958 in the aftermath of the Notting Hill Riots. Its intention was to represent West Indians as a whole to official bodies over matters which affected the West Indian communities in this country. As an umbrella organization WISC had a wide membership of groups but also of individuals.[9] WISC claims that it has worked for the elimination of 'racial discrimination (and) thereby promoting equality of opportunity for all racial groups and to cooperate with all other organizations where common interests coincide at local and national levels...' (WISC Constitution, 1981, p.1).

The organization celebrated its thirtieth anniversary in 1988. And this was no doubt a fitting moment for its present leadership to reassess the organization's past and future work. A reassessment of this kind would bring into sharp focus the problem of the prospects for a broker group such as WISC in the environment of the late 1980s and into the 1990s. In the past WISC has been criticized for its weak internal leadership and its supposed failure to influence public policy (Heineman, 1972, ch. 3). There is evidence of improved internal organization to indicate that some of these have been overcome since the 1960s but the question of whether the organization can *directly* influence public policy still remains. Groups such as WISC cannot, however, be judged solely by this criterion. They play other important roles – for example, keeping embarrassing questions in the limelight when the authorities would prefer to hide them. Moreover, some leaders of broker type groups would contend that others usually get the credit for whatever changes or new ideas the groups bring to public, and sometimes governmental, attention. No academic analysis of changes in British public policy regarding ethnic minorities would be unbiased if it fails to give proper credit to such broker groups as WISC.

Nonetheless, the organization faces other dangers. Indeed, the pointers are that broker groups such as WISC may become less relevant, at least in their present forms, and may therefore be doomed to extinction. First, it would appear that membership of WISC is not increasing amongst the young as it should be if the organization is to have a healthy future. The leadership in 1987/8 was almost entirely made up of individuals who would have experienced their early socialization in the Caribbean rather than in England. A sign of vitality must be the presence of individuals who have received their socialization in the womb of old England.

Secondly, the development of parastatal institutions, such as the CRC and the CRE, since the late 1960s, has drastically restricted the space for broker groups in Britain. Both the Community Relations Councils and the Commission for Racial Equality exist to coordinate the state's efforts in establishing a modicum of peaceful coexistence between groups perceived to be caught up in a conflict between different elements in civil society. These parastatals have themselves, not unexpectedly, assumed much of the functions of the broker. It is not surprising, therefore, that past leaders of WISC should have expressed the view that these parastatals have absorbed potential leaders of community-based broker groups such as their own. This last development was perhaps inevitable but it need not be seen in wholly negative terms as some commentators appear to do (Sivanandan, 1986, p.126). Fitzgerald, on the other hand, suggests that this is not the whole story and argues that there is little truth in the claim that black leaders have been 'creamed-off' by these parastatal bodies, because activists have continued to work in a variety of organizations (Fitzgerald, 1987, pp. 10–11). Clearly, this is a problematic situation. Nonetheless, one result of the development of parastatal institutions exclusively concerned with the management of the *effects* of racism seems to be, as Sivanandan's analysis suggests, the removal of much of the ground from under the feet of some groups. I would express this change rather differently, however: the *welfare* functions of groups such as WISC has increased over what was their main function – *brokerage*.

Third, the question may be asked whether in the light of recent developments, such as the more active participation of West Indians in mainstream politics, there is a need at all for broker groups and whether they will need to redefine their role. It is more than likely that the very useful critical role such groups play will continue to be relevant. After all, irrespective of their intentions, black members of parliament will not be able to respond to issues which affect non-white groups scattered throughout several constituencies. Altogether, however, the *welfare* functions of these groups seems most likely to outgrow or overshadow their broker functions as these are taken up by other functionaries who have thrown in their lot with the political parties and other leading mainstream British institutions.

These considerations invite comments on the more directly political groups to which I referred earlier.

Political Groups

There has been a variety of politically-oriented groups in the West Indian communities in Britain over the years but mainly during the late 1960s and the first half of the 1970s. It would seem that in the late 1970s a number of developments occurred which led to the demise of such groups but their contributions to the kinds of politics which have followed in the 1980s have been almost entirely overlooked by academic commentators. Before suggesting some of the ways in which these groups contributed to the public agenda I want to mention very briefly some of the other kinds of politically-oriented groups which have appeared from time to time since the 1950s.

These have been of two kinds. First, there have been branches of political parties in the West Indies such as the People's National Party of Jamaica, the People's National Congress and the People's Progressive Party of Guyana, and so forth. These groups inform people about developments in the Caribbean, receive political leaders when they visit Britain and provide ready forums during moments of political crisis (such as the invasion of Grenada in November 1983) and natural disasters (such as Hurricane Gilbert in September, 1988).

There is a second type of political group which is concerned with developments 'back home'. This is the largely single-cause type of group which seeks to highlight a particular issue or to nurture support for a specific cause. Prior to the 1960s these had to do mainly with the colonial question (Carter, 1986, chapter 3) but as political independence became the order of the day the focus changed to specific issues which were of concern in the region. An excellent example of the post-independence single-cause kind of group has been the Caribbean Labour Solidarity based in London. This group sets itself the task of informing the concerned about labour issues in the region as a whole (including the non-English speaking Caribbean) and seeks support for or against specific government measures. The group does not, however, restrict itself exclusively to issues of labour. Its radical orientation leads Caribbean Labour Solidarity to espouse a wide range of related issues. For example, one issue over which it has been very active since 1983 is the trial of Bernard Coard and his colleagues in Grenada for the alleged murder of Maurice Bishop, the popular New Jewel Movement prime minister after the 1979 revolution. In the 1970s, however, one of the group's main causes was to bring pressure to bear against the industrial relations law of the People's National Party government which was closely patterned on Edward Heath's unpopular 1971 Industrial Relations Act.

In the main, however, politically-oriented groups in the West Indian communities in the crucial period from the late 1960s to the late 1970s were concerned with events in this country rather than in events taking place 'back home'. This comment is not to belittle the inspiration they drew from developments abroad. The US civil rights and radical black power movements, the Caribbean expression of black power, particularly in the writings of Walter Rodney, the struggles against white entrenchment in Rhodesia and the Portuguese territories and, of course, the struggles of the Vietnamese people against the Americans were perceived to be parts of a concerted blow against imperialism. In this way the critical position over British society which these groups sought to articulate was not in isolation from a wider world view but their main concern was to relate directly to problems of their communities. These groups were concerned essentially with the question of *community-definition*, *people-identity* and a radical/marxist *critique* of the location of black people in British society.

These concerns were in sharp contrast to the kinds of political orientations which hitherto existed. Apart from those groups which were concerned with politics in the West Indies there were individuals who sought to locate themselves within existing political institutions and who, if only by virtue of being black, constituted some kind of West Indian presence. Lord Pitt of Hampstead and the late Lord Learie Constantine were of course the most well known of such individuals. But there were others, perhaps less well-known, who were members of the Communist Party and such left-wing fringe organizations as the International Marxist Group, International Socialist, and so forth. Additionally, the work of WISC, although essentially of a broker kind, also involved the organization in activities which were at least ostensibly political.

From the perspective of the relationship between such individuals and the West Indian communities these politics were mildly *patrician* in character. This is not to suggest that these individuals and the organizations they operated within were necessarily anti-democratic as would be expected in patrician type politics. Indeed, the contrary may be nearer to the truth in most instances because such individuals were attempting to work within organizations which took the tradition of British liberalism seriously. But insofar as they could be said to *represent* West Indians these individuals stood in the relationship of *patricians* to *clients*. Their claim to *leadership* was not based on any straightforward understanding of delegated or representative notions of democracy but almost entirely on a notional typicality: a black person in a given place is seen as a representative of other black people by virtue of a common blackness and presumed identical experience. There was also a class dimension to this form of representation. Most of these individuals carried something of the universally recognized middle-class' sense of the 'right' or 'duty' to 'represent' the case of the less fortunate fellow as they perceived this. And the vast majority of West Indians during the periods of entry and initial settlement between the landing of SS Empire Windrush in 1948 and the 1962 legislation which sought to bar black people from entering Britain, were indeed less educated than these individuals several of whom were professional men and women.

Patrician politics entailed emphasizing some aspects of the tactics of the *broker*. These tactics involved patricians negotiating with leaders of the majority white population on behalf of clients (the West Indian communities); establishing contacts with the liberal and more tolerant wings of the British socio-political leadership; making representation or registering protest on behalf of clients over matters which affected clients - but not necessarily leaders - in specific ways. The *patrician* sought to provide sincere leadership for West Indians but at a distance from the communities themselves. The leadership of the patrician appears to have rested on a *hope* and a *confusion*. First, there was the belief and/or hope that the integration of black folks into British society and institutions would occur smoothly. Secondly, there was a confusion between, on the one hand, individual success in gaining access to major institutions and social acceptability and, on the other hand, a declared willingness on the part of white majority society to treat other black people in much the same way as the few black professionals. It is well to remember that the presence of individuals of this kind, with higher professional skills, predates the entry of a sizeable body of black working people (Green, 1986) during the immediate post-World War Two period.

The dual search for *community-definition* and *people-identity* of the new groups which existed between the late 1960s and the mid-1970s rapidly developed into becoming the main force in the West Indian communities. It is perhaps the recognition of this fact that has led Gilroy to place as much emphasis as he does on *culture* in his account of how West Indians have been constructing a sense of *peoplehood* in Britain (Gilroy, 1987). Much the same emphasis is to be found in Pryce's contribution to this volume. In sharp contrast to groups of the *patrician age* these new bodies were very strongly community-based organizations and registered a sense of *belonging* to the wider society which was hitherto absent in the West Indian communities. This was, of course, paradoxical.

The first generation of West Indians felt that they were living out of suitcases and camping here before the return and at the same time had a strong sense of *belonging* here. This was because they regarded England as being the *mother-country*. *Afterall, a disproportionate large part of their schooling had been dedicated to nurturing an understanding of the glory that was England's, and some West Indians had fought voluntarily in two world wars for England's survival. The travel to England was, therefore, very much like the *internal-migration* both within the Caribbean region and within specific countries such as Jamaica and Guyana. This new wave of migration was part of a long history of physical mobility within a common British enclosure. The sense, however, of *belongingness* for this first generation of post-World War Two West Indians was soon shattered as the titles of some books on this experience suggest (Hines, 1966; Carter, 1986; Cross & Entzinger, 1988).

The natural response of partially withdrawing into themselves led, in turn, to a partial isolation of the majority of this first generation with their cares, concerns and fears. With time these helped to transmit, on the negative side of the account, a message of despair resulting in a sad complement of an increasingly marginal sub-culture of black unemployed and perhaps unemployable youth (Rex, 1988; Hall, et al., 1978; see, also Haskins, 1988). On the positive side, however, the despair gave way to the more hopeful voice of protest and although there is a limit to the politics of protest (Goulbourne, 1988b) with protest came engagement and the beginning of active participation in the mainstream democratic political process.

Following on from the experience of partial withdrawal and isolation, it was not surprising that in the early 1970s many parents failed to understand the frustrations of their children who were naturally experiencing difficulty accepting the lowly positions society had demarcated or earmarked, for them. Equally, many of the young felt that their parents did not quite understand the new situation. The new sense of belonging that was being articulated was not of the imperial kind the first generation knew; it was perhaps more attuned to the kind of belongingness white majority English people were themselves groping towards: the belonging which defines the condition of being the kind of *British* which is definable by the specificities of territory rights and homeliness. It was no longer enough to be British but with a home in Jamaica or Barbados; Britishness now meant being legitimately at home here in the United Kingdom. And this entailed changing, or at least questioning, the assigned inferior status of West Indians in British society. This, of course, was an entirely new dimension to life in Britain. It was new for the majority white population; it was new too for parents and managers of the state; and for the new generation who looked backwards, forwards and at the present with anger there was an insufficiency of the patience which nurtures an appreciation of a sense of the history into which the present was only one moment.

The politics of *critique* and informed protest which characterized these years did not allow for a ready or unqualified admission of the appellation 'British' to the activities of these groups. With hindsight, however, they very clearly were. And, in a sense, they were situated at a point in time between the first and second generations of people of West Indian backgrounds. The individuals concerned were nearly all born and received their early socialization in the West Indies. Some, however, were brought up in the United Kingdom. The connecting points between these sub-groups, however, were first a common experience of reassessment and youthful expectations. Few had any experience of the factory or the work process which had been the lot of the first generation and some of the young were either undergoing tertiary education whilst a few were just about to commence 'middle-class' employment of one kind or the other. Those who were directly from the West Indies tended to be from middle class backgrounds and those who were brought up in the UK had more formal education than their parents, that is post-elementary education. The *spokespersons* or *leaders*, as well as some members of the groups, were likely to be more sophisticated in the social weaponry necessary for survival in Britain than their parents had been in the 1950s-60s.

The groups I am speaking of here could be further subdivided into several types, depending on the nature of their political orientations, aims, tactics and so forth. I want, however, to mention very briefly just some of these.

First, there were those organized around the written word – bookshops and publications. Of the latter kind there was in the 1970s the **Black Liberator** under the leadership of Xavier Cambridge and Cecil Gutzmore; **Race Today** led by Darcus Howe, Leila Hussain and the poet Linton Kwesi Johnson in Brixton has been going strong from the 1970s. In North London the intellectual and poet John LaRose's **New Beacon** bookshop and publishing house has been in existence from even earlier, the late 1960s. And in West London Jessica and Eric Huntley's **Bogle L'Ouverture** publishing house and bookshop [10] have been in existence for a similar period. In nearly all these cases there were strong points of connections between those from the West Indies who travelled with some political experience and the new and fledgling generation.

These organizations and others like them have provided a wide range of services to the black communities in different parts of London. They provided forums for political views to be expressed; opportunities for young black writers to feel wanted; places where both black and white people in search of answers to large questions could turn without ever feeling that they were not wanted or that they were intruding. Additionally, these publishing concerns have worked closely with more broadly based community groups in their localities. For example, **New Beacon** has been intimately associated with the North London Black Parents Association and Howe and his colleagues have formed the **Race Today Collective** in the heart of Brixton.

There was a second type of political group during these years. Indeed, it was out of these more stridently political groups that **The Black Liberator** and **Race Today** (the two groups Hall, et. al. (1978) singled out, not entirely justifiably, as warranting serious analysis with respect to the 1970s), may be said to have grown insofar as the founders of these publications were first active members of one of the two most important political groups of the critical decade of the late 1960s and the first half of the 1970s. These were the Black Unity and Freedom Party (BUFP) and the Black Panther Movement (BPM). Both groups grew out of the United Coloured People's Alliance (UCPA) (Egbuna, 1971) which aimed to build a united black political front against both common and differential racism faced by Britain's ex-colonial peoples.

It is of these groups that Sivanandan wrote rather nostalgically but eloquently:

> We related both to the struggles back home and the struggles here, the struggles then and the struggles now, the struggle of Gandhi and Nehru, of Nkrumah and Nyerere, James and Williams, of DuBois and Garvey – and the ongoing struggles in Vietnam and 'Portuguese Africa', in Guinea-Bissau and Cape Verde – and the struggles for Black Power in the United States of America. They

> were all part of our history – a beautiful massive texture that in turn strengthened the struggles here and fed back to the struggles there – and of course we were involved in the struggles of the oldest colony, Ireland. And *black* was a political colour (Sivanandan, 1983, p.3).

If there is something of Sivanandan's hyperbolic style here it is nonetheless to be preferred to the tendency to underplay or outright deny the proper importance of these groups which has two quite distinct sources.

The first deny that these groups played any important role at all in the black communities. Those who hold to this view are not entirely ignorant of the groups' existence but there is a lack of appreciation of how they came to be of the order of importance I am suggesting they created for themselves. Trevor Carter's statement that these groups were 'hardly representative of a mass, class-based response from the black community' (Carter, 1986, p. 80) is perhaps typical representative of this perspective. It may not be intentional on Carter's part, but this kind of argument may be seen either as a remnant of the opposition within the black community itself to the philosophy of the black power movement of the 1960s and 1970s, or the argument may be reflective of the general ignorance which exists about these groups.

A second source of denial of a place for these groups is located within the academic community itself and is perhaps based more on ignorance than anything else. Now, the fact that West Indians protest over their conditions has been the cause of much upset to the British socio-political establishment. This is, of course, perfectly understandable; it would be most unusual for the political establishment not to be concerned about protest from any segment of the population. But less understandable has been the worry caused by specifically West Indian groups in Britain. This perspective informs the view of several leading academic analysts (for example, Dench, 1986) who consider the result of black protest in Britain to be rather counterproductive. Again, this position must be well taken and be separated from the kinds of polemics which seeks to denigrate academic debate and sinks it into a quagmire of intolerant and ill-informed squabble.

Two additional points may be made in response to both kinds of objections to the presence or legacy of such groups. First, without the work of such groups the kinds of participation of black people in the country's mainstream politics which are seen today may not have been possible. Secondly, it must be appreciated that nowhere in the diaspora have Africans and people of African descent been able to maintain a modicum of self-respect without *protesting* against the indignities inflicted daily against their humanity. Nor must it be forgotten that the first struggle of Africans outside Africa was to oppose the wholesale attempt to define and treat them as *non-human*. The struggle for human recognition may have been *formally* won with the acts of emancipation in England in 1838 and the USA in 1863, but these victories did not mean that the struggle to have the African in the diaspora regarded or accepted as a *person* was, or is, completely won. Protest is, perhaps sadly, likely to continue to be the major political tool for West Indians in Britain as long as discrimination acts as the major constraint against the emergence and development of a more equitable and just society for all irrespective of the colour or ethnic origins of people.

I want to suggest in very bald terms some ways in which the groups I am speaking of here contributed to the present situation in which West Indians have returned to mainstream politics in this country and may therefore overcome the drift towards the politics of despair which results in partial withdrawal.

It must be admitted from the outset, however, that not all the contributions of these groups to the present situation have proved to be of a positive kind. One example of the negative contribution of the politics of protest in the 1970s which has become evident in the 1980s is the feeling that it is legitimate to opt out of participation in some institutions. In the 1970s it was part of the politics of such groups to condemn individuals who sought to become active members in institutions of higher learning out of a fear that products of such institutions too readily abandon the black community. This was a simplistic reading of a complex situation but was, fortunately, soon abandoned. The same negative attitude towards joining the police force has not, unfortunately, been abandoned but, rather, nurtured into becoming a dogma as noted in the Introduction to this collection.

The West Indian community in Britain in the post-World War Two period, I would suggest, was however reminded of the crucial fact of the importance of protest in the history of black people outside Africa. The BUFP in particular was acutely aware of the limits of spontaneous protest into which the leadership of the black community seems to be sliding in the mid-1980s. The group did not embrace the then fashionable view that populist leadership could save the black communities in Britain. The group's position was that disciplined leadership was necessary and it therefore perceived protest as one of several legitimate ways of articulating the grievances of the oppressed and exploited. This, it was believed, had to be done in conjunction with other oppressed groups irrespective of colour (for example, the Irish) as well as the working class - when it awoke to the historical mission Marx had optimistically charted for it.

A third area in which a significant contribution was made was with respect to developing an awareness of black culture and pride. The long history of varied achievements, which has been vehemently denied by western civilization, had to be reconstructed and re-learnt from a new perspective. Lessons about African, Caribbean, Afro-American, etc., histories were organized outside the formal educational system. Cultural groups, which emerged in the later years of the 1970s, are developing this perspective but with the limitation that this kind of work is sometimes seen as an end in itself and not part of a greater whole. In other words, the present search for ethnic or racial differentiation was yet to be actively embarked upon. How, therefore, the 1960s-70s search for community-definition and people-identity contributed to this process needs to be examined.

These groups, furthermore, made a lasting contribution to the black communities by helping to ensure that some crucial issues were placed on the public agenda by the late 1970s and the early 1980s. Their work involved getting the West Indian communities to think more in terms of permanent settlement rather than an imminent return to the Caribbean. This was achieved, first, through an attempt to account for the presence of non-white peoples in Britain. Secondly, these groups itemised for the black community, the general public and relevant public bodies the specific questions of education, police brutality, black prisoners, the judicial system and black unemployment. The fact that by the late 1970s these had become commonplace items in public discussion owes a great deal to the work of these groups. Today, however, the prevailing wisdom would seem to suggest that these issues are being highlighted through the majority society or the state's desire to do the good thing by black people. This seemingly benign view of the situation denies black groups, particularly the highly influential BPM and the BUFP, their rightful place in the constellation of organizations which have worked for a better society in Britain.

This denial may be due to at least three closely related circumstances. As we noted in the Introduction, the sociological outlook in the literature on race relations in Britain has tended to dominate the field. Political analysis has not sufficiently been brought to bear on this area of life in contemporary Britain. Secondly, the mutual suspicion of researchers and members of such groups, particularly in the crucial decades of the 1960s and 1970s, meant that goodwill and access were not always forthcoming. Some analysts who have considered this question have made much the same point (Jacob, 1986; Ben-Tovim & Gabriel, 1982) but have not been able to point to ways of overcoming them.

A possible third reason for the implicit denial may be the fact that the influence of these groups were more *indirect* than *direct*. In other words, these groups did not set out to persuade or influence decision-making bodies or government over the issues raised. Indeed, there was much scepticism about this kind of politics, as reflected in the low voting intentions and turnouts shown in earlier essays. Instead, these groups sought to influence the thought and behaviour of members of specific communities on the problems they faced. This task was undertaken in the belief that if communities understood what was happening to their young people with respect to the schools, the police, employment and so forth, these communities would themselves attempt to change what was happening. The influence of these groups, then, on the public agenda of the late 1970s and the 1980s, must be viewed from the perspective of community action rather than in terms of direct relationships with the state, either at local or national levels.

Conclusion

It is important to construct a history or histories of these groups and thereby rescue them from the oblivion into which they have been abandoned. Such a history or histories would enable us to look more closely at the contributions of these groups to the kinds of politics West Indian people have participated in during the 1980s. A crucial aspect of this will undoubtedly be an appreciation of how the politics of identity and self-definition came to be transformed into the politics of involvement and engagement with the major political institutions in the land. To one degree or another this may be true for groups in other minority non-white communities in Britain but for various reasons not only may it be easier to identify the role of groups in other non-white communities but it is also much more necessary. Fortunately, it is not too late to retrieve what is an important element of these parts of the still ill-defined segments of the British population. If this is not done, then there is the possibility that much of our present ignorance or misunderstandings about the work of these groups and the nature of their contribution to politics will become the received wisdom of tomorrow. These notes are offered as a contribution towards a long overdue recognition and reassessment of a dynamic situation which partly established the basis for the kinds of politics which have become fairly commonplace in the 1980s.

Notes

1. The tone of this part of the book certainly runs counter to much of the good will Bourne and Sivanandan, correctly even if grudgingly and patronizingly, accredited to Rex in their general attack on 'the sociology of race relations' (Bourne & Sivanandan, 1980).
2. Howard's work contains an excellent bibliography on the 'black-led' churches in Britain as well as the churches in the Caribbean and elsewhere.
3. Charman estimated a growth rate of 5% (Charman, 1979, p.44) but it appears that this has increased (Howard, 1987, p.11).
4. Clive Harris' work on the released Cabinet Papers for the years of entry in the late 1940s and the early 1950s, is providing evidence of this (Harris, 1986).
5. It should be noted also that, as in America, it is in the black churches that many popular musicians first discovered and nurtured their talents & love of music.
6. Arif Ali's compilation is invaluable but it is not exhaustive because there are those groups which do not get a mention, no doubt because they do not want to be included in a collection giving information to a large and unknown general readership (Ali, 1986).
7. For a profoundly antipathetic and distorted treatment of West Indian cultural forms and efforts see Khan (1978).
8. Guyana and Trinidad are, of course, the exceptions. With the present coalition-type government of Trinidad and Tobago quite deliberately reflecting the African and

Indian groups in the country it is clear that West Indian leaders cannot afford to be complacent.

9. Heineman (1972) listed about 16 affiliated groups for 1966; in the June/July issue of the organization's journal **Team Work**, 31 groups are listed as members. These vary from associations of West Indian nationals to sports clubs, from occupational groups of teachers and medics to parents' groups; both radical and conservative groups are included as are groups concerned mainly with developments in the West Indies and those concerned essentially with conditions in this country.

10. The bookshop has been renamed after the distinguished Guyanese historian the late Walter Rodney who was tragically and cynically killed in Guyaana on Friday, 13 June, 1980.

8 Principles, strategies and anti-racist campaigns: the case of the Indian Workers' Association

SASHA JOSEPHIDES

Introduction

Distinctive characteristics of the Indian Workers' Association (hereafter the IWA) include its determination to form part of the British Labour movement whatever the obstacles and its great concern with the economic and political situation in India. These two areas of concern do not appear to be rivals but to enrich one another. Not only do we find, as with many immigrant leaders that the activists in the IWA had been politicised in India and brought that knowledge and experience with them, but in some cases people born here or who came over very young had their political consciousness fully aroused in respect of India.[1] The IWA's strong 'place of origin' orientation far from detracting from its work in this country, complements it. This is due to IWA members ability to draw on experiences of struggle in India, and to the fact that their political analysis is of the whole international system. Their political analysis is not at risk of becoming parochial because there is another country, ie. India, of which they have a special knowledge and to which they have a special attachment.

This leads to a third distinctive feature uniting the first two, which is that the IWA has a comprehensive political philosophy. A great deal of the IWA's work can be termed anti-racist but it is carried out in the context of their analysis of racism and is therefore quite broad. The significance of this is that although much IWA activity is clearly anti-racist and is a response to racism, it is not simply a reactive organisation. It has a political core and an agenda of its own. These aspects are part of its strength.[2]

Although I have been talking generally of the IWA this chapter is more specifically concerned with the IWA(GB). This group is to be distinguished from the IWA Southall which is a rather different type of organisation. The latter was set up in 1956 [3] and is not affiliated to the IWA (GB) although there have been linkages from time to time. The IWA Southall is also concerned with anti-racism and runs an advice centre, has a representational and campaigning role, and played a central part in 1979 when the National Front and the police invaded Southall. However IWA Southall deliberately avoids voicing any political positions and does not share the analysis of the IWA (GB).

For the rest of this chapter I shall outline the political analysis of the IWA (GB) as it relates to racism, and discuss how this analysis has predicated the type of relationship which evolved between the IWA (GB) and the Labour Party, as well as the IWA (GB)'s work on the industrial front in Britain. It is necessary to commence this discussion with a brief outline of the IWA's history.

Background

The IWA (GB) traces its origins to an earlier association by that name which was in existence in the 1930s. According to Desai (Desai,1963:pp.102–103) the first IWA was formed in the 1930s by a group of Sikhs and a few others who were mainly businessmen, students and professionals. It was confined in activities and membership to London (ibid). Most other sources consider the first IWA to have been created in Coventry in 1938. The IWA (GB)'s official account concurs with this view. Its founder members are said to have included Udham Singh, better known for having killed Sir Michael O'Dwyer at a meeting of the Asiatic Society and the East India Association at Caxton Hall in 1940 (Clark 1975, Sivanandan, 1982, p.3).[4] Hiro (Hiro, 1971, p.157) also names Ujjagar Singh and Akbar Ali Khan as co–founders. In interviews with IWA leaders, I was also given the names of Anant Ram, Kartar Singh Nagra, Abdul Hak and Babook Chima as founder members.

Other IWAs were also formed at around 1938. According to some published sources the bulk of the membership of these early organisations was pedlars (De Witt John, 1969:45). But there is also a mention of a business, a student and a professional membership (Desai, 1963, p.102–103). Udham Singh was himself an engineer and active trade unionist (Hiro, 1971, p.157).

According to most sources these early IWAs were largely concerned with the independence of India though there are different levels of emphasis as to the extent of this concern and on the differences between the IWAs and other Indian Associations (compare Desai, 1963, p.103 with Hiro,1971, p.157).

After the political independence of India and Pakistan in 1947 the IWAs in Britain went into decline but were reactivated in the early 1950s. Two reasons have been given for their reactivation (interview with Avtar Jouhal, 26.6.1985). One is that some members considered the independence of India to be a compromise between the representatives of the feudal lords and the colonisers and therefore felt there was still political work to be carried out in relation to India. The second is to do with helping Indian migrants in Britain. This help had two elements: the first was to deal with the problems of migrants who had not been issued with valid passports in India and came here on forged passports. This involved dealing with Indian officials and attempting to rectify this situation. The second element was dealing with the specific needs of Indians which are as a result of being in Britain.

As in most ethnic associations, IWA activists acted as 'social workers' for Indians, dealing with issues such as housing difficulties, the filling out of forms and so on. IWAs also served a social function showing films and providing cultural activities; and they provided a forum for political discussion with speakers, some of whom came from India and could give first hand accounts of the situation there.

IWAs were formed in all cities where sub-continental Asians settled, particularly in the Midlands. These IWAs were co-ordinated but independent until 1958 when they were centralised to form the IWA (GB).

According to most published sources the centralisation which was to occur in the IWA movement, came as a result of advise from Nehru when he visited Britain in 1957. He also advised the High Commission officials to help bring this about (Desai, 1963, p.104; Hiro, 1971, p.157). Although Nehru no doubt did give this advise members consider centralisation to have come about through a desire for unity and to be due to the efforts of IWA members.

Prior to centralisation the various IWAs were autonomous but had some links with each other and did similar work. Once centralised, local associations became branches of the national association, and the office-holders of the branches made up the General Council. The national office-holders and General Executive Committee were elected from this General Council. Policies and so on were decided on from the Centre and a third of the income of each branch went to the Centre. The aims and objectives of the centralised organisation in 1958 were stated to be
To organise Indians to:

i safeguard and improve their conditions of life and work
ii seek co-operation of the Indian High Commission in U.K towards the fulfilment of its aims and objects
iii promote co-operation and unity with the Trade Union and Labour Movement in Great Britain
iv strengthen friendship with the British and all other peoples in Great Britain and co-operate with their organisations to this end
v fight against all forms of discrimination based on race, colour, creed or sex for equal human rights and social and economic opportunities, and co-operate with other organisations for the same.
vi promote the cause of friendship, peace and freedom of all countries and co-operate with other organisations for the same.
vii keep its members in particular, and people in Great Britain generally, informed of political, economic and social developments in India; and to
viii undertake social, welfare and cultural activities towards the fulfilment of the above aims and objects.

Within the IWA (GB) political differences regarding India, Britain and the international scene eventually made themselves apparent. In 1967, the Naxalite uprising brought some of these to a head and split the organisation down the middle thereby bringing into being two IWA (GB)s; one led by Jagmohan Joshi, Teja Sahota and Avtar Jouhal (now known as the IWA (GB) Avtar Jouhal) and the other led by Communist Party of India <Marxist> members and sympathisers, (now known as the IWA (GB) Prem Singh).

Although after 1967 these two IWAs differed on a number of issues they also shared common ground and a common history. At the most formal level, the aims and objectives of the Prem Singh organisation as set out in the constitution remain close to the original constitution, although the item regarding co-operation with the High Commission has been removed. The Avtar Jouhal association's constitution has been totally re-written, giving more emphasis to anti-racist and anti-fascist work and reflecting its more militant position. In what follows I outline the position which stems from the Joshi faction and is continued in the IWA (GB) of Avtar Jouhal. I shall indicate the areas where there are differences with the IWA (GB) Prem Singh in context.

IWA (GB) Analysis of Racism

The IWA (GB) firmly recognises the earlier organisation of the same name by claiming the year of its own foundation as 1938. There are probably a number of reasons for this but the implied continuity between the Indian independence movement and the struggle against imperialism and racism in this country certainly fits in with the IWA analysis of racism. In their pamphlet of 1976 Smash Racialism and Fascism, the IWA (GB) sets out its position on imperialism and racism which relies on Marxist and Marxist Leninist analyses. The system of imperialism, the group argues, made it possible for the bourgeoisie of certain Western countries, through the super-exploitation of the colonised peoples, to make super-profits. They used part of these profits to 'bribe their own workers' in order 'to create something like an alliance ....between the workers of the given nation and their capitalists against the other countries' (ibid, p.2). With the crisis in imperialism, and the attendant need to reduce the wage bill through wage cuts and redundancies in order to remain competitive, it is necessary to convince the working class that it is the black immigrants who are bringing about the deterioration in their living conditions. The task of doing this belongs to the fascists. The group argues that it is:

> relatively easy for (the fascists) to spread the poison of racialism because racist propaganda has, over the centuries, been implanted in the minds of the working class by the colonialists and subsequently imperialist bourgeoisie in order to maintain its super-exploitation and plunder of the peoples of Asia, Africa and Latin America... the anti-black propaganda of the fascists is not an end in

itself; it is a means to an end, namely, (through creating divisions) to smash the working class movement and its organisations with a view to serving the interests of state-monopoly capital (ibid, p.3).

The IWA therefore consider the task of fighting racism to be inseparable from the creation of a strong united working class movement. Because of this, as well as organising around specific campaigns to do with racial discrimination of every kind, the IWA has put much of its effort into organising within the labour movement. At the same time they recognise that many working class white people are racists and believe this obscures the class nature of racism. Because many white workers have been corrupted and brainwashed and because black workers, through their struggle against imperialism in their own countries and their double exploitation in this country have become more aware, black workers must take up the initiative of fighting the enemy, the capitalist class. This is not only for themselves but also for white workers and white workers would join black workers in this struggle. They argued thus:

> We feel unity will develop in struggle. This does not in any sense deny the need for black workers to have their own caucuses in every factory and place of work. We do not advocate separate black unions; that would be to play the capitalists game of dividing the working class. (Report of the General Secretary, IWA (GB) Avtar Journal, 1970, pp.21-22).

The IWA also recognise that black people who are not workers are nevertheless the victims of racism and must not be excluded from the struggle, but consider the black workers to be the group destined to lead the fight against racism. Black workers have therefore to be organised and be united. This has to take place, however, within the context of the labour movement because although the initiative for the struggle rests with black workers, success depends on white workers uniting with them. IWA members, therefore, like to see themselves as strong trade unionists who welcome alliances with all other multi-racial, progressive groups.
This is one of the areas where the two IWAs have a different position. The IWA (GB) Prem Singh does not attribute a special role to black workers and considers that the initiative for the struggle has to come from the working class as a whole.

This analysis of the British and racial situation leads the IWA to believe that it is important to form alliances, particularly with other black groups. The IWA was involved in the general effort to create a coordinating Committee Against Racial Discrimination (CARD) in 1960/61 in which they worked with the Standing Conference of West Indian Associations, and several other immigrant groups. In 1968, in the wake of Enoch Powell's anti-black speeches the IWA was one of the founding members of the Black People's Alliance, and their then general secretary, J.Joshi, was the convener of the steering group (Guardian, 29.4.1968). The IWA has been involved in many other groups [5] and is at present involved with the campaign against racist laws (CARL).

Consistent with this position, the IWA does not involve itself with any of the bodies set up by what it regards as racist governments. Initially this referred to the National Committee for Commonwealth Immigrants and its various sub–committees and panels. As new bodies were formed, such as the Commission for Race and Community Relations and the Commission for Racial Equality, the same position applied. Their stand on this issue is as follows:

1. A principled stand not to be involved in anything that looks like a whitewash,

2. The belief that if these bodies are to exist the impetus for creating them should come from the immigrants themselves,

3. An objection to immigrants being invited as individuals; the IWA would only participate as representatives of their organisations. (from interview with Avtar Jouhal. 5 February 1987)

The reason for this position will become clearer when we look at Labour Party legislation and the IWA's response.

Relationship with Labour Party

It might be thought that the Labour Party would be a natural ally for the IWA but although some IWA (GB) members belong to the Labour Party and recently two IWA (GB) members have become Labour Party councillors, the IWA (GB) has not been able to give unqualified support to the Labour Party. This is because the Labour Party's legislation on race from 1965 was considered racist and so were the remarks of certain Labour MPs.

For example, while the 1962 Commonwealth Immigration Act was seen by many, including sections of the Labour Party, as racist, in 1965 Harold Wilson's ministry, far from repealing the Act, produced the White paper which confirmed the Act and further restricted Commonwealth immigration by limiting the numbers of migrants who could come to Britain. By doing away with 'C vouchers' the Labour Government also prevented unskilled migrants from the Commonwealth entering the country. At the same time the Government introduced the Race Relations Act of 1965. This Act brought the Race Relations Board into being and introduced limited legislation on racial discrimination.[6] The white paper also provided for the setting up of the National Committee for Commonwealth Immigrants (NCCI) under the Archbishop of Canterbury.

The logic behind this package was that the NCCI through its voluntary liaison committees would provide some form of integration and racial harmony while the race relations board would deal with complaints through its conciliation committees. However, there are more sinister interpretations which can be put on it. For example, Ramdin writes 'The thinking behind these bodies was to weaken the rising militancy in the black community by integrating the leading lights (in CARD) within the state's designs' (Ramdin, 1987, pp.496–7). The IWA has also voiced these views and it is probably this perception, that governments 'creamed off' black leaders, which has led them to the position to refuse to sit on committees in their individual capacity.

But their main objection at the time was that the NCCI was a product of the White paper. The IWA wrote of the NCCI that 'The National Committee cannot succeed. Because it is the product of a racialist document it has not the trust of the immigrant communities in Britain' (IWA, n.d., p.13). The document continues:

> The National Committee should be dissolved and a Conference of all immigrant and inter-racial organisations called. Race relations have now become a sizeable industry but the interests and views of the immigrant communities have been neglected. Only if the immigrant organisations are consulted can the government hope to know their problems and gain their cooperation in achieving racial harmony (ibid:14).

When, for example, Avtar Jouhal of the IWA was called upon to sit on the Employment panel of the NCCI he refused saying he could not accept an invitation in his individual capacity.[7] On another occasion the IWA and three other immigrant organisations boycotted a meeting of the NCCI saying it was a 'smoke-screen concocted very shrewdly by the Labour Government to cover state sponsored racialism'.[8]

The NCCI in any case collapsed a few years later when all 22 committee members gave their letters of resignation to the Archbishop of Canterbury as a protest against the introduction of the 1968 Immigration Act (better known as the Kenyan Asian Act). A newspaper story reporting the resignations added that: 'The NCCI has been disheartened and outraged by the Commonwealth Immigrants Act'.[9]

The IWA had more cause for dismay when Oscar Hahn was appointed Chairman of the West Midland Conciliation Committee and immediately after his appointment left Birmingham on a trade mission by Birmingham Chamber of Commerce and Industry to South Africa. The IWA stated:

> Mr. Hahn's visit to South Africa is objectionable because it implies double standards. On the one hand he is concerned with racial integration here, on the other trade with a segregationist state......A chairman who acts like this cannot have the confidence of the immigrants.[10]

Subsequent legislation, each time introducing more immigration controls and at the same time palliatives in the form of race relations acts and race relations bodies, made the IWA further disillusioned with the Labour Party.

Although the IWA has campaigned for some Labour candidates and has been instrumental in some Labour victories, it does not give blanket support to the Labour Party or endorse all of their candidates. In fact during the 1965 election campaign the IWA with other immigrant organisations drew up a statement urging all the voters in two constituencies where both Tory and Labour candidates had either made racialist statements or broken promises, to abstain from voting . They 'felt it was time to expose 'the lesser of two evils' theory which meant that the Labour Party, with a policy on the race question indistinguishable from that of the Conservatives, was getting immigrant votes' (Report of the General Secretary IWA (GB) Avtar Jouhal, 1967).

On the other hand, when an IWA member participates in Labour party politics he/she does not believe in separate organisations for black members. At the last Labour party conference, Bhagat Singh, a Labour councillor and IWA member, spoke against black sections saying they are not the real answer to people's problems and that certain individuals made them an issue and use them for their own purposes. He linked the movement for black sections to the attempt to form a black trade union in the past and recalls the position of the IWA at that time which was that separate organisation can lead to apartheid (Interview with Bhagat Singh 18.11.1987). Other IWA members, while sharing the position regarding the divisiveness of separate organisation, do not in any case see the point of the effort in getting more black people into parliament as Labour MPs. The president of the IWA (GB) Prem Singh queried whether there was anything to be gained in having Black politicians in parliament. People who are involved in Labour Party politics argue that there is a struggle to be mounted there too and they should be involved in that process. They also argue that there are no alternatives such as a revolutionary party and so black people must play their part in the Labour party – presumably, the next best thing.

Industrial Relations

Like all immigrants the first employment issue to effect Indian workers was finding work. Due to restrictive practices a number of industries were not open to Indians or only certain grades of work were available to them. One IWA member from Coventry described his experiences of trying to find work in the car industry around 1961 and stressed that the issue was colour and not merely being a newcomer to the area (interview, 5.7.1988).

> At that time people from Ireland, Scotland and Wales could come into Coventry and get a job in the car industry right away. We were of the feeling that we were also paying our rates and taxes so we should be entitled to jobs in any industry on fair grounds. So I went there and they told me there were three jobs. I said could I

> apply for one. Well they said as far as Personnel Department is concerned you can have the job the problem is with the union, there was a sort of closed shop, only union members could apply for the job. I said I am a union member. He said in that case you must go to Transport House, Union Headquarters in Coventry and get a card from them. That didn't apply to other people, only to coloured people. I went and asked them for a card. I didn't get a card. There was racial discrimination from the union and the employer. They couldn't give semi-skilled or any other job in the car industry (which was well paid at the time) to Asian immigrants. We in the IWA raised this issue from time to time.

This respondent had the same experience with Coventry City Transport:

> We couldn't get a job even as a bus conductor let alone as a driver. Normally they promoted drivers from bus conductors. But people from Ireland, Scotland and Wales could come here and apply for a job and get it straight away. So I applied for a job and didn't get it. Most of our people applied for jobs and didn't get them. For nine years we (IWA Coventry) kept going to the local council, which was Labour controlled, to put our case. Other councils in England were employing coloured bus conductors, why not Coventry? There was one convener who said as long as he was convener he wouldn't let any coloured people be employed as conductors. Eventually he retired.

Where Indians could find employment because of the strength and discretionary powers of white foremen and the frequent necessity to use Indian intermediaries, a system of bribery developed whereby workers had to pay for the privilege of getting work. This bribe would go to the foremen and sometimes the personnel manager (Aurora, 1967, p.81; Duffield, 1988, pp.43-44). The extent of the insecurity this created for Indians even once employed is stressed by Aurora who writes that 'even when the firm is keeping its workforce constant, some Indians are fired in order to employ in their place a fresh group for bribes' (Aurora, 1967, pp.81-82). A statement issued by Avtar Jouhal on behalf of the IWA stated that Indians had to pay up to £50 in order to get a job and then more in order to keep their job and be allowed to work overtime (IWA statement 2.3.63). The IWA claimed that it had been campaigning against the practice for the previous three years. Although calling for trade unions to take action against bribery and suggesting various punitive measures against the workers paying the bribes, the IWA statement and later interviews make it clear that they consider such workers to have been the victims of a racially discriminating society and the real problem to be combated to be that of discrimination (Express & Star 3.10.1963, Smethwick Telegraph, 4.10.1963).

The industry which did employ many Indian migrants was the foundry industry and in certain foundries large concentrations of Indians were allowed to build up. According to Duffield this situation developed because there were no strong unions in these foundries and therefore the 'gentlemen's agreement' which existed between unions, management and government and led to the control of the employment of immigrant workers and to their dispersal in other areas did not apply in the foundries. Paradoxically, although it was the lack of strong unions which enabled these concentrations to occur, the Indians, particularly those involved in IWA (GB), were determined to form powerful unions in their work place and the fact that they were there in such numbers provided them with the possibility of doing so. The reasons for wanting to unionise can be seen as twofold. To begin with, IWAs were committed to the labour movement as discussed above and therefore it was important in principle to join trade unions. Secondly, because of conditions at their work places it was imperative to have a strong voice.

The rise of the Indian shop steward movement in the foundries, the development of a racially segregated workforce and racially polarised trade unions are issues which have been analysed by Duffield (1988). Here I want to indicate the kinds of problems Indian workers were facing in these industries and the role of the IWA in mobilising around these struggles.

The strike at Coneygre Foundry in April 1967 is illustrative of a number of the issues which concerned Indian workers. Approximately 70% of the 500 strong Coneygre workforce was Asian. White workers were classified as experienced and skilled while Asians filled the semi and unskilled grades (Duffield 1988, p.86). In 1962 many Indian workers had joined the AUFW, the only union in the company, but found the white shop stewards inactive on their behalf. In 1966 those members and other Indian workers who were not yet union members all joined the TGWU and elected their own shop stewards (Ibid:87). In April 1967 due to falling orders, management closed one section and made 21 Indians redundant.[11] In an effort to avoid redundancies the Indians proposed work sharing as an alternative. The company rejected this. They then suggested using the 'last in first out' principle but this too was rejected (Ibid). The Indians, Pakistanis and one Englishman (in all between 350 and 370 people) walked out.[12] The TGWU did not make the strike official but gave its support.[13] The 150 AUFW members did not come out,[14] and a local AUFW official stated that his members 'were not involved in the redundancies and therefore not in the strike (Duffield, 1988, p.89 from, Express and Star 25.4.1967). The strike lasted four weeks and then the management gave in and took back ten of the 21. The rest 'did not wish to go back' (Duffield, 1988:89).

Besides its apparent success and the fact that it contributed to the growing realisation that Indian workers were not 'docile' other important features of this strike which were apparent in both earlier and later action by Indian workers were a) the ability of a union (the AUFW) to condone strike breaking when Asians were in dispute (see Duffield, 1988, p.88); b) the inter-union rivalry and racially polarised membership of the TGWU and the AUFW. This was to come to a head two to three years later in the same group of factories and formed an important part of the

Commission on Industrial Relations investigation and report (Commission on Industrial Relations, 1970); c) Finally, and this issue will be discussed further at the end of the section, the real and supposed influence of the IWA in instigating industrial action. Another form of racial discrimination or 'colour bar' the IWA worked to dismantle in earlier years, was the practice of providing separate toilets in factories for Asian and English staff (correspondence between IWA and AUFW, 1965–1966 relating to Midland Motor Cylinder Ltd). This issue, in at least one case, was taken up first with management and then with the union.

Many changes have come about since the heyday of the Indian shop steward movement in both trade unionism and in the foundry industry; indeed there is hardly an industry to speak of now. However IWA members still organise in the foundries and still encounter opposition to unionising in the smaller companies. D.C. Neville, now reopened as Goodridge Castings Ltd., is one such company (interview, 29.1.1988).

One new area in which the IWA feels it is necessary to organise workers is in the sweat shops, often Asian run, which are now proliferating in the Midlands. A case which received a great deal of publicity was the dispute at Raindi textiles and Supreme Quilting, both owned by the Raindi family. There had already been problems with low pay at the factories and the workers were attempting to organise within the TGWU. While the union was negotiating recognition, management sacked three TGWU members. The union gave the company a deadline for their reinstatement and recognition of the union. There was no response so the strike began, involving more than 180 of the workforce of 300. One of the directors said the strike was politically motivated and that the IWA had disrupted normally good relations between staff and management (New Statesman 17.12.1982). An IWA member said the workers (mostly Punjabi women and some lads) came to the IWA to ask for help and they put them in touch with the TGWU. Only 12–15 of the men took any initiative while 35–40 would not join the strike and broke the picket line. He and another IWA member stood with them on the picket line. They also went to their houses and spoke to their husbands and told them not to hassle the women or get in their way. (Interview 29.1.1988). Another sweat shop they were involved in unionising in the early 1980s was Sundring Khang. This was a much smaller company employing 27 to 28 people.

To return to the question of the extent of the influence of the IWA in these actions, it is very difficult to assess their precise role. One of the problems is that due to the paranoia of management which saw outside agitators in the form of IWA militants behind any unrest they publicly 'blamed' the IWA for all trade union activity. The IWA, for their part, were happy to take 'credit' for organising all activity, resulting in the press always publishing IWA statements on disputes and interviewing IWA leaders, particularly Joshi. So for their different purposes, employers, the IWA and the press make each dispute look as if it were IWA–inspired even when according to other sources the IWA had little or dubious involvement such as in the Imperial Typewriters dispute (Race Today Collective 1983). However, for the most part, given that in the sixties almost half of the Punjabis in certain centres in Britain were members of the IWA, these people were obviously adequately represented in these workforces, and therefore were bound to be part of any action, not as outside agitators but as part of the workforce.

The IWA's commitment to unionisation and collective action, as well as their political sophistication, would result in their members who were workers having a prominent role. In addition, the IWA as an organisation does attempt, whenever it can, to give leadership and support when there is industrial action, particularly when this action involves Indians or arises from racial discrimination. Examples of this have been given above and include raising funds, talking to other members of the community, arranging meetings, leafleting, putting workers in touch with the TGWU, standing on picket lines and so on. However, as various commentators have noted, while possibly playing a more prominent role than other organisations, they were not alone in giving this kind of support. Gurdwaras, for example, have also supported workers who were on strike (John, 1969, p.148).

A major issue is that the result of the IWAs reputation for being behind all industrial action and the fear of their influence, whether this was warranted or not, meant that they were able to threaten to utilise the strength of the Indian workforce nationally and thereby highlight possible consequences if it were to act in concert. For example, during the strike by Asian workers at Woolfs in 1965/66, although the strike had been organised by Southall IWA, Joshi of the IWA (GB) besides fund raising for the strikers, made it clear to the press that 'We are...asking all our members in local union branches, of whatever union, to get the factory involved blacked.'[15] During the Coneygre dispute he issued a press statement which made clear the possible unfortunate consequences. Besides the actual work carried out by the IWA in respect of any particular workplace, their reputation and the amount of newspaper space given them meant, particularly in the sixties and early seventies, that they were able to have an overall effect on industrial relations through spelling out the power of the Indian workforce.

General Anti-Racist Campaigns

The anti racist campaigns the IWA have been involved in have been extensive and cover many more areas than those outlined above. A particularly important campaigning area has always been on racist legislation and racist politicians. The IWAs have produced a great deal of literature and have also organised marches, demonstrations, pickets and meetings. For example when Harold Wilson, the then Prime Minister, visited Birmingham in 1968, the IWA demonstrated against the Immigration Acts (and two members were arrested on flimsy grounds. (Birmingham Post, 17, 18 & 19.6.1968) The IWA's have participated in, and often led, major demonstration on immigration, racism and apartheid organised and conducted in London in the last 25 years or so. They have also organised protests against Enoch Powell and the National Front both nationally and locally.

Although sceptical of the series of legislation introduced in 1965 and subsequently, about immigration and race relations in Britain, the IWAs have used legality to the full extent they could to fight racism. Calling for Enoch Powell to be prosecuted under the charge of incitement to racial hatred was one of the less successful attempts to use the available legislation. The IWA also campaigned on more specific and more local issues. One campaign which was widely reported in the press was the testing of the 1965 race relations act through immigrants acting as 'guinea pigs'. This particular campaign was co-ordinated by CCARD and involved groups of immigrants going into establishments in the Midlands known to operate a colour bar. If they were not served the establishment would be reported to the Race Relations Board. Public houses, hotels, restaurants, hairdressers and places of entertainment were the kinds of establishments visited (Mirror, Daily Mail, Guardian, 9.4.1965).

The IWA has also agitated over the problem of racism in education and housing. In education they called for the teaching of Asian languages in schools and have campaigned against the bussing of Asian school children. In terms of housing they have been active in objecting to rules which discriminated against immigrants acquiring council accommodation and in attempts to stop immigrants from living in certain areas. Another area of activity has been on the issue of illegal immigrants which the IWA has worked on, both as an issue and to help individuals threatened with deportation.

What is significant about the IWA is not the actual campaigns in which they have been involved. These are predictable given the areas in which racism has surfaced over the years. Rather, what has been significant has been the organizations' campaigning style which includes the ability to mobilise large numbers of people and to join with other groups. Equally important is their persistence. The fact that IWA leaders are extremely articulate people has also meant that they have been able to inform people of the issues likely to affect their lines through pamphlets and newspapers.

Conclusion

The IWA has been a particularly active black organisation with a strong political philosophy and an untiring leadership. It is always difficult to assess the extent to which particular changes are the direct result of the efforts of a particular group or a part of more general processes. In the case of the IWA there have been some clear victories such as in their work on the forged passports issue, their success in forcing specific unions to accept Indian members and in their campaigns for individual victims of discrimination. They have also added their voice to others in calling for things such as Asian languages to be taught in schools – something which is now becoming a reality. In fact many initiatives in which the IWA and other groups were involved and issues which they identified, have finally been taken on board by local authorities and other state bodies. Their work has therefore had an impact. Whether this spells the fruition or the death of the political importance of such initiatives is a different issue

More importantly, the IWA has consistently and systematically provided an organised opposition to racist parties and racist laws and to the erosion of the rights of working people. This work has had the result of raising the awareness of Indians and people in Britain in general and of establishing the IWA as an important political force.

Notes

1. For example one young man described being inspired by discussion groups held by Joshi (one of the most prominent IWA leaders) in the late seventies. He said that was the first time he heard of Marxism and wanted to see whether it held the answers to his questions. I asked him why he joined the IWA rather than one of the Trotskyist or Marxist Leninist groups. He said he was asking why people were so poor in India; why caste. He is now involved in anti racist work in Britain and human rights work internationally and sees relationships between the various questions he was asking.
2. Heinemann (1972, pp.221–223) makes the point that single issue organisations have shortcomings, while both Abner Cohen (1980) and Pnina Webner (1987) have suggested that successful organisations need a cultural or ideological base.
3. Report of the General Secretary of IWA Southall, 1974
4. Sir Michael O'Dwyer was the Governor of the Punjab at the time of the massacre of unarmed peasants and workers in Amritsar in 1919.
5. Many of these groups were formed to organize particular campaigns or as defence committees. For example in 1971 the IWA co–organised a march against racialism with the Action Committee Against Racialism; in 1979 they worked alongside AWAZ and other black womens' groups within the Black Peoples' Committee Against State Brutality. The IWA has also worked with the Afro–Asian Caribbean Conference, helping them organize a lobby in 1962, and have published with other organizations, in 1961 producing *Immigration* with the Pakistani Workers Association and the West Indian Workers Association.
6. Paradoxically, providing the legal basis for Michael X to be prosecuted on the charge of incitement to racial hatred.
7. Unidentified newspaper clipping filed in Resource Centre under NC1, Centre for Research in Ethnic Relations, University of Warwick.
8. Unidentified newspaper clipping filed in Resource Centre under NC2, Centre for Research in Ethnic Relations, University of Warwick.
9. Article by Adam Hopkins, unidentified newspaper clipping filed in Resource Centre under NC3, Centre for Research in Ethnic Relations, University of Warwick.
10. Undated Evening Mail article filed in Resource Centre under NC4, Centre for Research in Ethnic Relations, University of Warwick.
11. Article by David Haworth, unidentified newspaper clipping filed in Resource Centre under NC5, Centre for Research in Ethnic Relations, University of Warwick.
12. NC5 IWA Statement, Centre for Research in Ethnic Relations, University of Warwick.

13. NC5, Centre for Research in Ethnic Relations, University of Warwick.
14. NC5, Centre for Research in Ethnic Relations, University of Warwick.
15. Article by Malcolm Southam, unidentified newspaper clipping filed in Resource Centre under NC6, Centre for Research in Ethnic Relations, University of Warwick.

9 Culture from below: politics, resistance and leadership in the Notting Hill Gate Carnival: 1976–1978

EVERTON PRYCE

Introduction

The Notting Hill Gate Carnival in London has come to reflect the love–hate relationship that patterns the conflict between young Afro–Caribbean blacks and the established order in Britain. Within the Carnival experience the symbol of reggae–music is employed to express resistance against the police, who are seen by the youths as enforcers of institutional class rule and social control. The police for their part, have now reified their role within the event as that of 'performers' and Carnivalists (not law enforcers). But the feel of anxiety and agitation within the event still lingers, although there is the appearance of improved organisation, the containment of young blacks, and the absence of any vocal utterances by the leadership reflecting the hidden ideological and structural contradictions of the event. If the promotion of the Carnival can now be regarded as a 'success' then it is worthwhile examining at what cost this success has been achieved.

This chapter examines, therefore, the crisis of leadership within the London–based Notting Hill Gate Carnival (hereafter referred to as NHGC) throughout its most decisive years 1976–1978, as represented by the struggle between the two rival Carnival Committees, the *Carnival Development Committee* (CDC), and the *Notting Hill Carnival and Arts Committee* (CAC), against a background view of the nature of the Black resistance movement in Britain. The chapter describes some of the major events surrounding the struggle for leadership–direction of the Carnival, and the postures struck by the leading participants. The work proffers a tentative explanation for the conflict, based on an examination of differences in (a) ideology, and (b) social support–bases, and argues that ultimately the dual leadership's ideological divorce from the real sentiments of young blacks is itself problematic.

Carnival in Notting Hill Gate, 1966–1976

Carnival in Notting Hill began circa 1966 (Hall, 1979)[1] as a relatively multi-racial, if not multi-cultural affair, with the white residents playing the dominant role in its organisation. The organisers, most notably an English woman, Rhaunee Laslett, and an English man, Anthony Perry, were concerned with expressing 'black culture' in its ambivalent and somewhat conservative diversity. These organisers, backed by the North Kensington Amenity Trust (NKAT) – a social work agency operative within Notting Hill – promoted Carnival, with its calypso and steel band music, as a fun-loving event in which all and sundry could participate, including the police, who gained favourable publicity from the event. At its best, Carnival in Notting Hill Gate for the first several years, was nothing more than a caricature of Carnival in Trinidad, reflecting the organisers' perceptions of black culture in Britain, as that of a passive, fun-loving people. A Trinidadian nationalist element soon began to cohere around the Carnival; and by 1975 the *Carnival Development Committee* (CDC) was established, chaired by Selwyn Baptiste, a Trinidadian musician. By the late 1960s and early 1970s small conflicts surfaced as increasing numbers of blacks demanded control of the event.[2] These conflicts, up to 1972–1973, had no clear ideological orientation.

In 1974, however, Leslie Palmer, a Jamaican, armed with tremendous organisational abilities and an acute sense of timing, seized the initiative and co-opted the support-base of the NKAT, proceeding thereafter in the years 1974–1975 to give to the Carnival a *new* cultural orientation. He introduced into the structure of the festivities the cultural content of reggae-music, that which had been responsible for sustaining the newly-emergent *street-culture* of black youths in Britain. The result was a dramatic increase in the number of people converging on the streets of Notting Hill; especially young blacks with allegiances to different reggae 'Sound Systems'.[3] In terms of the numbers, Carnivals 1974–1975 were spectacular successes.

But the Carnival's very success, especially in 1975, was problematic. The serious neglect of the event's administrative requirements fanned the flames of opposition. Local white residents in Notting Hill Gate, the local borough council, and the police of North Kensington, sought to have the Carnival removed from the streets of Notting Hill and imprisoned in the White City Stadium. Typical among the complaints from the opposition forces, were: the noise emanating from the newly featured reggae sound-systems, the lack of sanitary facilities, inadequate crowd control, and the increased need to police the event. The question of the role of the police polarised the competing forces within the Carnival, especially since the summer and autumn of 1975 had seen a series of confrontations between the police and young blacks in Brixton, Lewisham, Peckham, London, and Chapletown, Leeds, which had cast grave doubts on the future of good 'race relations' in Britain.[4]

The preparations for the 1977 and 1978 NHGC assumed the form of a highly politicised contest between the two rival Carnival Committees, the CDC and CAC about the ideology of Carnival, the scope of involvement of young blacks, and the nature of policing. What ensued was the mobilization of public opinion – by both the dominant white and 'subordinate' black media – on: 1) the idea of mass participation on the streets of Notting Hill Gate for the two Carnival days, and 2) the political mileage to be gained out of the struggle for political leadership within the black community.

The NHGC, however, is best understood as the two days of the year when many black people in the United Kingdom consider themselves to be in the *majority*. It is essentially an occasion when many black people come together to *assert* their presence culturally, politically, socially, and if needs be, violently, in symbolic affirmation of the mood of agitation endemic to the existence of black people in an overwhelmingly white milieu.

The Afro–Caribbean Diaspora and Cultural Resistance

Active defences of the cultural institutions of Afro–Caribbean blacks continued throughout their passage to Britain – from settlement (in the 1950s) to the establishment of communities (in the 1970s). As blacks in exile, they brought with them the objects and forms of their cultural practices; but these were to come under renewed intense pressure in the new multi–racial setting.

Beginning with the 'Race Riots' in Notting Hill and Nottingham in 1958, Afro–Caribbean blacks, as a set of communities, met the challenges of the manipulators of racist violence – the *British Union of Fascists* and their Teddy–boy working–class supporters – on a large and organised scale (Jones, 1978 pp.28–37). The black organisations however, were relatively short–lived. The decade of 1965–1975 saw many 'Black Power' and affiliated black organisations de–stabilised; and many blacks came to interpret the use of the legal charges of *affray* and the *Vagrancy Act of 1824* against them, throughout this period, as challenges to the Black communities. State action included systematic police harassment and attacks upon Black cultural venues and events, and upon black persons, political organisations, and cultural institutions. This was in spite of the fact that the culture of Afro–Caribbean blacks was represented then – in the main – in extremely 'private' ways, the content of its representational mode being, through black churches; multi–racial 'friendship' associations; clubs–shebbeens; 'roots'/ basement restaurants; private gambling dens; and private homes. Nevertheless, the confrontations produced, *inter alia*, the murder of Nigerian David Oluwale (1971), the Mangrove raid and trial (1972); the *Carib Club* police attack and the *Cricklewood 12* trial (1974–1975). The major raw *fascist* attack on the Afro–Caribbean communities in the period, occurred in 1980, in the form of the Sunderland Road bombings in Lewisham.[5]

If the intention of both state action and racist attacks against black cultural organisations had been to effect the repression, if not co-option of such organisations, the strategy achieved only partial and temporary success. The cultural presence of Afro-Caribbean blacks in Britain had been relatively 'dormant' over the period 1965-1971, but in 1973-1974 a *new* phenomenon occurred: the emergence of the UK-based *Rastafarian* movement (Campbell, 1980; Cashmore, 1979; Clarke, 1980).

Parallelling the emergence of Rastafarianism was that of militant *reggae-music.* Reggae music at this conjuncture played the role of linking the *style* and *form* of Afro-Jamaican street-culture to the *style* and *form* of the *street-culture* of young Afro-Caribbean blacks in Britain. And with the Rastafarian movement, these gave black youths an *orientation*, in that both *reggae* and *Rastafarianism* (Dread), assumed together, the appearance of and overt and mutinous *force* or *power* which the state - its concerned institutions and personnel - came to regard as a *threat* or as *potentially* threatening. this new development had permanently changed the qualitative content of black culture in Britain, and the agents of history that constituted this culture 'brought a distinct quality to struggle at the cultural level in their new metropolitan home' (Gilroy, 1982, p.285).

The re-emergence of black resistance in 1975 in the form of the NHGC, played the role of a decisive and challenging force against the state throughout the years 1976-1978. This black 'majority' asserting itself at Carnival time, affirmed the existence of a fragmentary political base of disaffected black youths whom black leadership - such as the rival Carnival Committees - seemed impotent to direct. A Black leadership, in the main, unprepared and politically ill-equipped to lead this actual or potential power-group, merely made flacid gestures of support for a category called 'the youth' in the belief that if this power were to explode such token support would guarantee its own political legitimacy.

To describe the leadership of the NHGC throughout this 1976-1978 period thus, is to admit at once that there exists a crisis of leadership within the black resistance movements of the late 1970s and early 1980s; it is to admit also, that both community-leadership and resistance-leadership within the black communities converge on the NHGC, and then diverge into serious dissension.

The Wind of Change: 1976-1978

The CDC of 1976 was composed of West Indians of various backgrounds, professions and political persuasions. The majority of its members were Trinidadians: steel-bands men, musicians, poets and actors. There is some contention surrounding the claim that these men are responsible for establishing a carnival tradition in Britain (Race Today Collective, 1977). This committee became in 1976 the victim of its own success when its organisational skills were severely tested. The tasks involved in organising an event such as the Notting Hill Carnival are immense especially when complicated by attacks from 'without', as was the case in 1976, which persists even into the late 1980s with a vengeance (Kirsch, 1988; Taylor, 1981).

In April 1976, the CDC met with the local authority of the Royal London Borough of Kensington/ Chelsea Council (KBC) and the police to discuss: 1) the proposed shift of venue to the White City Stadium, 2) the nature of the policing of the event, and 3) financial arrangements for the promotion of the festival. By late June and July of 1976, these matters remained unresolved, and the Committee proceeded with its plans to have the Carnival in Notting Hill over the August Bank holiday weekend. Senior police officers who had been engaged in the negotiations, decided to increase the number of police on duty over the two days from 60 in 1975 to 1,200 in 1976. Their decision seemed well informed, for a grotesque battle ensued in the streets of Notting Hill between the police and a section of the 250,000 revellers, most notably the younger West Indians. Carnival 1976 'provided a shock for the nation'.[6] Reports of the battle were relayed on television screens throughout the world, thus giving to the event political implications beyond the intentions of its organisers.

This occurrence brought with it mounting criticism from the CDC members against its un-elected chairman, for his lack of organisation of the event. The chairman, Selwyn Baptiste,[7] violently responded to the criticisms by vacating his post, with the intention of creating his own committee. In May 1977 the indictment of fraud was laid against Baptiste by the chairman of the liaison committee of the borough of Kensington and Chelsea, councillor Michael Cocks, in a letter to the Kensington News and Post (27 May, 1977). A subsequent widespread dismantling of Baptiste's remaining Committee occurred in the form of resignations, when it was further alleged that £1,500 were unaccounted for from a grant made to the 1976 CDC by the NKAT. Baptiste assertively responded to the allegations made against him by Michael Cocks saying that they were obstructionist 'tactics' (West Indian World, 3-9 June 1977; Laureen & Smith, 1977; Kensington News & Post, 3-17 June, 1977). Having protested his innocence, he receded into temporary obscurity.

The failure of the CDC leadership to provide a coherent explanation for the violence at the 1976 Carnival, and its paralysis in directing the resistance, together with the allegations of fraud and Baptiste's defiance, led to a widespread national feeling that incompetency and irresponsibility lurked within the Carnival Movement. The CDC's handling of 'private negotiations' with the police for the 1976 Carnival was belligerently attacked by Darcus Howe, then editor of the political (black) journal Race Today. Indeed, it was left to forces outside the Carnival Movement to provide explanations for the August 1976 debacle.

The process began with an attack upon the structure of West Indian leadership, by the then Labour MP for Teeside, Middlesbrough, Arthur Bottomley, who was quoted thus:

> West Indian leaders have not exercised as much authority and influence as they should. It is time they took over full responsibility

for the West Indian community and did not leave it to some elements of the Black Power Movement. (The Times, 1 September 1976)

The West Indian family structure was also seen as the root of the problem by The Economist

> Parental control within the West Indian community is ... breaking down ... In the aftermath of the Notting Hill Carnival, sensible black and white adult Britons must not minimise the black teenage problem that many urban Britons now face, and that even more now virulently resent. The special obligations on black adults ... should be to co-operate with the police against any sort of bogus soul-brother solidarity with muggers that can so easily take root. (The Economist, 4 September 1976)

There was much sympathy for the police. In a letter to the editor of The Daily Telegraph, a sullen resident of Notting Hill hinted at Britain's moral indignation at the heavy casualties that the police had sustained at the 1976 Carnival.[8]

Responding to the call for upright leadership of the Carnival Movement, the CAC emerged from the breakaway members of the CDC of 1976. In January 1977 it held a series of 'public meetings' in the borough of North Kensington to elect its members. Many ex-members of the splintered CDC were co-opted. Participants int he CAC election process were broadly-based: local community groups, members of the police, the Community relations Commission (CRC), the KBC, the NKAT, the Black Peoples Information Centre (BPIC), the Notting Hill Social Council (NHSC), and many other political, cultural and social work agencies (Gutzmore, 1978). The support-base of the CAC reflected the ideology of its chairman, Louis Chase, a Barbadian-born graduate of Oxford University, and a resident then of Notting Hill. Chase insisted that all members of a Notting Hill Carnival Committee ought to be residents of Notting Hill, and that there should be substantial representation of local black community groups on the committee. Because of the 'inefficiency, extremism and ugliness' (interview with Louis Chase, 8 April, 1978), of the deposed CDC, Chase felt that it had not been able to adequately manipulate the political issue of the Carnival, which to him, and his Committee, centred around the plight of the young blacks who revolted. Furthermore, the CDC, in his opinion, had not sought a 'mandate' from the people of Notting Hill to continue its existence; it had grossly underestimated the fact that the political dimensions of the Carnival stemmed from the image it ought to project of black people in Britain.

The CDC, in a last ditch scramble to regain respectability, regrouped under the intellectual leadership of Darcus Howe - a Trinidadian - and his collective. Howe, who had entertained doubts about the character of the CDC leadership[9] was subsequently elected chairman of a new CDC by the remaining members of Baptiste's faction. Howe pledged the support of Race Today in 'educating carnival enthusiasts and the interested public about the build-up to the festivities and the festival itself' (Race Today, Vol.5, No.71, 1973). Race Today (as a propaganda organ and political 'force' within the black community) had become for the new CDC the 'organisation and the platform to winning a police-free carnival and to placing before the Black community the democratic structures through which its cultural and political struggles would ... be extended' (op.cit. p.2). Through its Bulletin, Mas, the CDC stated its manifesto:

> We the steel-bandsmen, mas men and sounds men of the Carnival Development Committee wish to inform all that we are responsible for Carnival 1977, for without us there can't be a West Indian Carnival (Foot, 1977).[10]

This pro-Trinidadian, calypso-cum-Carnival posture of the CDC led to a massive intake of Trinidadians whose loyalties were to Carnival, Trinidad and a reinstated Baptiste now Director of the revamped CDC. The combination of the political orientation of the *Race Today Collective* and the cultural nationalism represented by Baptiste resulted in the consolidation of a firm ideological position within the new CDC.

The Response of the Rival Carnival Committees to Black Youth

In the years following 1976 - the year of 'defeat' of the police by young blacks at the Carnival; the year also that the history of the event changed in terms of demonstrating the potential power of blacks to resist cultural oppression by urban revolt - the police took the view that they had a responsibility to maintain 'public order' in the face of mass (Black) cultural presence on the streets of Notting Hill. The police effected a highly sophisticated campaign in crowd control at the Carnival in 1977, 1978 and 1979. Resistant young blacks were contained over these years. The divergent explanations of the political behaviour of young blacks at the Carnival, offered by the rival leadership of the event, denote a bifurcation of ideological/ political consciousness. Neither Committee had an adequate explanation for the persistence of the resisting behaviour of young blacks. But with the weight of public opinion, and the dynamics of state/sub-state funding agencies firmly demanding an explanation,[11] the 'forces' within both Committees moved with zeal to provide one.

At a general meeting at the headquarters of the CAC on 24 May, 1977, Louis Chase explained that his Committee's policy was based upon an understanding of the politics of confrontation between the police and young blacks in the black communities over the period 1974-1976:

> The Notting Hill Carnival cannot be seen as a non-political event - a mere cultural and artistic extravaganza. For it must clearly relate to some of the other needs and concerns of this community.

> It is political for we are dealing with the lives of a minority whose disadvantage has led to frustration ... (Chase, 1977).

The CDC leadership, by contrast, failed to acknowledge the political nature of black youth resistance to the police. Remaining true to its own interests, it indicted the police for being provocative and over-reactive (Race today Collective, 1977, p.13). Furthermore despite previous assertions that Carnival was not a mere cultural extravaganza (ibid), the CDC, when confronted with suggestions for changes in the organisation and management of the event – especially in relation to black youths – resorted to the notion that the Carnival was primarily cultural. 'The Carnival', according to one CDC member, 'is the theatre of the streets ... it makes no distinction between the performer and the spectator. Everybody is free to join in and have fun, and freak out'.[12] 'Carnival', said the CDC's Director, Baptiste, 'is all year round; it is a learning process for all of us. We learn dignity and we hope to gain respect. But we have no respect for those who hurt Carnival ... As musicians we feel that to use Carnival as a political platform ... is to hurt Carnival'.[13]

In the eyes of certain forces within the CDC, to 'hurt Carnival' – to focus on politics – meant devaluing the prestige inherent in the ability to control the most calypso/steel-bands on the streets of Notting Hill throughout the two Carnival days. To diminish the kudos of the competition between the bands, amounted to knowing 'nothing' of Carnival, which was equal to being anti-band, and anti-Trinidad, characteristics of 'dem Jamaicans' who sought to 'brok-up Carnival'. This same force within the CDC subsequently articulated a propaganda campaign in favour of the disbanding of the CAC because of its alleged failure to meet the requirement to 'produce a band'.

By contrast, the CAC's over-riding policy towards the event was that the Carnival should reflect the needs and aspirations of young blacks, since they bring to bear upon the event their latent frustrations and deprivation. Carnival, it insisted, is 'a celebration of the black community' (Chase, 1978). More important, black resistance within the Carnival experience is symbolic of an attack against the British state, and is therefore *political*.

The CAC, therefore, saw the need for the containment of this *resistant* force of youth by instituting preventive measures within the structure of the event: the provision of entertainment – predominantly competing reggae sound-systems – *on the ground*, which could give to the leadership a lever of control in police-youth confrontation. On this issue of containment of a 'disruptive element', both Committees were agreed. And though the problem was essentially one of the effectiveness of leadership/direction, both Committees handled it in terms of another question: what form of 'control' ought to be applied to the 'disruptive elements' within the corpus of young blacks at the Carnival?

The two Committees, in effect, wanted practical control of rebellious young blacks, but they differed in their conception of the institution of Carnival and thus, in the ideology/politics of youth leadership. For the CAC, the spirit of Carnival was best realised within a community-based

Carnival movement, responsive to the needs of young blacks, and focusing on preventive measures to contain potential rebellion within the Carnival experience:

> The Notting Hill Carnival is only the stage on which the youngsters act out the drama of their lives ... (it) dramatised the magnitude of something that has been minimised for years and further neglect and the absence of preventative action can only forecast, not hot summer's days as have taken place at Notting Hill during the past two years, but hot summers which will not be events for mediocre street celebrations (Chase, 1978, pp.4–27) [14] (emphasis added)

For the CDC, by contrast, the displaying of the cultural/artistic component of Carnival in venues divorced from the black community and rebelling youths (such as the Commonwealth Institute), was not perceived as antithetical to the spirit of Carnival. Indeed, the rebellion of the young, the CDC asserted, was symbolic of the generalised violence of the British state, and could not be contained by the kind of preventive action envisaged by the CAC within the Carnival structure:

> The state is aware that an energy which makes spontaneous battles and turns them into politically supported defences in court, is capable of generating fierce organisation in class combat ... Until land unless British society ensures that this growing section of the population gets what it needs and demands on its own terms, it will have no option but to turn up, looking for the main chance at public gatherings ... (Race Today, Vol. 5, No.11, 1973, p.17).

The CDC's position reflected a virtual abdication of practical responsibility for the behaviour of young agitating blacks.

On 8 June, 1978, Louis Chase resigned as chairman of the CAC out of the 'frustration ... experienced at the hands of the authorities and the lack of administrative facilities to carry out (his) functions.' (Interview with Louis Chase, 23 July, 1978).[15] The CDC was to manipulate the revelation to their advantage with bitter pique. Chase was roundly attacked as a 'Carnival Clown' and his involvement in the Carnival since 1976 condemned as an act of opportunist intervention. His Committee was also attacked as a conglomerate of 'political scamps' determined to make 'political capital' out of the Carnival.

Afro–Caribbean Identity in Britain

The crisis of leadership direction for the Carnival suggests not only the conditions under which Afro–Caribbeans struggle, but also the quality of their lives and their impact on British society. There is a crisis of Afro–Caribbean identity fulfilment in British society, which has its basis in the colonial complex of their background, and which, though determined economically, is nevertheless defined culturally (Allen & Smith, 1977; Allen, 1971; Moore, 1975; Miles, 1978; Hiro, 1971). The most significant dimension of this reality is the relationship that Afro-Caribbeans have to one another, that depth of involvement and unspoken recognition of shared experience which create a way of life. The isolation of the Afro-Caribbean within his own group is clearly illustrated, for example, in the initial disintegration of the CDC and in its inability to respond to criticism from within the community. Such situations which demand the taking of decisions and the defining of political and cultural objectives within the Afro-Caribbean community often generate contradictions and intragroup rivalry.

The *cultural* assertions that define the dominant directions of the Carnival's dual leadership, can be seen as a way of contending with the class-ascriptiveness of the wider British society, a form of adaptation. This on-going reification process explains how it was possible for both Committees to grandiloquently affirm the positive character of Carnival in ameliorating the status of Black people in Britain, while simultaneously engaging themselves in a divisive struggle for its leadership. The leadership of both Carnival Committees failed to adequately comprehend the nature of its own social group. Since the Afro-Caribbean community possesses few 'institutional' or 'model' leaders (Collins, 1957; Pryce, 1987)[16] and individual Afro-Caribbeans hardly accept those few members of the group in the traditional professional and political elitist framework as models for emulation, the Carnival Committees' rhetoric of Afro-Caribbean group solidarity via the Carnival evaded the problematic question of why the community leadership of the Carnival was itself fragmented.

Several factors account for this fragmentation of leadership. Firstly, there is the sociological argument which maintains that a less developed pattern of migrant leadership is evident among Afro-Caribbeans - as opposed to the Asian community, for example - and less opportunity for the minority to exert its own controls over its members (Banton, 1974). Secondly, such migrant leadership as does exist, tends to draw its support from loyalty-patterns based on island origin - relations voluntarily entered and maintained, rather than prescribed by factors like extended kinship. Thirdly, we may perceive struggles for positions of leadership within the Afro-Caribbean communities in Britain as expressions primarily of narrow self-interest and lust for power - despite the rhetoric of seeking to articulate the grievances of the less fortunate members of the black community. This does not seem to be merely an 'immigrant problem', as Bentley maintains (Bentley, 1970), which will disappear through a process of 'integration' or 'assimilation'.

In the specific context of the Carnival Movement, the fragmentation of leadership of the Afro-Caribbean community can be grasped via an examination of their divergent support-bases, underpinning ideologies and pragmatic strategies.

All the major groups involved in the Carnival (throughout the period under discussion) at the local level, have varying degrees of preoccupation with the racial question, and differing modes of operation. The CAC's support-base - the Black Peoples Information Centre (BPIC), the KNAT, the Notting Hill Social Council (NHSC), and the Community Relations Commission (CRC) - constitutes effectively, 'local political collectivities with wide ranging interests relating to the areas of North Kensington'[17] and Notting Hill per se, and differ accordingly from the support-base of the CDC - the Race Today Collective and other nationalist-oriented individuals/ organisations.

The support-base of the CAC's inter-racial mix naturally has much to do with 'race-relations' in Britain, though their activities may be defined as conducted within the narrow context of social work, counselling, advice-work, and self-help. This social support-base, in effect, represents and constitutes a long and shaky historical compromise in community solidarity in the Notting Hill district, when in the mid-1960s 'scores of joint white-black formal associations were formed ... under essentially white leadership' to fight campaign battles on housing, public service, and amenities issues, but always serving the 'limited interests of small groups, and quickly disintegrating' (Cohen, 1982, p.29).[18] In the absence of any systematic representation of the views of these groups vis-a-vis the Carnival crisis, however, we may say that they contributed the *community-leadership bloc* to the conflict.

The support-base of the CDC on the contrary, has a wider frame of reference, relating generally to the activities of Afro-Caribbeans in Britain, and to developments in their home countries.[19] The Race Today Collective's radical disposition daily becomes more sophisticated and receives legitimacy from black and white liberals alike who have found 'consciousness', and from grass-roots politicians who seek votes, and, perhaps, unity. To this end they further the intellectual creed of middle-class liberals who believe in a multi-racial society and the assertion of the dignity of the black man. The Collective, furthermore, has a long track record of providing militant leadership and organisation for the black community.

As a social force, the Collective is governed by a problematic theoretical and strategic appraisal of black politics: since the social relation, in its view, is multi-dimensional - involving politics, ideology, exchange, property, distribution, production, etc - the class struggle itself becomes multi-dimensional. There is strong support for this view in Stuart Hall's analysis of the representative positions of The Black Liberator and Race today (Hall, et al., 1979, ch.10).[20] Elsewhere Hall extends the analysis by arguing that Race Today supports 'the autonomy of class resistance and its necessary separateness just now', and that this characterises it as a 'Gramscian party in a sense', although 'It's not an organised party, but it has a formative and educative relationship to the black community' (Ibid, p.12). The political consequence of this, Hall points out, is that it 'lead(s) them into some very serious mis-analyses and cul-de-sacs. It leads them to take on a kind of sectarianism, in relation both to other currents in the black struggle and in relation to the white working class' (Ibid). When in 1977 then, the Race Today Collective (which publishes Race Today) assumed the position of spearheading the CDC, it was fully aware of its relative political strength, and knew that its policies on behalf of the CDC were likely to win mass support from different quarters within the broad political spectrum of Britain. Race Today, as a Collective, contributed the resistance-leadership bloc to the NHGC conflict.

These distinct profiles of political support-bases, when intersected at the point of the NHGC, further inspired dichotomous ideological perceptions and conceptions of the racial and class position of blacks in Britain.

The Ideological Dichotomy

The CACc's ideology vis-a-vis Carnival, subscribed to a notion of race-relations that would subordinate 'blackness' to the requirements of a national identity and acceptance in Britain, as the country which afro-Caribbeans have adopted. There was a 'Euro' identification in its aims, which ultimately determined the strategy it envisaged most effective for alleviating the depressed and frustrating conditions of young blacks within the Carnival. Its constitution as a community-leadership *tour de force*, held out for the operational-ization of its strategy, in political terms, a negative response to the problem it addressed, representing a 'response to the threat posed by alienated black youth'.[21]

The CDC, although in convergence with the CACc's assertion for the reinstating of black pride, clearly did not accept that the subordination of 'blackness' to the requirements of a national identity was a feasible strategy for alleviating the malaise of young blacks as expressed within the Carnival. Ideologically, the CDC was suggesting that the genesis of identity fulfilment must emerge from within the Black community and embrace a universal 'Black Brotherhood'; it is not blacks who need changing, but the social systems in which they exist. Hence the CDC's notion of *solidarity* as opposed to *change*. Ultimately it was not *what* the CAC demanded that invited the belligerent rebuke of the CDC, but *how* the CAC envisaged that its goals would be realised. The affected radicalism of the CDC exemplified a belief in a multi-racial *society*, as differentiated from a multi-racial *personality*, the character of the latter being the reinforcing of black inferiority feelings and the consolidating of presumptuous white overlordship. Conversely, the conservative-moderate CAC, and race-relations industry folks, similarly concerned with the image of the black man as equal to the white, assumed the acquiescent posture of respectable decency as defined by whites.

Both of the above ideological positions vis-a-vis the elements of resistance within the Carnival experience throughout 1976-1978, are manifestations of political bankruptcy, emanating from a historical, though not easily recognisable, entrenched political contradiction, probably unique to the Afro-Caribbean community in Britain: there is very little evidence that *political* as opposed to *cultural* achievement, is the dominant concern of Afro-Caribbeans, especially among their leaders. What is indeed evident is that political leadership elicits deep-seated aversions within the

Afro-Caribbean community against the politically ambitious, despite that leadership's vociferous claims that it advocates the cause of the community. This contradiction, seen in terms of the struggle between the CDC and the CAC, suggests that expressions of political extremism, conservatism or moderation are equally opprobrious to the cynical, especially the black youth whose particular place in British politics – as native Britishers, not migrant labourers – is yet to be decided.

This contradiction can explain the general inability of the political forces within the Afro-Caribbean communities, and those who sporadically make academic interventions into black politics, to translate racial awareness into class politics in Britain. Afro-Caribbeans necessarily bring to the class struggle in particular instances two racially determined ideological imperatives: 1) rejection of racial oppression, and 2) resistance to cultural hegemony, which distinguish them as a group from the indigenous white working class, and which make the attempt of neo-Marxists to articulate race and class in a non-reductionist mould problematic.

The contribution of Paul Gilroy to the debate should be briefly considered, since he denies that race and class are mutually exclusive concepts (Gilroy, 1982). Gilroy begins his analysis from the curious premise of firstly, accepting the independence of race relative to class and class struggle, and secondly, of trying to bring them into articulation. His attempt to do this consists essentially of arguing that black protest and resistance are reduced to class struggle in *racial appearances*, and he thus denies their formerly asserted independence. He therefore uses the concept of race as a social category without the necessary qualifications. The serious problem that this line of argument creates for Gilroy, and , indeed, other neo-Marxist thinkers (see Sivanandan, 1982, ch.I; Pryce, 1983, pp.194–195). is that while accepting the political category of *race*, he fails to demonstrate its role in areas of political struggle, choosing instead to sacrifice its independence by assimilating it to an untheorised concept of *class*. Gilroy's line of argument creates ruptures in analyses designed to label aspects of the social milieu of Afro-Caribbean blacks as 'middle-class' (Foner, 1979; Pryce, 1981, pp.136–8) or classically 'working-class' (C.R.C., 1975) without qualifications.

By contrast, I suggest that there is evidence in our portrait of an instance of black politics and resistance – the NHGC – for an analysis of blacks in the British class structure that argues for their characterisation as a *black* (racially differentiated) political category with different sets of relationships to the economy and polity, *autonomous* of other classes (Cambridge & Pryce, 1974/5; 1980; Rex & Tomlinson, 1979; Rex 1979). It must be stressed that the on-going debate on the dynamics of race and class seldom makes specific reference to concrete instances amenable to testing theoretical postulates, or wherein political contradictions are manifested, and tensions between *aims* and *tendencies* given a content.

The ideological contradictions elaborated above probably account for the Janus-faced politics of the 'forces' within both Carnival Committees vis-a-vis young Afro-Caribbean blacks. For the predominantly Trinidadian CDC, being 'pro-youth' was compatible with *control* of the 'resisting' young blacks at the Carnival – this category being synonymous with 'dem Jamaicans'. Furthermore, being 'pro-youths' was also compatible with being 'anti-youths', 'anti-Jamaicans' and 'anti-CAC'. How was this possible? The simple answer is the politics of 'divide and rule'.

In their political thinking, the CDC linked the anti-youths element in the Carnival to the existence of a *structure*, the CAC, and this facilitated the call for the disbandment of the CAC. The CDC therefore, hardly needed an elaborate policy on how to police the Carnival: what would there be left to police, if the very structure which supposedly sustained the presence of resisting young blacks – the CAC – were dispersed?

The CAC's contrasting policy of 'preventive measures' was indeed problematic: the CAC offered the youths little more that a structure of entertainment – the sound-systems. This token gesture of support defeated the logic of the enterprise, especially since reggae-music and resistance are intricately linked. The substance of young black's cultural expression in Britain, is their cognitive perception of the current national economic decline, and the attendant crisis of social relationships that it engenders. Reggae music articulates the tragedy and suffering, the ideals and aspirations of the ghetto. In militant reggae music the concept of a just society is affirmed. Thus, black youths see reggae music and resistance as a marriage which must be made and consummated in the interest of transformation and development; this suggests that should resistance, and/or rebellion explode around a structure that perpetuates this music form, it would signal in an idealistic vision of what might be accomplished.[22] To attempt to 'control' such a movement of resistance, while courting it, is therefore to deny black history in the making.

Resistance, not acquiescence, is the core of Black cultural autonomy in white racist societies, and black youths within the Carnival experience understood this concept well. They demonstrated their resistance to racial oppression and cultural hegemony and containment, in violence against both the symbols of white institutional class rule and social control, and the ambiguous black CDC/CAC leadership of the event.[23] In raising the sight of struggle from the narrow confines of cultural-race-relations, young blacks now seek *political direction*, as is made clear by their willingness to introduce political themes into their conflicts with the police, irrespective of their having been no prior 'intentions' to do so. Here, we must uphold Gilroy's criticism of certain sections of the independent 'white left' for persisting in omitting this reality from analyses of the unity-in-diversity character of the class struggle in Britain, and for failing to 'see any need to situate the culture of young Afro-Caribbean people on the political terrain' (Gilroy, 1982 p.280). But I view as misguided and dogmatic, Gilroy's perception of the process of resistance as revolutionary.

The *politics* that informs the culture of young blacks is derived from the requirements of survival on the streets, and narrowly distinguishes between crime and politics. Overt political definitions can hardly be applied to the symbols of resistance of young blacks, as Gilroy unsuccessfully attempts to do (Ibid). Young blacks' cultural symbols of resistance are best defined as reducible to the terrain of the politics of *critique*. The shift from popular cultural-politics of critique to the politics of *participation* requires more than the manipulation of symbols (Pryce, 1983). This distinction suggests why it was that young blacks at the Carnival were unable to identify with the leadership, and why the leaders in turn flinched from the responsibility to provide political leadership for the potential power of resistance of the young. When young blacks at the NHGC throughout the period under discussion pulled and used knives, bricks and bottles against the multi-racial make-up of the symbols of authority,[24] the politics of black liberation was no longer confined to cultural politics; this was the reason why the leadership's *culturalist* assertions lost sight of the basis of the young people's political independence.

Rastafarianism, reggae music, 'herbs', or 'kally-weed', 'hustling', 'sticksing', 'kiting' or 'frontlining' are all everyday aspects of black culture and for many black youth, these denote their autonomy from domination by capital; these practices constitute the 'fruits' of their history, and in turn determine that history. Black history and black culture therefore, define black resistance and rebellion in the historical moment. This suggests that the practice of black resistance cannot be eliminated by the traditional leadership strategies of simply retreating into blind and naked ignorance, or proffering limp gestures of support. The manifestation of resistance among black youths must clearly now be seen as an autonomous social force in British politics.

Conclusion

The daily distortions and debasement of black youth's political reality continue to lead them in consequence to consider themselves *victims*, and as such deny themselves good leadership, whenever and wherever it occurs. One very important insight to emerge from our findings, is that the rebellion of the young at the Carnival in 1976-1978 superseded any one territorial boundary, and in this sense validates to some extent Louis Chase's claim that it 'dramatised the magnitude of something that has been minimised for years' (Interview with Louis Chase, 23 July 1978), although the basis on which he made this assertion was a slight misrepresentation of the attitude of the young.

Equally, Darcus Howe was perceptive in recognising the political undertones of the young people's behaviour, but dogmatic in dismissing the phenomenon as of no concern within the context of the Carnival. Young Afro-Caribbean blacks persist in being non-hypocritical in their attitude of defiance, and in their every stride of life reject the definitive socio-political labels used to describe their existence which would relegate them to a peripheral relationship with British society. Their struggle within and beyond the parameters of the Carnival crystalises 'the struggles of the oppressed to contest and transform the categories of their oppression into a source of political strength' (Gilroy, 1982, p.289), and this affirms optimism in their 'survival' game in Britain.

This was an issue overlooked by the CDC: the forces within this leadership spoke through the organ of Race today, from above, rather than directly to, the social reality of young blacks. This further highlights the autonomy of young blacks on the political stage in their communities, especially when we consider that they, much more than their parents, cannot look forward out a return 'home' because they *are home*, and as such will be more bitter than their parents about blockages to advancement and about racial prejudice and state harassment.

The form of their rebellion at the Carnival in 1976–1979, contained the seeds of what was to follow by way of political revolts, in Bristol in 1980, and Brixton, Toxteth, Liverpool 8, Moss Side and Southall in 1981; its aim was to achieve a sense of political potency (Kettle & Hodges, 1982). The specifics of these revolts by young black militants, regenerating the guerrilla politics of their slave ancestry, enhanced a thirst for political participation and representation, but, it should be stressed, was in no way revolutionary.[25]

The NHGC invariably tends toward expressing two opposing tendencies within a unity of form; one toward a symbolic affirmation of the status quo, and the other toward expressions of mass resistance, protest, and violence. To this extent, carnival constitutes 'an ambiguous symbolic formation that camouflages and mystifies a contradiction (Glukeman, 1954; Cohen, 1982 p.37). The NHGC throughout 1976–1978 encompassed both acquiescence and resistance, with resistance being the dominant theme, given the on-going tension in the relationship between Black and White Britain. The nature of this relationship, as expressed in the behaviour and attitude of young Afro-Caribbean blacks, changed the precarious balance of the event in more way than one.

While young blacks can be said to have given the practice of resistance within Carnival in Trinidad from 1784–1918 (Hill, 1972) a certain continuity, the form of their relationship to the event in its new multi-racial setting must be noted. They did not appear in 1976–1978 to be overt supporters of this cultural form, but tended rather to view the event as a vehicle for achieving certain particularistic and individualistic ends, which were not reducible out cultural goals. The youth's participation in the experience of the Carnival *en masse* since 1976 focussed attention on the basic demands sought by the black masses in Britain in the process of cultural-political-economic and social liberation.

Reggae music at this conjuncture, has superseded calypso as the weapon traditionally used to symbolise resistance against state oppression - although an uneasy alliance prevails between these two music forms in the British setting. Reggae, and the drama that occurs around it within Carnival in Notting Hill today, has become the Freedom Procession, or the 'Canboulay' (ill, 1972; Rohlehr, 1984) of young Afro-Caribbean blacks. The message therefore, that eluded the leadership of the Carnival throughout 1976–1978, was that young Afro-Caribbean blacks do not consider the solution to their unspoken dilemma to be preserved within the beating of steel-drums and masquerading costumes, nor in the posturing of Afro-Caribbean professionals. Carnival, which nevertheless is part of the cultural heritage of many, allows for a demonstration of the extent to which their relationship to British society is literally and morally a *blood relationship*.

What is additionally instructive about the Notting Hill Gate Carnival, and the politics and leadership that emanate from it in the late 1970s and early 1980s, is that it is indeed the contemporary reality of British black youth sub-cultures - not cultural nostalgia - which provides Carnival with its *raison d'etre*. The political consciousness that young Afro-Caribbean blacks brought to Carnival in the years 1976-1978, was that as a mass black cultural event, it could only claim to be expressive of resistance against cultural domination by virtue of its advocacy of a youth sub-culture. The Notting Hill Carnival will help realise the potential power of the black masses as a subordinate minority striving for solidarity-resistance within the deeply racist structures of British society only when the youths themselves gain control of its organisation, and transform the symbolic resistance power manifested at carnival time into actual political power in the British state.

Notes

1. In my investigation into the historics of the NHGC, I necessarily relied a great deal on oral history in determining some of the sequence of events. Other commentators have, however, arrived at different conclusions with regard to the actual beginnings of carnival in Notting Hill (See A. Cohen, 1982; Gutzmore, 1978).
2. Abner Cohen comments on some of the wider political frictions within the community in Notting Hill Gate that formed the backdrop to the take-over bid of Carnival by blacks in the area. He also offers some interesting explanations for these early conflicts (Cohen, 1982, pp.27-34).
3. For populist appraisals of the 'Sound System' phenomenon to black culture in Britain, (see McGlashan, 1973;Salewics & Peel, 1983; Fletcher, 1983, p.5).
4. For a full account of these incidents, see, inter alia, Time Out (London), 21-27 July, 1972, and Race today (London), passim.
5. See Race Today, relevant years.
6. See The Editorial, The Times (London), 1 September, 1976. Between 1976 and 1978, the NHGC attracted an estimated 700,000 people, 948 injuries were sustained by both police and civilians; over 600 crimes were reported to have been committed; well over 100 steel-bands and floats paraded the streets of Ladbroke Grove; over 95 arrests were made for a variety of offences ranging from 'mugging' to drunkenness, followed by numerous convictions; and the overall financial turnover was well in excess of £750,000.
7. For a brief account of Baptiste's first involvement in the 1976 Carnival, see Cohen (1982).
8. 'I believe the most terrible responsibility rests with all of us who allow such a task to be thrust on our police. We did not have the moral courage to say 'No', so we gave way, and in doing so put several hundreds of London's police at terrible risk'. Peter Kirwan, 'Letters to the Editor', The Daily Telegraph (London), 2 September, 1976.

9. It seems somewhat opportunistic that Howe, having attacked the CDC leadership of 1976, now sought to take over the leadership of this faction. In an open-letter reproduced in (30: 17-18), Howe had said:

   One quarter of a million black people on the streets of Britain in 1976 is a political event. That is how the state sees it. It is not simply an artistic festival of fun-loving West Indians ... We understand that you are calling on the Home Secretary to institute an inquiry into the events of Sunday and Monday. Wo what end, we ask? Who will inquire? ... you were outwitted and out-manoeuvred at every turn by the Metropolitan Police ... no one, bar no one, expected so many police officers until the week before the Carnival. You must have known, you ought to have known what the plans of the police were. After all you were in negotiations with them for eight months...you remained silent. We suspect that you were too paralysed to act... (See also, Race Today, vol.5, no.11, 1973).

10. There is the implication deriving from the CDC's manifesto that Carnival in Notting Hill is predominantly a West Indian affair that should not be influenced by British-based reggae-music and its symbols.
11. See the following selected press reports: Robert Parker, 'Clash over who runs *Notting Hill Carnival', The Times, 12 May, 1977; John Clare, 'Cut Back on Carnival Police, Rees Asked', The evening Standard (London), 11 May, 1977; 'Carnival Disaster Warning', The Evening News (London\0, 13 May, 1977; T.A. Sandrock, The Daily Telegraph (London), 13 May-3 June, 1977; The West Indian world (London), 29 April-5 May, 1977; The Paddington Times (London), 14 May, 1977; and the Kensington News and Post (London), May 6, 20/27, 1977.
12. Larry Forde, quoted in Time Out (London), 1 September, 1977.
13. Selwyn Baptiste, quoted in Time Out (London), May-June, 1977.
14. See also, The Kensington News and Post (London), 20 May, 1977.
15. See also, The Wet Indian world (London), 19 June-22 June, 1978.
16. As a result of the General Election in Britain on June 11, 1987, two Afro-Caribbean Blacks, one Black of African parentage, and on of Asian background, were elected as candidates of the Labour Party to serve as members of Parliament in the British House of Commons. It was the first time in 57 years that Blacks were elected to Parliament in Britain (see Pryce, 12987).
17. According to Vince Whyte, former dispatch-worker with the BPIC in personal communication.
18. See also, The New Statesman (London), 18 June, 1960, and 5 November, 1960.
19. See any number of copies of the journal Race Today.
20. The Black LIberator, to date, probably Black Britain's best theoretical and anti-imperialist journal, ceased publication in 1979.
21. For a discussion on the social control function of self-help groups within the Black Community in Britain, see, John (1981).
22. In this context, Gutzmore's essay (Gutzmore, 1978) stands as the most graphic description to emerge on *thenature and quality of the violence at CArnival in Notting Hill Gate in 1976 and 1977.
23. For pictorial accounts, see, inter alia, The Daily Telegraph (London), 31 august, 1977; The Daily Mail (London), 30 and 31 August, 1977; and The Sun (London), 30 August, 1977.

24. Carnival 1977 saw the use for the first time of black stewards in conjunction with the police, in the business of the 'policing' of the young. Cf. also, fn. 23 above.
25. See Taylor (1981) for an excellent summary of some of the main approaches to the study of violence and their possible use in explaining the riots in Britain.

10 Misunderstandings?: policing, reform and control, co-optation and consultation

MICHAEL KEITH

Introduction

In 1981 Ira Katznelson entitled a book about urban politics, 'City Trenches', after a comment by Gramsci that

> 'civil society' has become a very complex structure and one which is resistant to the catastrophic 'incursions' of the immediate economic element (crises, depressions etc). The superstructures of civil society are like the trench–systems of modern warfare (Quoted in Katznelson, 1981, P.iv.).

The generalised suggestion that adjustments to political systems tend to be constructed to conjure up more the symbolic appearance of change than the substantive reality of reform is both analytically plausible and politically powerful. Reactions to any putatively reformist political initiatives must immediately address the charge that change is targeted more at the co–optation of specific groups than at the resolution of material conflicts.

In the Police and Criminal Evidence Act (PACE) of 1984 statutory consultation between the Metropolitan Police and the 'communities' of the boroughs of London was introduced in the wake of major incidents of uprisings or riots and amidst a major political controversy about the changing face of policing in Britain. This chapter, which is based on a much broader project, looks only very briefly at a couple of instances in which such charges of co–optation were levelled.

In doing this there is certainly no suggestion here that the *reforms* embodied in statutory consultation can be taken at face value. The political processes which lay behind the ostensibly more liberal elements of the PACE Act constructed police/community consultation as a political symbol of good intent rather than a credible exercise in police reform (Keith, 1988; Murji and Keith, 1989). As with many political initiatives in general (Edelman 1985, 1988) and the history of so many policy changes in the field of 'race relations' in particular (Solomos, 1985, 1988), the introduction of statutory police/community consultation in London allowed the state to be seen to be doing something. More specifically, in public exchanges and political debates the measure was a rhetorical token used as a public acknowledgement of a political agenda set by the Scarman report of 1981 (Keith, 1988).

The contention here is that whilst recognising the potential abuses of the process as a medium through which institutional practices are legitimated, consultation should be an important component of **all** relationships between **all** bureaucracies and the state apparatus, whether it is a housing department of a local authority or the police in a particular city.

The fact that institutions are erected in palpable bad faith as part of a system of city trenches does not invariably mean that their sole use will be the defence of those bastions of the establishment they were created to conserve.

The Case Against

> *The state must be a transparent robe, clear as water, that clings close to the body of the people. Every ripple of the sinews, every tensing of the muscles, every swelling of the veins must be imprinted on its form.* (Buchner,1835)

The notion that the state acts as an independent arbitrator, society's honest broker in the resolution of conflict, has long been discredited (Poulantzas,1973; Lukes,1974; McClennan et al,1984), but there remains necessarily little or no agreement on the actual form of this elusive entity. Hence the position of all minority groups in a multi-racial society will in theoretical terms be as dependent on the preferred conceptualisation of the state as on the empirically defined position and circumstances of the minority groups themselves. Whether reforms such as statutory consultation are seen as genuine change, or as accommodations by one (relatively autonomous) element in the structure of society in order to protect economic fundamentals, is similarly answerable only by reference to levels of theoretical abstraction it is not possible to address here. Yet significantly, such competing conceptualisations rationalise the historical experience of migrant communities in Britain and are frequently the source of opposition to institutions like the police/community consultative groups.

The critique is in many ways a powerful one and is best understood from an account of the other government aid institutions that stand at the interface of popular mobilisation and the state (see Diagram 10.1). These include both the area based groups such as the Inner City Partnerships and the specifically race related organisations such as the Commission for Racial Equality and the local Community Relations Councils (CRCs). The relationship between the state and these groups is one of patronage/sponsorship and so they can never venture outside the strictly circumscribed limits set down by government policy. In short their working practices are dominated by the *social problems ideology* that is

Diagram 10.1 Systemic problems of 'Popular movements' and 'Ethnic' mobilisation

Success Criteria

a) Need to be neighbourhood based to enlist popular support

b) Need concrete achievements to sustain support

DIVIDE AND RULE EFFECT I

'Neighbourhood' interests may conflict with 'issues' that divide movement (eg construction jobs v opposition to redevelopment).

Must subscribe to 'social problems' ideology to be accepted in dialogue with

i) RACE RELATIONS INSTITUTIONS

DIVIDE AND RULE EFFECT II

II) GOVERNMENT AID INSTITUTIONS

'Ethnicity' as a divisive influence

DIVIDE AND RULE EFFECT III

Fiscal and de facto control

i and ii act as institutional buffer, shifting debate into competition for government funds

Patronage and Sponsorship

THE STATE

The description in the flow diagram contains no casual mechanism. Every effect does not have a premeditated cause (i and ii may effectively act as an institutional buffer but are not necessarily designed to do so). Each element of the diagram cannot necessarily be treated as a historical actor because of the relationship between intentionality and action.

their very *raison d'etre*. The relationship between the institutions and popular (ethnic or racial) mobilisation (eg. migrant associations, residents' or tenants' associations) is primarily financial.

In order to sustain their own support, neighbourhood and community groups need to show material successes in either combating racial injustice (involving the expenses of law suits) or in compensating for racial inequality (eg the provision of amenity facilities such as youth clubs and community centres). To gain this success the popular groups must conform with the social problems ideology of the aid institutions and place their case for financial support in the arena of comparative need in a competition for scarce resources. This serves to 'divide and rule' popular groups because antagonism is inevitably built up within the aid institutions in this competition. In racial mobilisation the distinct backgrounds of different migrant groups exaggerate this effect, an influence that is behind Sivanandan's renowned vilification of the divisive facet of 'ethnicity' (Sivanandan, 1982).

As well as defusing popular mobilisation via the tool of ethnicity (Sivanandan,1983; Ben-Tovim and Gabriel,1982, Messina, 1987), the CRE and the CRCs are alleged to co-opt members of racial minorities as symbolic tokens of progress in organisations which have little or no reforming power and also act as an institutional buffer between race based groups and 'genuine' reform (Castells,1983; Ben-Tovim et al,1986). As Friedland (Friedland, 1982, p.167) remarked in the North American context,

> In short, they (the local state) could not solve the Blacks' problems but they could manage them.

The very institutions that were ostensibly created for the benefit of racial minorities may be the instruments of their continued suppression. At its most insidious the political goal of the elite is no more than a fraudulent exercise in the extension of hegemony. Put at its most cynical 'the critical issue is what it will take to persuade blacks that the system is fair' (Altshuler 1970 p.03).

Though it is not possible here to assess the validity of this account of the relationship between state and the political agenda of 'race', the dangers of co-optation, the potentially divisive role of ethnicity and the ambivalent patronage (and implicit control) of aid institutions by the government are all plausible, if not proven, criticisms of state funded organisations. For the purposes of this analysis it is important to make two points in particular.

The first is the renewed significance of the distinction between description and explanation. The radical critique of the race relations industry may provide a useful description of reality but can not serve as the sole basis for explanation. The problem with conspiratorial analyses is that the ontology of the component parts of the description is not considered, failing to recognise that the model in the diagram is synchronic, in that it describes a conjunction of structures at a particular point in time, described from one particular angle. The strength of this vision is that in such essentially structuralist work a viewpoint transcending that of the actors that are the living realisation of the description can reveal the unacknowledged conditions of action of those same actors. The result is, in Habermas' sense of the term, emancipatory, validating the social need and theoretical power of critical theory. Typically, in his use of the (Gramscian) notion of 'City Trenches' Katznelson claims that in the USA

> At issue was the attempt to take the radical impulse away from the politics of race by the location of mechanisms of participation at the community level that had the capability to limit conflicts to a community orientation, to separate issues from each other, and to stress a politics of distribution - in short to reduce race to ethnicity in the traditional community-bounded sense (Katznelson 1981 p177).

In the descriptive sense it matters little the machinations behind the design of the city trenches if their configuration so effectively silences protest without giving away 'real' power.

Yet this analytical strength is also potentially the model's greatest weakness, because, just as an object may be photographed from many different angles, this description is only one of many valid descriptions. In particular, problems arise when analysis ascends to causal explanation, tacitly assuming that this description defines a monistic whole, is sufficient for understanding behaviour. Consequently, the tendency is to transform the descriptive structure into a cast of social actors with implausible powers. The inevitable result of such methodology is that analysis moves inexorably towards some form of conspiratorial functionalism because of the failure to recognise that explanatory accounts must be potentially reducible to individual actions and must therefore take into consideration the major problems of philosophical intentionality. Cause and effect are in this way conflated. That the effect of reforming institutions may be detrimental is not disputed, quite possibly it is a valid criticism of both 'the race relations industry' in general and the new consultative groups in particular. But the functionalist argument assumes that the prescient state was aware of these effects, a level of planning and co-ordination that would be remarkable.

This raises the second important consideration for analysis of the police/community consultative process. This is that regardless of the social reality the **perception** of the relation between community organisation and the state will implicitly or explicitly determine the reactions of individual actors to the consultative process as a whole. Hence it would be perfectly possible to support the descriptive power of the diagram without impugning the integrity or devaluing the efforts of those who invest much time and work in consultation. For these individuals are only involved because tacitly or openly they espouse a liberal/democratic vision of society which stresses that any problems between police and community stem in the final analysis from misunderstanding, from a failure to communicate. Conceptualisations of *social problems* structure individuals' actions and set the agenda for committee discussion.

This is exemplified by the number of times at both Islington and Lambeth police consultative groups reference was made to the 'rotten apples' in the police force, without whom everything, it was implied, would be fine. That there might be a deterministic foundation to the confrontation between the police force as representatives of white bourgeois social order and the Black community (Mingione,1981) as many on the Left might suggest, or that alongside this materialist configuration conflict was also a historical product, deeply rooted in the places and experiences of the British Black community, as suggested here, simply does not and can not enter into this notion of rotten apple racism. Yet such considerations are simply not open to discussion in the context of the committee room liaison committee. This is why the police consultative groups themselves selectively include only those who are prepared, in the committee room at least, to subscribe to a *social problems ideology*.

However, such a position alone does not guarantee the validity of diagnoses of co-optation. For there are a great many similarities between the police and other major bureaucracies in developed capitalist economies, all of which are vulnerable to powerful critiques on the question of accountability. There are many who would, whilst recognising the very limited power embodied in consultation, suggest that it remains inconceivable at present that major service provision bureaucracies such as housing, gas and water would open themselves up to the public scrutiny involved in the consultative process. However, as Barbara Roche, head of the Hackney Police Committee Support Unit for much of the 1980s stressed (personal interview), the comparison with many local authority services does stop with the democratic accountability of the Borough Council.

Moreover, for those who genuinely believe in the analysis suggested by the diagram, one possible strategy is not only to refuse to co-operate with the consultative process (the policy of Hackney Council), but also to attempt to destroy any group that is established. I would suggest that it is this latter course of action that was adopted, initially by accident but increasingly as strategy, by Lambeth Council between 1985 and 1987.

The gradual withdrawal of Labour Party representatives from the Community Police Consultative Group for Lambeth (CPCGL) from the mid 1980s onwards occurred principally through apathy, partly through constituency party pressure and partly through the exigencies of local politics from 1982-85 (see Cansdale,1983). In June 1982 the GLC Police Committee published a report which stated that,

> borough level accountability will also be important. It will be necessary to oversee the operation of the Metropolitan Police local districts/ divisions and accountability at this level should be based on borough councils. (Except where specified, this and the following quotations are from Keith, forthcoming).

Setting the tune for some Labour groups across London, the report went on the suggest, 'The proposed new consultation groups (liaison committees) would be a step in the wrong direction.'

These views were echoed by Richard Allen, a member of the Lambeth Council Police Support Unit from February 1984 and the acting head of the unit from 1985–1988. He quite clearly saw the CPCGL as having no impact on the police and believed there was a danger of the Metropolitan Police extending their power in London by manipulation of the Consultative Groups. He stated (personal interview) that for him one of the main aims of the Lambeth Police Support Unit was to 'push back the frontiers of multi-agency policing', suggesting that the Council should play the dominant role in organising crime prevention, only involving the police force at a much later stage in the process. He also rejected the idea that the consultative group could serve as an arena in which the police were called (verbally) to account, claiming that 'they (the police) just obfuscate'. Hence not only did he see 'no point in co-operating with a group that has failed' but also in answer to the question, 'Because you say the consultative group causes damage do you see a need to destroy it?' he replied, 'We do not need to destroy it, only to marginalise it.'

> It is in the light of these views that the relations between the CPCGL and Lambeth Council in 1985/86 are most readily comprehensible. In mid 1985 the council circulated those voluntary bodies receiving council funds or using council facilities, stressing the need to avoid legitimation of the CPCGL by taking part in consultation. The hostility that was by this time growing rapidly was brought to a climax on 20 May 1986 when the recommendation of a CPCGL sub-committee inquiry into the disorders of the previous October that 'plastic bullets should only be used as a last resort'

in public disorder was passed by the full committee, amid much concern from two of the senior Black representatives, Astel Parkinson (the chairman of the group at the time) and George Greaves (head of Lambeth CRC). There was also uproar among several Black members of the public present, who claimed the CPCGL were supporting police militarisation.

The reaction of the council was swift, issuing a press release that in condemning the possible use of plastic bullets in Lambeth stated that,

> the Consultative Group is now supporting the use of these lethal weapons against the residents of Lambeth. The Council has long ceased to take part in the Consultative Group because the Group has failed to represent the interests of those who experience most in the way of bad policing.

The press release also called for people to leave the consultative group and announced that the council would henceforth withdraw all facilities (photocopying, use of town hall for meetings) from the group. From this point onwards hostility from the council toward the CPCGL intensified, with the new leader of Lambeth Council, Linda Bellos, regularly making statements in press and media interviews attacking the CPCGL.

In this situation the considerable mutual antagonism which built up was such that even though both Astel Parkinson's successor (Greta Brooks) and senior police in Brixton were keen to emphasise the importance of council involvement, they readily admitted that any change of position on the part of the council was extremely unlikely. The critique of the diagram had been taken to its logical conclusion and the council were now engaged in a policy which quite deliberately tried to discredit the CPCGL.

The Consultative Process and the Triumph of Bureaucracy

I want to suggest that community consultative groups are neither panacea for police/Black antagonism nor calculating and fraudulent exercises in co-optation and public relations. Instead they are a flawed reform, institutions that cannot satisfy one of the main functions for which they were created because of the salient characteristics of their design. This is so because their role of 'talking away conflict' is contradictory, because their structure incorporates a fallacious notion of 'community', because the power of committees is often largely illusory, and because of the nature of bureaucratic procedure itself. Not all these issue can be addressed here but it is intended to illustrate some of these points anecdotally from work carried out across London between 1984 and 1988.

Contradictions in the Concept of 'Taking Conflict Off The Streets'

The reasoning behind Scarman's recommendation of statutory consultation was that at the heart of the *disorders* in Brixton were real grievances felt by an oppressed Black community, grievances which had no other outlet than violent street protest; essentially an echo of Martin Luther King's comment that riots are the language of the unheard. In providing an arena for such expression the implication was that in the consultative group the Black community could be heard, and could explain their plight in person to senior officers. In this sense it was hoped to institutionalise conflict, taking it off the streets and into the committee room.

On three occasions in London in the period after 1981 it could be said that this goal was achieved, if not always in formal consultation, then in informal organisations which were close approximations to the official consultative structure. In 1984 in Notting Hill and in 1983 in Brixton, rising tensions which had escalated to the point of nascent public disorder were partially defused after public meetings on All Saints Road and Railton Road, respectively, when senior police officers (Whitfield in Notting Hill; Marnoch in Brixton) held public meetings where they explained the police position amidst general hostility and abuse.

A third occasion occurred in Brixton on Tuesday 1st October 1985, when in the wake of the widespread rioting that had followed the police shooting of Mrs Cherry Groce (a middle aged Black woman), a public meeting of the CPCGL was seen by members of the group itself, by senior police officers and by press present at the time as acting as a peaceful outlet for the anger of local people. Yet it is possible, without contesting this general description, to suggest that this meeting, rather than being the exemplary success of the CPCGL, highlighted the flaws that handicap its very existence.

Astel Parkinson was at the time chairman of the group. He has lived in Brixton since 1959, been a youth worker since the mid-sixties (full-time since the mid-seventies) and his son Horace was one of the Brockwell Park 3 in 1973. This was one of the many *causes celebres* in the Brixton history of clashes between the police and the Black community which served as a grim *leitmotif* to local *police/community relations*. Parkinson had been active in the campaign protesting about police behaviour. Friendly and generous, he could talk with authority on the history of the area because this sort of 'local knowledge' is for him no more than autobiography. He is certainly no 'mouthpiece' or 'puppet' of the police and was one of the few members of the group who was well-known and respected on Railton Road, where he was chairman of the Afro-Caribbean Community Association (ACCA). He was also a friend of the Groces and at the start of that night's meeting introduced one of the members of the family to those present, whilst making a moving speech for serious but controlled discussion of the emotive issues that had occurred in the preceding few days.

The public gallery in the committee room of Lambeth town hall that was being used for the meeting had rapidly filled up and before business opened there had already been heckling of the police present. Within seconds of the start, three Black people (two men, one woman, all in their late twenties/early thirties) in paramilitary gear, shoved into the room, snatched the microphones from the committee table and began to harangue both Parkinson and the police. Every time either he or Commander Marnoch, the senior police officer present, tried to speak they were shouted down by the slogan chanting of the intruders. Whenever Astel Parkinson tried to retaliate he was drowned in a chorus of 'Uncle Tom, Uncle Tom, Uncle Tom' from the three paramilitaries, who had now placed themselves strategically around the room and controlled all the microphones. Their amplified vilification was often echoed from the floor and they frequently demanded that the meeting should be stopped because of the futility of even talking to 'filth' like the police. About fifty people filled the room and a great many more had been locked out of the town hall and were noisily demanding to be let in.

The assembly continued fitfully in this vein for about half-an-hour until a group of about fifteen to twenty from outside the town hall overpowered the security guards and demanded that all those outside be allowed into the meeting. The leader of this group made a scathing attack on Astel Parkinson, labelled him a parasite on other people's misfortune and a toady to the police. Visibly upset, Parkinson lost his cool and a further row followed. The back door to the committee room was now open. With the numbers of this second vociferous protest faction growing rapidly, the collapse of the gathering was avoided only when a council official allowed the meeting to move from the committee room into the main Lambeth function room, where between two and three hundred people filled the hall, many covering their faces to prevent identification.

There then followed a meeting more reminiscent of the tribunals of revolutionary France than the protocols of the twentieth century committee, a gathering so intense that by the end of the evening as an observer, I felt emotionally drained, after the most sustained display of mass anger I have seen inside a single room. It was not the self-righteous anger of politics. There was rhetoric, but not much. Only a small minority indulged themselves. It was the anger of the indignant, the wounded, the shocked. There was a feeling of incredulity, 'How could they have done this?', and over everything a fury at the police that regularly surfaced in overt and palpably sincere hatred.

In the larger hall the paramilitary group stepped back and Parkinson's authority as chairman was again usurped, this time by Tony Morgan, a local young member of the Black community better known for self-publicity than for 'street credibility', who openly abused the members of the committee on which he had once served. Assuming command with a shout of 'We're taking this meeting over Astel,' it was under his aegis that the rest of the evening took the approximate form of a public interrogation of Marnoch, with individuals taking turns to come to the microphone to say their piece. Sometimes Marnoch was given a chance to reply.

Throughout this time a series of minor scenes were enacted just off the main stage. A television cameraman was bundled out of the room, not without force, after an impromptu vote ruled against his presence, whilst John Clare, the BBC correspondent, hid his tape recorder under his jacket and looked nervous. A group stood on one side of the room chanting, 'Fire, Fire, Fire'. Occasionally the flow of the meeting would be interrupted. Once somebody ran into the room, advanced on Marnoch and accused him of having the building surrounded by police. Hostility and tension increased dramatically and the numbers of those present who had kept on their anorak hoods and wore scarves over their faces, notably increased. At another time somebody interrupted the meeting with the cry, 'Toxteth's on fire' to the prolonged cheers of the gathering.

Throughout all, one person after another came up to the front of the hall and explained their experiences and feelings of the last three days or the last thirty years. Their hurt and their bitterness turned the night into an abridged, but moving, account of a racist society. Occasionally this would become personalised. Two individuals threatened to kill Marnoch and another announced to the audience that the Lambeth Police Commander was responsible for jailing him eight times and that, 'I will get you before I die, Marnoch.'

In replying, Marnoch made some outspoken comments that included declarations of support for any public inquiry into the shooting of Mrs

Groce and a democratically elected police authority in London, as well as the statement that,

> I have stated several times in the past, and I still believe, that it will not be possible to have peace on these streets with the current high levels of deprivation.

But eventually it was all too much. Briefly, Marnoch broke down and was visibly in tears. Tough, gregarious, very large and very tall, the senior policeman in Brixton stood in front of a couple of hundred people in Lambeth Town Hall and cried. 'Crocodile tears', somebody standing a foot away from him shouted in his face.

Neither Marnoch, nor Parkinson, nor the rest of the committee, who for the most part had remained silent throughout, could assuage the anger of those present at the horrific shooting of Mrs Groce; in fact most of their statements seemed instead further to rouse most people. At about 9.45pm a lady from the 'Black Parents' support group strode to the microphone and demanded that everyone walk out of 'this fiasco', at which point the meeting broke up in disarray.

In private interviews several months later both Marnoch and Parkinson suggested that this meeting was successful. The number of registered informants on Railton Road doubled within two days, which Marnoch took as a sign of some public support. The police had been called to account, in Parkinson's mind. Yet in reality both men had been trapped by the contradictions that undermine the whole value of consultation as a mechanism for the resolution of conflict between the police and Black communities in London. The roots and nature of this conflict were simply not susceptible to being talked away. Their remarkable actions might have served to buy time but not to resolve conflict. Astel Parkinson's exemplary and principled position may well have persuaded many to be more reluctant to take to the streets. Marnoch's courage may have won friends and informers on Railton Road. But the level of sustained abuse and the public humiliation of both men revealed that such successes were tokens buying time at enormous personal cost.

Parkinson did not stand again as chairman of the CPCGL and told me that he saw his prominence in police/community affairs in Lambeth diminishing in the near future. Marnoch had a breakdown. When interviewed six months later after prolonged medical leave he still looked physically and mentally exhausted. Fine words can not gloss over the fact that these two individuals had achieved so little yet paid so much. Certainly, antagonism between police and community had not 'diminished', almost certainly their equals in calibre could not be found in Brixton. As individuals they could not have invested more in the consultative process but they worked within an institutional structure that could offer only occasional palliatives to a social schism.

The Power of Committees

Though limited in formal powers the actual power of the police consultative groups is moot. The GLC commented in 1982 that,

> in essence large voluntary committees with no clear lines of accountability to the community, no clear relationship with the police, and whose function is no more than an exchange of information or views, on terms solely dependent on the police, are not likely to meet current demands.

In contrast, the view of Islington Council was that it was possible to subvert the apparently powerless status of the new consultative groups by forcing senior officers to account for themselves in a public forum. It is certainly the case that senior police officers in both Brixton and Hackney confessed in private interviews that they feared 'interrogation' in the process of consultation. It is also certainly the case that in Conservative dominated Merton, Kensington and Chelsea and Wandsworth the predispositions of the majority of representatives on the committee often made the claims of the 'Left realists' look slightly thin, as criticisms of the police were drowned in a chorus of indignation (although see 'new critics', section 3b).

Yet both of these arguments overlook the fact that the police force is an institution that is characterised by the paradoxical structure of ostensible regimentation in a formal hierarchy in which the real powers of senior ranks over junior ranks is strictly circumscribed by the nature of 'the Job'. Quite possibly these two elements of police organisation make the relationship between police practice and any committee, however powerful in statute, a tenuous one.

In the most obvious sense, the discretion of the junior ranks allows ample room for redefinition of managerial objectives, license for the expressive realm of personal criteria to dominate the practical realm of professional policing laid down by senior ranks. That the police who appear at the consultative groups have authentic control over police practices is not as straightforward as the clear chains of command would imply.

More subtly, the rank structure can cut across those matters that are of greatest interest to the consultative group. In removing the District tier of organisation from the Metropolitan Police the Commissioner removed the one level of management that most often covered the same geographical area as the London Boroughs on which consultation is based. This angered the consultative groups of Lambeth and Islington, who in 1985 and 1986 both registered official notes of protest with the Home Office about the failure to consult before this reform was announced. Significantly, only divisional staff were to be represented at the consultative meetings, with the result that each group would be faced not by a single set of officers in a clear cut hierarchy but with two or more parallel sets of management, one coming from each division in the borough. In Hackney there were two divisions (Hackney and Stoke

Newington), in Lambeth four (Clapham, Kennington, Streatham, Brixton) and in both cases the contact at inter-divisional level within the police service was necessarily limited. Exceptionally, in Lambeth, the flagship of the new groups, a police Commander continued to attend meetings, though by 1986 Commander Lloyd's attendance at CPCGL was not as consistent as his predecessor, Commander Marnoch. In all other cases the most senior officers regularly present would be the Chief Superintendents in charge of each division. The effect of this was to downgrade the level of authority which dealt with the police consultative group.

Again, it is impossible to know if this was a calculating move by the Commissioner. Yet its benefits for the police rapidly became visible in hindsight and Newman's senior officers were not slow to take advantage of this change. DAC Jones, talking about police representation on consultative groups, cited one example where the police Commander in charge of the District (borough) of Tower Hamlets had, 'said something which is now providing bullets for the council to attack us with' (private interview).

For Jones, the removal of the Commander from the consultation process guaranteed that major policing issues which arose at consultative meetings could be considered carefully within Area management, with the official responses passed back to the borough level groups, rather than having policing commitments extemporised or pledges 'on the record' forced out of senior management in the heat of public debate. Again there is ambiguity, the corollary of this sort of 'considered management' being the potential to emasculate consultative groups, to defuse the calling to account of police in a public forum.

The most clear cut example of this phenomenon occurred in Islington in the wake of what became known as 'the Holloway incident'. In 1983 five boys were assaulted by officers from a police van on the Holloway Road in Islington. An official inquiry by the Police Complaints Authority recognised the validity of the complaints of the five, but failed to establish the identity of the officers responsible. Only the actions of the local MP, Chris Smith (an active member of the Islington group) ensured that this result met with a blaze of publicity. On 14 February 1986 the London Standard led with a banner headline, 'POLICE THUGS' and an editorial condemning the Home Secretary for claiming that nothing more could be done about the incident. The Islington consultative group met on 18 February 1986 for the first time with no officer of higher rank than Chief Superintendent. At this stage the Commissioner was alleged to have reported to Tory back benchers that there was no point in taking the matter further and the Home Secretary had told Chris Smith that the incident was closed, two positions that infuriated the committee.

To the surprise and disbelief of almost all present, the police who came to the meeting that evening said that they had nothing to say about the incident and at one time Detective Chief Superintendent Meek commented, 'Those reports in the press, you read the same as I do, I know nothing more about this matter than you do.' The group were furious. Councillor Calnan, who was regularly the most astute exponent of Islington's policy of bringing the police to account in consultation, but who was to lose his seat in the 1986 local elections, claimed the police were putting up, 'a wall of silence that does more justice to the Mafia than to the Metropolitan Police,' going on to state,

> The fact that there is nobody here to answer to us tonight makes a mockery of the whole function of this consultative group ... this crisis is the worst yet for the group.

Similarly, the leader of the council, Margaret Hodge, scathingly remarked, 'Why do you come here saying you know nothing when the issue is quite clearly on the minutes?' The dismay was such that there was talk of withdrawing the council from the consultative process altogether.

Yet the Mafia allusion was perhaps misleading. At one point in the evening a senior police officer said in an aside to one of his colleagues that he had not even known that the Home Secretary was holding a press conference that evening on the Holloway incident. It was not less alarming to realise that the police present were not deceiving the consultative group, only being used as canon fodder for their superiors.

Deputy Assistant Commissioner (DAC) Richards, responsible for the Area, pointedly refused to come to this and subsequent meetings of the Islington consultative group. Though the group protested, the Home Office reply (read at the meeting on 15 April 1986) stated that the Commissioner's policy was for Chief Superintendent only to attend consultative meetings, unless matters of policy were at issue. In the event, the official inquiry into the Holloway incident was reopened amid further front page publicity on the 19 February 1986 and by the 24 February 1986 four PCs had been charged with the offences. But by September 1986 DAC Richards had still not appeared before the Committee.

The Micro-sociology of the Committee

A ubiquitous social-psychological facet of committee practice is that the procedural niceties of meetings may at times become more important than the issues which are being discussed. Occasionally, Harre's liturgical metaphor for analysis of social behaviour (1979) seemed appropriate in all consultative groups. The protocols of recording minutes, moving motions, setting up sub-committees and voting on the most insignificant procedural matters often gave consultative meetings a rigid, almost ceremonial, structure that was familiar to all committee members but arcane to members of the public who would occasionally come to air grievances. This was particularly resented in Lambeth on the limited number of occasions when representatives of the young
Black community came expecting a less formal and more visceral discussion of the reality of police/Black relations in Brixton. In these circumstances certain officers of consultative groups, caught up in the ceremony, clearly overestimate their own significance.

There is also a more insidious, connected problem that stems from the relationship between 'committee officials' and the police. This was most clearly seen when on 24 July 1986 the police staged a massive raid on the Railton Road Afro-Caribbean Community Association (ACCA), in what was known as 'Operation Condor'. Commander Lloyd stated several times in television and radio interviews that he had consulted with 'community leaders' before the raid. Astel Parkinson was shattered. As Chairman of ACCA and a vigourous anti-drugs campaigner he had himself arranged for the club to be shut down over the bank holiday weekend a few weeks earlier, recognising the rising tension on Railton Road. In spite of this, Lambeth Council, heavily involved in financing the centre, insisted that it was reopened and Parkinson was actively involved in trying to clean up the very real problems of criminal activity that were developing there. However, he knew nothing of the police raid in advance yet he told me that after Lloyd's public statements not a single person on the *Front Line* would believe this. He felt that his credibility had possibly been destroyed by the police. For him, his own alleged co-optation, once risible, had become a more plausible accusation.

The construction of co-optation is haphazardous. It is difficult to locate the elusive '*they*', the personification of the power-bloc, the anonymous managerial 'controllers' of fictional dystopia. At the level of the consultative process itself such Machiavellian types rarely, if ever, exist. If some of the police I observed and interviewed recognised pragmatically that 'community relations' was 'in vogue' and a promising promotion channel 5, the majority were working within a vision of society that incorporates the common sense notion that if only everybody 'understood each other' then the bitterness of police/Black conflict would dissolve. As it happens, this is a vision which is profoundly alien to both the personal views of the author and all the findings of the research project from which this chapter is derived.

The institutionalisation of the police/Black conflict, the sedimentation of antagonism in time and place, and the social context of racial injustice all undermine such ingenuous notions; the rhetorical assassinations of Alec Marnoch and Astel Parkinson were the product of this contradiction of common sense. This in no way negates the sincerity of many police involved in consultation. If co-optation was designed into the consultative process, it was designed in such a way to deceive police as well as public. More plausibly, the flaws of functionalist sociology are once more exposed, cause and effect confused. In these circumstances co-optation may be an incidental facet of the consultative process, an equally alarming phenomenon. The case of Parkinson and the raid on ACCA is a clear cut example of this contingent property, yet this was produced by the insensitivity of the local Police Commander rather than by the institutional imperatives of the consultative process, though the result is no less unfortunate. In pairing the living tragedy of conflict with the protocols of the committee room only the body bureaucratic can triumph.

Conclusion

Police community consultative groups have become political issues in their own right. Functional significance is commonly overwhelmed by political symbolism. Both participating members and non–participating opponents tend to play up the importance of the consultative groups to the detriment of all. The groups are cited as major reforms (by the police) or as the locus of co–optation (eg Hackney and Lambeth councils), when in fact they are not **necessarily** either.

In this context it is important not to base a justification for consultation on the suggestion that it is 'a staging post on the way to accountability' (Jock Young 28/5/88, ALA). Unfortunately, and paradoxically, the conflict that underwrote the events of 1981 which provided the impetus for 'reform' remains a principal legitimation of the consultative process The historical depth and social basis of the conflict between police and Black communities ensures that consultation cannot provide any 'solutions' to this conflict, whatever such 'solutions' might look like, but it does not mean that consultative groups invariably fail to provide useful arenas through which interests can come together.

Generalisation is elusive because personalities matter. A pragmatic, gregarious Commander of police dealing with one consultative group in one sensitive part of London may be replaced by an officious, pedantic successor. The chair of he same group may be at one time a sincere community activist with first hand knowledge of some of the unpleasant realities of inner city policing, at another time a moral entrepreneur playing at social science and politics.

More depressingly, study of one aspect of consultation confirms that the nature of police/Black conflict is beyond polite discussion, contradicting images of liberal–democratic Britain, institutionalised in the social divisions of the racist nation.In the context of American Civil Rights struggles of the 1950s and 1960s Friedland has suggested that strategies of reform were doomed from their inception because 'they could not win enough, even as their victories told them that they were right to struggle in the first place....the urban system, its genetic codes, could not be touched.' In watching the hypocritical antics of the Thatcher government in the field of race *relations over* the past ten years it is easy to see the relevance of such comments to 1980s Britain.

However, there is also a danger that critical analysis sets up easy oppositions between the cynical pessimism of a diagnosis of institutional buffering and the naive optimism of visions of progressive incorporation in the political process. The search for analytical clarity by (principally white) academics may trivialise the complex reality of political experience.

11 Black Sections in the Labour Party

KALBIR SHUKRA

Introduction

One new development in mainstream British politics has been the growing recognition of the Black presence. In recent years, Black Labour party members have set up bodies such as the Asian Labour party Alliance, the Afro-Asian and Caribbean Alliance for Labour and the Standing Conference of Afro-Caribbean and Asian Councillors. None of these has, however, excited as much passion and media coverage as the attempts to establish Black Sections in the Labour party. This chapter attempts a detached analysis of the political impact of Black Sections. It is therefore worth considering how the debate came into being, what impact it has had and what trajectory it has taken. To examine the formation of Black Sections it is important to situate this discussion within the general context by which it was significantly influenced.

The Historical Context

As some of the earlier chapters in this book have shown, Black people in Britain have historically supported the Labour party more than any other party (Fitzgerald, 1987, pp.5–7). One initial reason for this lay in the early local relationships forged between black individuals and Labour representatives. When black people first came in significant numbers to Britain in the post Second World War era, they were concentrated in inner city, Labour controlled, working class areas. Locally and nationally the Labour party had already established close relations with the British working class, which the majority of black people emigrating to Britain became a part of. The result was that their main access to people with political power was through the Labour Party. Issues in education, housing and social services were decided chiefly through Labour-controlled local authorities and local MPs in areas of black settlement also tended to be Labour. Thus if black people wished to participate in the decision-making process which affected their lives, whether on matters of representation, immigration or education, the channel available was the

Labour party. This situation tended to encourage black individuals and community groups, which soon developed, to cultivate alliances with local Labour party branches. There were thus black activists operating within the Labour Party long before Black Section was formed.

Founder members of Black Sections were therefore existing Labour party activists who recognised a need to organise as a pressure group within the party in order to influence it. The reasons for which they joined the Labour party vary according to individual experiences and political views. They were nearly all, however, black trade union or community activists. With the exception of Sharon Atkin, who joined in 1966, most of the founding members of Black Sections joined the Labour party from the mid 1970s onwards. There was a sense of change in the party during the seventies and early eighties which attracted new members,including black people, in larger numbers than before (Wainwright, 1987, p.164). The changes were chiefly a result of the left-wing Campaign for Labour Party Democracy's (CLPD) attempts to democratise the party and the rise of Bennism. Sharon Atkin was involved in CLPD whilst Hassan Ahmed, Chair of Nottingham black section in 1987, joined the Labour party because 'there seemed a chance to have an influence' (Wainwright, 1987, p.164). Similarly, other leading figures such as Chris Khamis and Philip Murphy, were attracted by the 'growth of left and democratic changes being made (which) created a hope amongst black people' (Interview with Chris Khamis, November 1988). Bernie Grant (elected MP for Haringey in June 1987), a trade-union activist, also joined the Labour party to help the left make changes from within. This was part of a general tactic being pursued by left wing trade union activists from the mid seventies which involved building a stronger left-wing base within the party. Grant joined Tottenham Labour party as a delegate from his union branch which 'had people joining all over the place in London, because if you join you can get onto the General Committee and you can challenge the MPs and vote in the selection' (Interview with Bernie Grant, May 1988).

Most of the black activists who joined at the time and became active in Black Section, joined in order to bring about changes within the Labour party and attempt to help change society. For those who 'believed in the policies of the Labour party' (Interview with Keith Vaz, 19 April, 1988) like Keith Vaz and Paul Sharma, the decision to join was logical and painless. For radicals like Marc Wadsworth, Chris Khamis and Linda Bellos, however, the decision was more difficult. Wadsworth was one of the activists who was also influenced by the Black Power movement and, therefore, black separatism. Khamis was associated with the left outside the Labour party and Bellos with 'Revolutionary Feminist groups, Black Women's groups and Women Against Violence Against Women' (Guardian, 11 May, 1987). Nevertheless, when the left was in its ascendency these individuals joined in order to extract maximum resources for black people via local government and organise black people to make an impact in mainstream party politics. Generally, black activists began to join Labour because 'they believed that the old structure was breaking up and that they could reshape it to fight for a kind of socialism which would mean liberation from the oppressions of race and gender as well as class' (Wainwright, 1987, p.165).

Leading Black Sections activists have been influenced chiefly by trade union and socialist struggles on the one hand and black separatism and anti-imperialist movements on the other. Although the balance of these ingredients varies and they overlap, all Black Section activists remain, or have become, staunch proponents of the Labour party. Their common objective is to influence Labour party policies and structure in an effort to effect change in society. Before discussing the changes being pursued, it is worth examining aspects of the politics of the emergence of Black Sections.

The decade preceding the establishment of Labour Party Black Sections witnessed increasing official concern about the potential consequences of unbridled discrimination against black people. There was no shortage of reports indicating that racism was rife in Britain. The Political and Economic Planning (PEP) of 1974 had shown that while discrimination against black people with qualifications had declined, unskilled workers would meet discrimination in between one third and one half of all applications for jobs (Gordon, 1983, p.19). In 1975, the Runnymede Trust pointed to extensive discrimination in the allocation of houses by the Greater London Council. These reports went on to show the results of repression also. In 1976 the Metropolitan police complained to the Parliamentary Select Committee on Race Relations and Immigration of the tendency of black youths to combine against the police in efforts to rescue arrested friends. Furthermore, a government white paper, Racial Discrimination, published in 1975, expressed continuing concern about 'the immense danger, material as well as moral, which ensues when a minority loses faith in the capacity of social institutions to be impartial and fair' (Gordon, 1983, p.19). With the spectre of rebellion in America haunting British governments, the White Paper suggested that in order to contain the anger of those victim to racism day in and day out, efforts to increase the confidence of black people in British officialdom would need to be made:

> It is vital to our well-being as a society to tap these reservoirs of resilience, initiative and vigour int he racial minority groups and not allow them to lie unused or to be deflected into negative protest on account of arbitrary and unfair discriminatory practices (Quoted in Gordon, 1983, p.19).

The authors of the government report recognised that the alienation of black people resulting from racism could be dangerous and therefore black anger would need to be contained by involving black people in mainstream society.

Such warnings were heeded by the Labour government which passed the 1976 Race Relations Act and in the following year embarked on a comprehensive expansion of the urban aid programme. Both of these enabled local authorities to involve black activists in state funded community groups and projects. Section 71 of the Race Relations Act placed a responsibility on local authorities to make 'appropriate arrangements' to ensure that their functions were carried out in such ways as to eliminate racial discrimination and promote equality of opportunity for all racial groups (Layton-Henry & Rich, 1986, p.36). Labour's enhanced urban programme also indicated the high priority given to dampening urban anger. The White Paper on the matter promised to give this new initiative 'an explicit priority in social and economic policy, even at a time of particular stringency in public resources' (Layton-Henry & Rich, 1986, p.36). Fear of social unrest was such that the Labour government was prepared to pass legislation and raise spending in an effort to increase black people's confidence in official institutions, hoping to dampen black anger resulting from the experience of racism.

Building the confidence of black people in the social and political system also entailed integrating black people into mainstream electoral politics. Until 1974, black people appeared to be too small in number for their votes to be of concern to the political parties. As have already been noted in earlier chapters, the two general elections of 1974 changed this as the number of marginal seats made every vote important. This in turn stimulated interest in the electoral importance of black voters, as reflected in the Community Relations Council's publication entitled The Participation of the Ethnic Minorities in the General Election of 1974. It was the first major study of the voting behaviour of black people in Britain. Their concentration in particular inner city areas, black voters were given more electoral importance than their actual numbers would have warranted. By indicating the potential of the black vote in determining the outcome of elections, the report highlighted the possibilities open to the political parties if the black vote was registered, wooed, secured and won. This was further refined in the Commission for Racial Equality's study of the 1979 General Election (Commission for Racial Equality, 1980). It was through such studies that the notion of the potential importance of the black vote began to be re-evaluated.

After the publication of the CRE's study, the main political parties made special efforts to recruit black members, encouraged them to register and began to compete for their votes at election times. Election literature, manifestos, and election addresses were translated into various Asian languages and bilingual party workers were used during the election campaigns. By 1978 the press was reporting on 'How Tories are wooing immigrants' (Sunday Telegraph, 24 September, 1978). Whilst the Conservative Party began to set up an Anglo-Asian Conservative Society and an Anglo-West Indian Conservative Society, the Labour party established the Labour Party Race Action Group in 1975 (LPRAG). LPRAG acted as a pressure group to educate and advise the party on relevant issues. It distributed a leaflet, *Don't take black votes for granted* to all Constituency Labour parties (CLPs). The leaflet referred to the CRC's study and suggested ways of attracting black support in the 1979 election. The Home Affairs and Organisation Committee of the National

Executive Committee (NEC) also began to examine the issue of the black vote and produced a document, Labour and the Black Electorate, which was circulated to all CLPs in February 1980. This document suggested to the CLPs how black people could be involved in the party. The Labour party was consciously attempting to attract both the black vote and black activists for itself.

The electoral threat to the Labour party posed by the National Front from the mid-seventies, resulted in anti-fascist campaigns to attract black voters and consolidate white support (Layton-Henry, 1984, p.155). Anti-fascist organisations such as the Anti-Nazi League and branches of Campaign Against Racism and Fascism were formed, particularly in response to National Front demonstrations and electoral success. Local Labour parties were actively involved in anti-fascist campaigns and demonstrations. Grant, was one of those active in setting up ALCARAF (All London Campaign Against Racism and Fascism), organising counter demonstrations in Lewisham and Haringey. Atkin was also an active anti-fascist. Such activities facilitated links between black activists and the white left, which was particularly active in these campaigns, both inside and outside the Labour party.

From the mid-seventies, several developments coincided to place the issue of black representation on the political agenda. Local authorities began to aid black community groups and mainstream political parties competed for black votes. The Labour left was preoccupied at this time with party democracy and anti-fascist activity. Consequently, black activists within and without the Labour party began to discuss the issue of black representation in both local authorities and parliament. However, it was not until 1981 that black activists were able to begin to make their voice generally heard on the issue (Howe, 1985, p.11).

The explosion of black anger in the urban ghettoes of Britain in 1981 provided black activists, who had been arguing for greater black representation for some time, with the leverage and opportunity needed to place the issue on the mainstream political agenda. This coincided with the rise of left-led Labour councils concerned about equality of opportunity and policies that would 'most benefit working class people' (Wainwright, 1987, p.97). One of the ways in which the new left-wing councillors hoped to benefit working class people was by 'opening up' to local people and local 'control'. One of the first of these left-led councils to emerge - the Greater London Council (GLC) - implemented its philosophy to open up decision making by trying to involve people they thought were directly affected by the work of the respective committees. As part of this process, the councils began to involve a small layer of black activists in a set of elaborate networks of consultation. Black representatives were co-opted onto council committees, race relations committees were formed, race advisers employed, and grant aid distributed to community organisations (Prashar and Nicholas, 1986, pp.12-25). The result was that black activists were successfully able to argue for greater representation and increased resources through local authority organised conferences and working parties.

As grant-aided organisations and race advisers became reliant on council funding or specific political priorities, young black professionals began to consider it pragmatic to join the local party which supplied the grants and services. Some activists joined their local parties in order to influence individuals and policies which would contribute to success in their application for grant-aid. Lobbying increased as local government cuts began to bite and resources became more scarce. With the demise of campaigns against the cuts and abolition of the GLC, Labour party membership and activity, became necessary for those who needed to secure their funding or work.

For most activists there was little distinction to be made between salaried work and political activity as they regarded their jobs to be consistent with their political objectives. Furthermore the opportunity could be used to build up contacts and networks of like-minded activists. Grant, a Haringey councillor, was able to make contacts through the Black Trade Unionists Solidarity Movement (BTUSM) for which he was a development worker in 1983 and subsequently through his work as an Equal Opportunities Officer in Newham. Narendra Makanji, elected chair of Black Sections in 1988, worked for the GLC Industry and Employment committee and was a Haringey councillor. Russell Proffitt worked for Brent Council, chaired the Race Committee in Lewisham and was a founder member of SCACAC. Diane Abbot, Hackney North MP, was chief press officer for Lambeth council and a Paddington councillor. Philip Murphy worked for the CRE and became a Birmingham councillor.

In general, then, the network of contacts and activists facilitated the formation of Labour Party Black Sections. From the mid-1970s, factors affecting the rise of the Black Sections movement were emerging. At the same time that the left was gaining ground in the party and attempting to democratise it, the mainstream political parties were chasing the black vote. Both of these were important factors in the recruitment of black activists to the Labour party. The rise of left-led Labour councils increased black community reliance on Labour patronage, and thereby strengthened the close relationship developing between black people and the Labour party. It was not until the inner-city rebellions in 1981 against racism, however, that emerging and existing black activists found the lever they needed to fight for more representation and resources for the black community. These demands were articulated from within the Labour party by Black Sections when it was established in 1983.

Why Black Sections?

There have been two main approaches to the formation of Black Sections. On the one hand, some supporters of Black Sections have argued that the key motivation to the establishment of the group has been the view that although black people have consistently voted for Labour over the decades, this was not being reflected in party policies, priorities or its hierarchy. By organising as a section within the party, black Labour party members hoped to involve increasing numbers of black people so that party policies and structures could be changed to take account of black needs. Thus the needs of the black communities in Britain and the electoral support needed by the Labour party would be mutually realised.

On the other hand, for many of the founders and present activists of Black Sections, black political self-organisation has been an organisational principle (Interview with Marc Wadsworth, 7 October 1988). For Black Section activists autonomous organisation within the Labour party was a logical extension of such bodies within unions and workplaces. Thus Grant believed that the existence of black sections would be a 'continuation of the BTUSM in the Labour party' (interview with Bernie Grant, 5 May 1988). Abbot acknowledged in a round table discussion on black sections that 'black sections ... must be seen in the context of the emergence of parallel demands for black sections in the unions' (Marxism Today, September 1985, p.31). Stuart Hall rationalised this perspective in the same round table discussion thus:

> The worst thing for people who are involved in the Labour Party/trade union area is to operate there without autonomous organisation, simply to submerge themselves and the black experience under the agenda set by the predominantly white male organised working class (ibid).

The alternative to being submerged is to organise as a pressure group, or caucus, to transform the organisation by operating from within. Black Sections attempts to do this but also fights for formal recognition within the Labour party.

It is sometimes argued that constitutional recognition as a Black Section has been its overriding objective from the beginning. In 1983 a meeting of existing black activists within the Labour party came together to discuss the merits of setting up a pressure group within the Labour party. After debating the form it should take, it was agreed to demand constitutional recognition along the lines of the Women's and Youth sections. For those who currently argue for compromise with the party to form a socialist society, it is important that the demand for a Black Section began as a tactic in order to achieve some form of recognition from the Labour Leadership (Interview with Paul Sharma, 21 October 1988). Although initially obstructed by Militant activists, a resolution in support of taking this demand to the 1983 Labour Party conference was passed. LPRAG used one of its mailings to circulate a 'model resolution' for annual conference on their behalf and, in September, the Greater London Region of the party allowed them to use its headquarters to launch the campaign (Fitzgerald, 1987, p.32). A composite resolution on Black Sections tabled at the 1983 conference was remitted at the request of the NBC, so that a working party could be set up. On behalf of the NEC Jo Richardson, MP for Barking, promised that 'sympathies are with the aspirations which are behind the composite and we will look carefully at those proposals and any others which come forward through the working party' (Fitzgerald, 1987, p.32). However, what became very clear was that the Black Section initiative was going to come up against passive opposition from the party leadership.

The Labour leadership has consistently opposed Black Sections with the exception of the occasion in April 1984 when Neil Kinnock was reported to have insisted that he was 'open to persuasion' on the matter and 'would seriously consider any recommendations made by a working party on the topic' (Guardian, 11 April 1984). To the surprise of Black Section activists, the leader of the party is on record for saying that 'there was a genuine case to answer that the existence of Black Sections would invite more people from the ethnic minority communities to participate in political activities' (Guardian, 11 April 1984). However, the working party failed to reach any conclusions within its first year. Instead, it produced a discussion document entitled *Black People and the Labour Party*, outlining the case for and against Black Sections. The document was circulated for comment to constituencies and affiliated organisations.

Meanwhile, the Black Sections campaign held its founding national conference in June 1984 in Birmingham. This conference, attended by over 200 people, endorsed a clear demand for the creation of a constitutional Black Section within the party (Times, 11 June 1984). The day concluded with agreement on the formation of Black Section rules and an extended steering committee including more regional members. The overriding argument at the conference was that Black Sections were necessary to challenge Labour taking 'its black members for granted for too long, relying on a few 'Uncle Toms' and 'Godfathers' to deliver the black vote at election time' (Times, 11 June 1984). The activist and journalist Darcus Howe of Race Today, identified their weaknesses at the time as a lack of political orientation and policy which only served to create suspicions of opportunism (Howe, Sept. 1985, p8). Indeed, the campaign had been formed on the basis of fighting 'for greater representation. It was as limited as that' (Interview with Paul Sharma, 21 October 1988). Consequently, the Black Sections Movement brought together a range of black activists with diverse political perspectives united under the banner of representation of black people in mainstream Labour Party politics.

Later that year, however, Black Labour Activists Campaign (BLAC) was formed to 'promote left politics in Black Sections' and develop Black Section as an organisation (*Campaign Black Links – The Way Ahead for Black Section*, July 1985, as amended May 1987). This campaign addressed the criticisms of A. Sivanandan, Director of the Institute of Race Relations, (Race & Class, Autumn 1985 pp.72–4); Darcus Howe from the Race Today Collective (Howe, 1985); and Labour Party members who supported the Militant Tendency, a left wing political group within the Labour party. Sivanandan, Howe and Militant all challenged Black Section for its lack of policies and direction. The response was that:

> The current strength and weakness of Black Sections is that we were originally just about black representation in the Labour Party.

> That got the debate going. But once the ball was in motion it was inevitable we had to decide its direction – 'left', 'right' or 'centre' (*Campaign Black Links – The Way Ahead for Black Sections*, July 1985, As amended May 1987).

Such 'direction' was believed to be essential when it became clear that the Labour leadership would not tolerate nor recognise Black Sections for fear of alienating the white electorate. Although the Black Section leadership up to 1985 could have been relied upon to support Kinnock (Interviews with Paul Sharma, 21 October 1988 and Marc Wadsworth, 7 October 1988), the possibility of losing white voters made recognition for Black Sections untenable. As formal recognition became increasingly unlikely, resignations and realignments took place. BLAC activists finally gained control at the 1985 Black Sections conference when Atkin took over as chair from Russell Proffitt, with a slate of BLAC candidates, supporting an alliance with the Labour left. The future direction of Black Sections was becoming clearer: alliances would be forged with the left of the Labour party and policies would need to be developed. The links with the left further isolated Black Sections from the more moderate to centrist Labour leadership and some early supporters of Black Sections resigned. These included Ben Bousquet, then prospective parliamentary candidate for Kensington and Vidya Anand, then prospective parliamentary candidate for Folkestone and Hythe. By August 1985 Bousquet was publicly accusing leading Black Sections activists of opportunism in criticising Kinnock on South Africa (Guardian, 15 August 1985).

From 1985, the leading lights of Black Sections were organised around BLAC. At national level they included Marc Wadsworth, Narendra Makanji, Sharon Atkin, Diane Abbot, Bernie Grant, Paul Sharma, Keith Vaz and Chris Khamis. Having identified Black Sections with the Labour left, they looked to the left in the CLPs to support their pursuit of recognition and representation. With the process of reselection and selection of parliamentary candidates underway, BLAC identified fourteen safe seats where large black electorates could be found, and called on 'genuine anti-racist, white hopefuls to look elsewhere'; the group also called for CLPs 'with large black electorates to invoke short-lists for selection which consist entirely of 'good' black candidates' (Caribbean Times, 1 February 1985). BLAC activists had led up to this demand carefully, using the media to make maximum impact. They warned the party that it risked losing black voters by failing to give blacks representation in the party structure (Times, 29 September 1984). In October Abbot claimed some opponents of Black Sections were racist (Times, 4 October 1984) followed by a Black activist's claim that Labour could win the next election if it secured the black vote by providing greater black representation in the party (Times, 5 October 1984). Although conference had recognised the need to develop policies, energy was still predominantly channelled into demands for recognition and representation.

These demands were articulated through the lobbying of constituency parties. Between 1983 and 1984 this increased the number of resolutions to Labour party conference from 4 to 18 in favour of Black Sections, with 7 amendments and only 1 resolution against. At the 1984 Labour party conference, the NEC requested remission until the outcome of the consultation was known. The movers of the composite resolution in favour of Black Sections refused to remit and were heavily defeated on a card vote. The resolution against Black Sections, however, was carried. Support for Black Sections was just as scarce at its Labour Party conference fringe meeting. Out of the 200 people at the meeting, 'fifty of them (were) black. Of the blacks, the majority were militant supporters hostile to the platform' (Howe, 1985, pp.6–10).

The left–led Black Sections continued its campaign into 1985 by calling for white middle class males representing constituencies with large black populations to stand down in favour of black candidates (Times, 21 January 1985). Since white males formed the majority of parliamentary candidates and MPs, any attempts to increase black representation in parliament would mean a decrease in white male candidates. The campaign also began to win support from London constituencies to set up Black Sections (Times, 22 February 1985). By April, six constituencies had declared their support. In response the party leadership intervened in opposition (Times, 15 March 1985). The NEC was able to gain the support of the country's most prominent black union official, Bill Morris, who told a Tribune fringe meeting in September 1985 that he was opposed to Black Sections (Guardian, 3 September 1985). Later that month, Morris won the post of deputy general secretary of the Transport & General Workers' Union (TGWU). The Labour Party leadership, of course, welcomed Morris's appointment in the light of his opposition to Black Sections (Times, 18 September 1985). The leadership of the party was wary of the new left leadership of Black Sections and its formal links with the left. But, before the working party had reported its findings (which supported the principle of Black Sections) in June 1985, people had become entrenched in the positions they held.

Under pressure, the leadership of the party made various attempts to find a compromise solution to be presented to the 1985 party conference. In June 1985, for example, Kinnock supported the formation of a black rights group in the Labour Party, but made it clear that such a group would not be exclusively black. In July 1985 the NEC rejected by 15 votes to 7 the report of a working party calling for Black Sections. Even a compromise motion proposed by then chair of the Labour Party, Eric Heffer MP from Liverpool did not win support. The NEC defeated his plan for black groups to affiliate to the party by 16 votes to 8. Although the leadership sought a compromise, their parameters remained strict.

By the time of the party's conference in 1985, the political climate within the party had changed. The 1984 miners strike had been defeated and left–wing Labour councils' opposition to ratecapping discredited. Both the miners strike and the local authority resistance to ratecapping were associated with the left. They were also seen by the Labour leadership as an obstacle to electoral success. Consequently, Kinnock decided to whip the left into line. Black Sections did not escape the onslaught, from the leadership. Conference voted five to one against amending the party constitution to provide for separate Black Sections. The compromise forwarded by the leadership and adopted by conference was a new 'Black and Asian Advisory Committee' with black members drawn from the regions, CLPs and trade unions alongside representatives of the NEC. Conference also backed a proposal to appoint a new party official with special responsibility to service the committee and to advise local parties on 'improving the position of Black and Asian peoples in the party and for monitoring progress' (Fitzgerald, 1987, p.331). This indicated that the Labour leadership recognised the importance of its relationship with black people but also feared a white backlash which could lose votes. Although Labour was pursuing black votes, it did not wish to alienate its traditional white working class voters. The Labour leadership was attempting to balance the two conflicting pressures in order to win maximum votes.

Black Sections activists refused to compromise but continued to fight for recognition. Despite the defeat they emphasised that conference had increased threefold its support for the idea since the 1984 debate on the issue (Times, 1 October 1985). Black Sections activists attacked the Black and Asian Advisory Committee, and well into 1986 Black Sections threatened boycotts and mass resignations. Wadsworth, who asked the 12 members elected to the committee to resign, argued that it could never substitute for Black Sections which would ensure automatic representation at every level of the Labour Party (The Independent, 3 October 1987). Indeed, the BAAC received little support. The Labour leadership was forced to recognise this in 1988 when discussions were sought with Grant and proposals for an affiliate society were supported at Labour party conference.

Black Sections' refusal to cooperate with BAAC resulted in further acrimony between Black Sections supporters and the Labour leadership. Compromise proposals in 1986 continued to be opposed. An NEC meeting in July 86 rejected a proposal by Eric Heffer and Tony Benn for black people to be allowed to form their own affiliated groups with representation on the NEC (Guardian, 16 July 1986). A few months later Roy Hattersley, MP, played a prominent role in opposing the creation of a Black Section in the constituency of Birmingham Sparkbrook, which be represented. The subsequent conflict in Birmingham resulted in the expulsion of Amir Khan and Kevin Scally from the Labour Party. Supported by the Labour left, Black Sections campaigned successfully for their reinstatement.

The more Black Sections was isolated from the party leadership, the more it was forced to turn to the left for support. In September 1986 Black Sections became a founder member of the campaign Forum of Labour MPs launched as 'an Alliance for Socialism', bringing together groups on the 'hard' left of the party. Such alliances, in turn, alienated Black Sections from the party leadership. Isolation and links with the left made campaigning and policy work increasingly important areas of development.

In May 1987 a Black Sections internal document from July 1985 was amended. It identified two options. The movement could either concentrate energy on forcing change through party conference or place greater emphasis on extra-party activities based on links with the black community to 'prioritise joint campaigning and joint platforms with the black single-issue protest groups' *(Campaign Black Links - The Way Ahead for Black Sections*, July 1985, As amended May 1987). The March 1987 Black Sections AGM in Nottingham had indicated that substance would be given to policies and campaign work. The theme of the AGM was Going on the Offensive with the Black Agenda (Chair's report to 1988 Annual Conference) and the conference adopted policy positions on a number of key issues, including the police, immigration, law, education and parliamentary activity. In 1988 these were amongst the policies incorporated into the document The Black Agenda examined below.

Another development which became clear in 1987 was the gradual separation between those Black Sections supporters who were elected to office and those who were not. A tension was emerging over the issue of recognition caused by the success of the demand for greater representation. Those elected to office remained under pressure to maintain a Black Sections perspective. Some of those elected appeared less enthusiastic than before. At the October 1987 Labour Party conference in Blackpool, leading Black Sections activists and MPs Grant and Vaz made public their opposition to maintain the fight for constitutional recognition. Two resolutions calling for Black Sections to be adopted were overwhelmingly rejected but Grant made clear that he was 'opposed to us coming back next year and saying we want Black Sections recognised by the Labour Party' (Independent, 3 October 1987). Grant, backed by Vaz, stressed that he continued to support the principle of black representation but suggested some form of affiliation. This was contradicted by Marc Wadsworth, chair of National Black Sections who reiterated, 'We are here to fight, here to stay and will be back next year' (ibid). Those activists who did not seek office, tended to remain committed to the fight for recognition as a section.

Paul Sharma, who left Black Sections in May 1987, also publicised his newly favoured option of a socialist society (New Life, 16 October 1987). Sharma lobbied Bill Morris, who subsequently wrote an article for *Tribune* supporting the idea (Interview with Paul Sharma, 21 October 1988). The debate on the form of recognition that should be pursued continued to be conducted through the media from October 1987 to the 1988 Black Sections AGM. Bill Morris, Paul Boateng MP for Brent and Kingsley Abrams appeared on television whilst Paul Sharma made his views public in the Asian Herald, (22-28 March 1988). At the conference debate on 'The Way Forward', Wadsworth reported that Black Sections supporters' commitment to the fight for constitutional recognition had not abated. A consultation exercise launched in November to establish the views of the 'rank and file' outlined five options but 'Not a single submission proposed (sic) we cease making our case at Labour party Conference' (National Committee Report of Strategy Consultation, February 1988, p1). Consequently, conference agreed that:

> should a precise proposal come forward which meets our criteria and has the support of significant unions and/or Labour's national executive our national conference be recalled to decide whether or not to accept. Irrespective of this, we should continue as before but with much greater emphasis on deepening our roots in Black community struggle and more attention to trade union work (National Committee report of Strategy Consultation, Feb. 1988, p.3).

Throughout the 1988 conference delegates recognised that issues such as the poll tax needed to be addressed by Black Sections and speaker after speaker agreed on the need to strengthen Black Sections locally. Nevertheless, conference concluded that constitutional recognition, in whatever form, should be negotiated by Grant and Kinnock. The two chief tasks of recognition and campaigning were not contradictory since both were rooted in the objective of change through the Labour party.

Direct negotiations between Grant and Kinnock's representative proved fruitless. Nevertheless, the party's conference in October 1988 passed a motion from Glasgow Pollock CLP resolving to instruct the NEC to bring proposals for the establishment of an organisation for black people modelled on Labour's socialist societies to the next conference. Whilst Sharma and Morris support the idea, Black Sections remains sceptical since its experience of the Working Party led by Jo Richardson in 1984/5. According to a Black Sections press release, 'We shall be redoubling our efforts in the coming year to win recognition for Black Sections' (Black Sections, Press Release, October 1988).

The difficulties faced by the movement in its relentless pursuit of black representation via constitutional recognition in the Labour Party are evident in the experience of Birmingham Black Sections. Roy Hattersley and the Black Sections movement have always been opposed to each other. Black sections supporters and Kevin Scally, Secretary of Sparkhill ward, appeared in a Channel Four programme, shown on 26 September 1985, alleging recruitment irregularities in Sparkbrook. Hattersley opposed the setting up of the Sparkbrook CLP Black Section (The Birmingham Post, 21 September 1985). At the Party's conference that year he passionately opposed Black Sections once again. By 15 October, however, 35 Labour members in Birmingham CLP were requesting admission to Black Sections as a result of a CLP meeting which reselected councillor John O'Keefe as the candidate for the next city council elections (Daily News, 15 October 1985). Scuffles broke out at the meeting where Hattersley was branded a 'racist' for supporting Councillor O'Keefe. Mohammed Rafique, the constituency's membership secretary argued that although he had stood, he was not given a fair chance to fight for the position and would join Black Sections to 'fight for justice' (Voice,

2 November 1985). The upheaval within the CLP resulted in the expulsion from the Labour party of Mohammed Rafique, Amir Khan, and Kevin Scally for bringing the party into disrepute (Birmingham Post, 27 November 1985; Evening Mail, 11 December 1985). Khan, a Birmingham city councillor and Rafique claimed that it was a 'witch hunt' against Black Section supporters.

Despite their treatment at the hands of the Labour party, some of the expelled members were determined to be reinstated. Indeed, Black Sections was central to the 'Campaign to Reinstate Amir Khan and Kevin Scally'. Other ex-Labour party members led by Mohammed Quereshi, however, formed another party in January 1986 - the Democratic Party. In February it had 500 members - 70 of whom it claimed were former Labour Party members. One newspaper then claimed that the 'split from Labour was triggered by the expulsion of two Asian councillors from Sparkbrook Labour Party for conduct considered to be not in the best interests of the party' (Birmingham Post, 3/2/86). Nevertheless Khan, expelled from the Party, sympathised but refused to join: 'I shall remain loyal to the Labour Party whatever happens' (Birmingham Post, 3 February 1986). In 1987, Khan went further than this and buried his differences with Hattersley to campaign for him in the general election (Guardian, 3 June 1987).

Black Sections commitment to the Labour party at any cost also became clear when Black prospective parliamentary candidates in the 1987 General Election found that their association with Black Sections placed their candidacy in jeopardy. In the wake of the Greenwich by-election the Labour leadership began a clean-up campaign within the party ranks. As well as stepping up the campaign against Militant, the 'loony left' and gay activists, Kinnock made his intentions towards Black Sections clear. He secured majority backing from the NEC for a resolution which threatened disciplinary action against future 'separatist' activity. The six black prospective parliamentary candidates, who belonged to Labour Party Black Sections, were told not to subscribe to statements of Black Section policy which differed from the general party programme (Guardian, 26 March 1986). Black Section's response to such a forthright attack from the leadership was a defensive one: 'There is no question of caucasing against the Labour party. We are part and parcel of the Labour party' (Guardian, 26 March 1986).

The Labour leadership had no intention of smashing any moves towards black representation. What it sought to do was to contain and incorporate these demands in an acceptable form. It knew that black representation could be used to its electoral advantage. The Labour leadership maintained sufficient opposition to show white voters who could be alienated by Black Sections, that the leadership remained in control. It also asserted control whenever it needed to remind Black Sections what the acceptable parameters were. Thus Atkin's deselection in 1987 operated as a disciplinary device which warned the other black candidates of the penalties of challenging either the leadership's priorities or the party's racism.

It is against this background of events that an unofficial Black Sections movement has operated within the Labour party. The following pages examine the work and the achievements of Black Sections locally and nationally in order to assess the impact and effect of Black Sections' electoral work, policies, campaigning and form of organisation.

Black Sections as a Pressure Group

The efforts of Black Sections within the Labour party can be broadly divided into electoral work, which has won members to the party and resulted in the election of black councillors, and MPs; policy and campaign work, to build community support; and the organisational development of the movement itself.

Electoral Work

The objectives of Black Sections have formally been in line with those of the Labour Party leadership, 'To secure the support of black people for the principles and policy of the Labour Party ... To recruit black people into the Labour party and to give all possible help, as far as may be practicable, to achieve the principles and aims of the Labour Party' (Labour Party Black Section, *Rules for the Labour Party Black Section*, Draft as amended in March 1987', p.1). In attempts to secure black votes for Labour, Black Sections coined the slogan 'Registration, Recruitment and Representation' in 1984 and organised around it. Black Sections led registration drives through councils, encouraging thousands of people to place their names on the electoral register. In the council elections in Haringey, for example, the result according to writer and researcher Hilary Wainwright was a rise of 20,000 names on the electoral register, most of whom were black. This was reflected in an increase in both the turn-out of black voters and the size of the Labour vote (Wainwright, 1987, p.196). When the Greater London Labour party launched a major drive for black electoral registration in the run up to council elections in May 1986, leading Black Sections supporters, like Grant and Abbot, who had benefited from such work in the past, helped with its launch even though officially Wadsworth, as chair of National Blacks Section condemned the campaign as a 'cynical vote garnering exercise' (Voice, 28 January 1986).

As well as enfranchising black people, Black Sections activists encouraged black people to join the party. A membership drive among the Asian community in Southall, for example, turned the Glebe ward into the biggest Labour ward in the country. Recruitment was used as a means of ensuring the selection of black candidates. In Southall the work was intended to facilitate the reselection and replacement of Sid Bidwell (Video of 'Reporting London', 1985, courtesy of Atkin). In Nottingham, it was possible for four black candidates to be selected to 'winnable' council seats in 1987 where before there were none (Wainwright, 1987, p.194). This was possible because there were 27 black delegates to the General Management Committee and four or five Black Sections supporters as chairs of their ward parties with Hassan Ahmed as chair of the constituency.

The new black members and black voters provided the pressure and machinery that Black Sections needed to have black candidates short-listed, selected and elected to office. By 1986 a number of black councillors had been elected to Lambeth council as a result of local Black Sections pressure. These included Kingsley Smith, Linda Bellos, Irma Critchlow, Sharon Atkin, Amelda Inyand, Janet Boateng and others. At various points they became committee chairs, Bellos became leader of the Council and Kingsley Smith became mayor. The performance of Black sections in Lambeth was a result of the local branches making use of opportunities such as the suspensions from office over ratecapping which made candidates hard to come by.

Not only have recruitment and registration drives amongst black communities provided leverage for Black Sections to increase black electoral representation, but they have also been useful in strengthening Labour's position in important inner-city wards (Jacobs, 1988, p.82). Jacobs indicates that moderate Labour party members have supported the Black Section call because they recognise its usefulness in this respect. Similarly, black Labour candidates have been selected in areas where they can usefully win seats for the Labour party (The Next Step, 10 – 17 July 1987, pp.10–11). In the 1986 local election, Labour fielded 168 black candidates, nearly all of them in areas of high black concentration – 148 in London alone. Black candidates were particularly concentrated where Labour wanted to win black votes from the Tories. Thus Labour fielded 24 black candidates in Brent, which had a minority Tory council before May. In Hackney, which also has a high black population but is a safe Labour borough, there were just nine black Labour candidates (The Next Step, 10–17 July 1987, pp.10–11). The Labour party appeared to be using Black Sections' electoral machine in order to win seats for Labour rather than to promote black representation. Indeed, the Labour leadership's decision to deselect Atkin and replace her with Aslam in the 1987 General Election, was further indication of Labour's cynical manipulation for electoral gain. The replacement of a radical black candidate with a more moderate black candidate had the effect of silencing other black candidates afraid of losing their own candidacy if they spoke out. The Labour leadership was happy to allow black candidates in the General election as long as they operated on NEC terms.

Black Sections has always emphasised the need for electoral gains; in 1986 Black Sections stressed that:

> Four years ago we predicted there would be a threefold increase in the number of councillors elected in London alone and, with the total now standing at more than 200, that has come true. The 45 strong ruling Labour group on the newly-formed elected Inner

> London Education Authority has nine black members. In a quarter of the selection processes the Black Section was involved, and Labour's national leaders were forced to back down and accept our participation. That sets an important precedent (Labour Party Black Sections, Newsletter, Autumn 1986.)

The consequence of such electorally oriented politics, however, has been to turn political issues and black anger into a question of black faces in office. The creation of a black electoral machine to pursue black representation has been at the expense of mobilising black community support around issues. The success of electing hundreds of black councillors and four black MPs has reinforced the view that black representation, rather than mobilisation, can achieve change for black people.

The importance placed on electing black people to office because they are black may result in the neglect of candidates' political positions. Given the broad range of political views held by black councillors and MPs, political conflict has been inevitable. Local government cuts has been one of the issues over which black councillors and activists have been in dispute. After the third Labour defeat in Parliament in 1987 and the experiences of Liverpool and Lambeth over ratecapping in 1985/6, the Labour left had reflected on whether or not the government could be confronted over the cuts at all. The result was a split between the 'hard' and 'soft' left in the party. Supporters of Benn, believed in opposing the cuts but the soft left took its cue from Kinnock and adopted a 'dented shield strategy' of side-stepping the issue of cuts by defending the most 'deprived'. The split in the Labour left was reflected amongst Black Section councillors in 1988. In Haringey, Grant and Ossamer were at odds on the issue. Lambeth leader Linda Bellos defied the anti-cuts position of her local Black Section, even though Sharon Atkin had been surcharged and suspended from office in 1986 for her opposition to ratecapping. The pursuit of black representation has now resulted in black councillors implementing cuts in jobs and services. For example, £17 million of cuts made by Brent's black councillors in 1988, made newly Tory controlled Bradford council's proposals of £5 million of cuts appear insignificant.

With black councillors firmly in place, it was logical for Black Sections to argue for black representation in Parliament. Although several black prospective parliamentary candidates (PPCs) had been selected for Labour in 1983, they had all been standing in predominantly white middle class areas. In 1985, when the selection process was underway, Black Sections targeted constituencies with a high proportion of black voters and then worked with supporters in the CLPs to ensure trade union or branch nomination of someone from their 'blacklist'. Black Sections claims direct responsibility for the selection of black Labour PPCs and, consequently the four MPs. There were, however, other factors involved in the selection of the four candidates that won the election. Perhaps the greatest pressure on Tottenham CLP to select a black candidate arose from the revolts on Broadwater Farm, which had to be contained. In Brent left-wing support ensured an all black short-list. In Nottingham, Atkin was encouraged to stand by the local women's section, and in Leicester pressure had been placed on the Labour Party by the 'massive abstention of black electors in 1983 when they were so disgusted that Labour selected a London lawyer instead of a black candidate to fight Leicester east that they abstained. That allowed Peter Bruinvels the Tory to win' (Interview with Paul Sharma, 21 October 1988). In order for Labour to win Leicester in 1987, black votes through a black candidate was essential.

Once selected, the candidates were under pressure to distance themselves from Black Sections in order to maintain the backing of the Labour leadership. At the 1986 Black Section AGM, a proposal to produce a black manifesto for the June 1987 General Election was put forward. The Labour Party NEC responded with threats of expulsion and increased the pressure by deselecting Atkin for publicly describing the Labour party as 'racist'. Atkin's deselection indicated dramatically that the Labour party would treat black activists like any other party members: they could only participate in its ranks if they remained within the parameters defined by the leadership. Kinnock's efforts to strengthen his own authority by marginalising the hard left affected Black Sections because it was closely allied to the left and could upset white voters. Hence, Black Sections did not escape the deselection of candidates and expulsion of individual members. When Grant, Abbot, Proffitt and Boateng not only remained silent over Atkin's deselection but signed a statement pledging allegiance to Labour it became clear that the candidates had accepted the Labour leadership line on party unity (Race and Immigration, May 1987). For Race Today this revealed that because the candidates were 'parliamentarians of the old sort, not different from most benchwarmers of all parties, we cannot expect from among them one to emerge as a black Bobby Sands or Bernadette Devlin (Race Today, June/July 1987). That is, rather than using their position in parliament as a platform for black liberation and exposing the limitations of parliament, they would become part of the parliamentary machine. Leading Black Sections activists have expressed similar concerns:

> It was a statement to black people that when push comes to shove, the party comes first ... we do not have black MPs. We have Labour MPs who happen to be black (Interview with Marc Wadsworth, 7 October 1988).

The commitment to Labour and its potential effect is shown most starkly by Diane Abbot. When Britain's first black woman MP, spoke in defence of Labour Party colleagues in Brent, she indicated quite clearly the potential demobilising effect that the black MPs could have. Addressing Brent Nalgo's October 1988 AGM, Abbot argued that council staff should not attack Labour councillors (Public service, December 1988). In a borough where black councillors have led cutbacks in jobs and services which affect black people, Abbot's concern was the defence of the Labour local authority and not the defence of local jobs and services.

One effect of Black Sections work has been to create a flexible electoral machine, pinning all hope of liberation away from the streets and workplaces and onto the election of black 'tribunes'. Even Wadsworth acknowledges that for these tribunes, the Labour Party takes priority above issues of Black Sections or black people. The pursuit of black liberation is equated with the achievements of black MPs and councillors rather than the active resistance of ordinary people against every manifestation of racism. A year after their election, the 'tribunes' appeared in the press and on television arguing that there was little that they could do as four new MPs in opposition (City Limits, 16–23 October 1988). At the same time, marches and revolts against racism are at an all time low. It could be argued that the pursuit of black representation, and its success, has channelled black anger and militancy into the official political machinery and neutralised it. Black anger is rendered harmless because it is directed away from effective mobilisation against racism and directed towards bureaucratic political machinery.

Policies and Campaigning

Although the development of policies that could be taken into the Labour party was initiated by BLAC activists and agreed at the March 1985 Black Sections conference in London, the first policy position did not emerge until the 1986 AGM agreed a paper on South Africa. Serious attempts to implement the new direction towards policy and campaign work did not occur until March 1987. One hundred and sixty delegates representing 48 sections attended the 1987 Black Section conference. The theme was 'setting the black political agenda'. As noted earlier, policy positions on a number of key issues, including the police, immigration, law, education and parliamentary activity were adopted. This continued in 1988 when the AGM agreed on a position paper on education. These policies were brought together in the form of <u>The Black Agenda</u>, published in 1988 to 'form the basis for debate among anti-racists inside and outside the Labour Party, paving the way for a firm set of policies decided by Black People to be finally put into practice by British local and national government' (Black Section, <u>The Black Agenda</u>, 1988). However, as Sivanandan pointed out:

> The Black Agenda is meaningless to me and to you as an agenda unless it is the agenda of a political party which can deliver the goods. If it is not part of a political party that can deliver the goods then the agenda cannot be activated. If the agenda cannot be activated then what are those responsible for Black Section doing at the grass roots level? (Interview with A. Sivanandan, 25 October 1988).

As Black Sections and its agenda are not recognised by the Labour Party in opposition, there is little hope of the group's policies being incorporated into a national party strategy. Nor can Black Sections rely on local Labour councils since they increasingly refuse to implement policies which require challenging the law or overspending. Sivanandan's question suggests that if it is not possible to ensure the policies are put into practise by the Labour party, then the approach which remains is one of mobilising black people to campaign for such policies.

Nevertheless, Black Sections continues to look to the Labour Party to implement the demands outlined in the document. The Black Agenda recognises that 'State Racism' in the form of immigration controls, policing and social policy is a key problem (Black Sections, 1981 p.6). In their current form, however, the demands in the document are not based on a strategy to eradicate racism. Even where the bipartisan approach to immigration is cited, the ten demands are 'short-term' ones which tackle the effects and not the causes of racism (Black Sections, 1988, pp.22-24). This is likely to remain the case for as long as Black Sections relies on the Labour Party to implement these demands whilst simultaneously recognising both Labour and Tory needs for immigration controls.

The need to strengthen roots in the black localities by conducting campaigns in them, has been identified and repeated since 1985. In practise, Black Sections' involvement in community campaigns has included work on the Broadwater Farm Defence Campaign and Handsworth Defence Campaign from 1985; Newham 7 and Justice for the Pryces campaigns in Newham in 1985; Viraj Mendis in sanctuary in Manchester; sacked workers at Kenure Plastics in Middlesex in 1986; Wheelers Restaurant; Diamond Four in 1987; Clinton McCurbin in Wolverhampton in 1987; Trevor Monerville in Stoke Newington from 1987; Harwich Ferry Refugees in 1987; Dewsbury in Kirklees in 1988. Nevertheless, Black Sections qua Black Sections has not been able to mobilise significant numbers to such rallies. In many of the campaigns where leading support has come from Black Sections supporters, they have been working in other capacities. On Broadwater Farm, for example, Martha Ossamor and Bernie grant operated more as councillors than as Black Sections activists.

Many of the campaigns which Black Sections has been involved in are not based in mobilising wide community support. Campaigns such as those to reinstate Khan and Scally in Birmingham in 1986; support Kingsley Abrams for the Young Socialist place on the NEC in 1986; attempts to unite with Militant Tendency to oppose alleged witch-hunts; Suspensions in 1986, Abolitions and the 65% Campaign in Birmingham in 1987, are like the Black Sections campaign itself. That is, they are about internal Labour Party matters. These campaigns have not mobilised black communities but have succeeded in consolidating Black Sections' links with the Labour left. This culminated in Black Section support for the hard left's unsuccessful challenge to the leadership in 1988 which was led by Tony Benn and Eric Heffer.

Nevertheless, a new layer of black activists has been attracted to Black Sections as a result of its efforts to campaign and its association with the Labour left. These include Kuomba Balogun and Unmesh Desai, longstanding critic of Black Sections (Marxism Today, September 1985, pp.31–36). Although it was hoped that Desai's co-option onto the campaigns committee of Black Sections in 1988 would facilitate campaigning, Desai's energy went into standing for selection as Labour Party candidate in a Newham Council by-election. By joining Black Sections, Desai and others have taken the risk of 'becoming machine politicians' at the expense of mobilising the black community (Interview with Sivanandan, 25 October 1988).

As noted earlier, one of the founding members of Black Sections, Bernie Grant, also began his career as a trade unionist and political campaigner. He soon learned that since the objective during a General Election campaign is black representation in Parliament, rather than mobilising against racism, black prospective parliamentary candidates could not afford to be seen as electoral liabilities. The crude test was whether the black votes they could gain would outweigh the white votes lost. Similarly, once in Parliament, Grant recognised the need to operate carefully. As he told Darcus Howe:

> If the black community says that we need representation in parliament, well then they have to expect that I will act as a parliamentarian. They can't expect me to act in the same way I did when I was the leader of the Black Trade Union Solidarity Movement ... Your situation changes and then your approach has to change with that (Race Today, Jan/Feb., 1988).

This is not treachery or selling out but the logical conclusion of pursuing a strategy of representation rather than mobilisation. Unless there is grass roots pressure, the only way that representation can be maintained is through manoeuvring and acceptability to those in control. Black Sections activists have been integrated into Labour party politics and the MPs into the parliamentary process. The message is: do not challenge the system when you can have a stake in it.

Despite Black Sections success in increasing Black representation throughout the mainstream political process, the Labour party does not present anything very positive to its black supporters. Its policies on immigration and policing, key issues for black people, continue to maintain racism. Black Sections cannot change these without sufficient pressure from outside the Labour party. Although it intends to campaign for policies in black communities, Black Sections will face the same problems: it will only be allowed to operate on the Labour leadership's terms. And the promotion of confrontational policies could result in another leadership assault on Black Sections.

Organisational Structure

The nature of Black Sections has ensured that its key achievements have been at an organisational rather than a political level. Black Sections was formed on the demands of recognition and representation and not a policy programme. Therefore, it has never been a movement attempting to mobilise people against racism, although racism is identified by Black Sections as a key problem. It is a pressure group or a political coalition of individual activists seeking change in the Labour party. It is therefore logical that Labour Party Black Sections is organised to almost shadow the structure of the Labour Party. For example, according to its rules, local Black Sections must be constituted so that 'The area to be covered by the Constituency Labour Party Black Section shall correspond to the area covered by the Constituency Labour party' (Rules for Labour Party Black Sections, March 1987). The 'Objects' of the 40 local Black Sections (Ali, 1988, pp.147–151) also correspond closely to the structure and operation of the Labour party. The sections support and nominate black members for Parliamentary and Local Government selections as well as elections for Party officers. Local Black Sections AGMs elect delegates to the General Management Committee of the CLP, a delegate to the Executive of the CLP and delegates to the Local Government Committee 'on the same basis as that adopted by the Constituency Labour Party' (Rules for Labour Party Black Section, March 1987). This structure enables local sections to maximise their imput into local CLPs. Similarly, Regional Labour Party Black Sections correspond to Regional Labour Parties. They cover the same area and a key function is to advise the Regional Council of the Labour Party.

The supreme body of Black Sections is Annual National Conference, just as the supreme body of the Labour Party is Annual Conference. According to the 'Rules for the National Labour Party Black Section' (Rules for Labour Party Black Section, March 1987, p.9), Black Sections Conference should nominate two representatives to the Labour Party National Executive Committee. Despite the Labour Party's refusal to recognise Black Sections, two nominations were made in 1988. Diane Abbot was Black Section NEC candidate for the Constituency Division and Martha Ossamor for the Women's Division. Ironically, NEC nominations which are not recognised by the Labour party created the greatest stir at National Black Sections conference in 1988.

Between conferences, decisions on policy and the running of Black Sections are taken by the National Committee. This comprises two delegates from each Black Section, at least one of whom must be a woman. In turn, this committee appoints regional organisers. National Conference also elects a National Executive consisting of eight officers. These range from Chair to National Campaigns Organiser. Also represented on the National Committee and Executive are the Parliamentary Black Section; Black Section Councillors; Women in Black Section; Black Section Youth Committee.

The key demands of Black Sections are articulated through this structure: recognition and representation at all levels of the party. The structure is also appropriate to recruit black people to the Labour Party. The campaign's primary purpose, however, has been to apply pressure for constitutional change within the Labour Party. This concern has necessitated the development of an organisation which broadly mirrors the Labour Party structure, embellished with rules which they would like to see adopted by Labour. Such embellishments include the rules relating to the full participation of women in delegations and on committees. Campaigning around policies was not, however, reflected organisationally until the 1987 Conference decision to establish a Campaigns Committee and National Campaigns Officer.

Although Black Sections is well organised to affect all forums of the Labour Party, its founding national conference in 1984 was 'shambolically organised...with shouting and chaos' (Interview with Chris Khamis, 2 November 1988). Unhappy about both the direction of Black Sections and its weak organisational form, BLAC set about trying to put it 'on a firm footing and get ourselves organised with a proper constitution, elected officers and a tight knit group' (Interview with Chris Khamis, 2 November 1988). BLAC supporters elected as Black Sections leaders in 1985, ensured the organisation's development. Although attendance at these conferences declined from over 200 at the first national conference, 168 delegates in 1987 to 50 in 1988, the matters were efficiently dealt with.

Black Sections has consistently emphasised the importance of bringing people of Afro-Caribbean and Asian descent together in the organisation. It has united Afro-Asian people under the banner 'Black', opposing ethnic divisions and rivalry. According to Sivanandan, the notion 'Black' had been the result of organising as 'communities of resistance' in response to racism. Having lost its 'political culture' and become a 'cultural colour' rivalry between ethnic groups for resources and representation was set to spread (Interview with Sivanandan, 25 October 1988). Sivanandan describes how 'Black, as a political colour, was finally broken down when government monies were used to fund community projects, destroying thereby the self-reliance and community cohesion that we had built up in the 1960s (Race and Class, Autumn 1983, p.4). He recognises that although Black Sections try to reconstitute 'Black', it is changing 'Black as a grassroots struggle...to black as a parliamentary struggle' (Race and Class, Autumn 1983, p.4). Since Black Sections do not mobilise 'communities of resistance', Afro-Asian unity remains at the level of internal, organisational or electoral achievements.

Black Sections cannot mobilise 'communities of resistance' because that is not their *raison d'etre*. The nearest Black Sections can get to mobilising is 'the mobilisation of Black people into the Labour Party and Black Party members into the Black Section movement' (Black Sections, Rules for the Labour Party Black Section, March 1987). Once inside the Labour party, members are constrained by the Labour leadership. Achievements are then a result of Black Sections ability to organise and manoeuvre effectively; through interventions and fringe meetings at Labour party conferences, organising within CLPs, and gaining maximum publicity. The emphasis on organisational matters has the effect of making political debates secondary to organisational questions.

The broad range of views held by Black Sections supporters has resulted in on-going tensions and conflict. For example, the pledge of allegiance to the Labour party from four PPCs put 'great strain on Black Section unity at a time when it was most crucial' (Ali, 1988, p.149). These tensions inevitably occur because of the different pressures on individual supporters. At the Birmingham meeting, Atkin was under strong pressure from black separatists and responded by acknowledging Labour's racism. The four candidates, however, were under greater pressure from Labours Headquarters on Walworth Road to sign a statement or risk deselection. Having been selected through manoeuvring within the Labour Party rather than through pressure from the black community, when a crisis developed, the candidates were isolated. Lack of community pressure strengthened the Labour leadership's grip. The root conflict is between Black Sections' commitment to Labour and, ultimately, Parliament on the one hand and its commitment to fight racism on the other. Black Sections supporters readily acknowledge the racist nature of the Labour Party and yet try to reconcile the irreconcilable: Black liberation through the Labour Party. The very premise of Black Sections is rooted in a political contradiction. The same contradiction is apparent in Black Sections attitude towards Parliament and its structures. On the one hand the official political process is decried racist and on the other hand Black Sections seeks to use it to fight racism. When political conflicts arise, they can only be dealt with organisationally.

For as long as Black Sections is committed to the Labour party, its primary purpose will be to provide us with more black representatives. Racism will not be eradicated, however, by electing more MPs. Any serious opposition or mobilisation against racism would mean opposition to the racism of all political parties and parliament. Opposition to racism would mean opposition to the Labour party itself since it has been part and parcel of the development of racism in post-war Britain. Anti-racism means mobilising people against the causes as well as the effects of racism. For black struggle this means building an organisation that fights to defend black people's rights. Such an organisation would not blame the white working class for racism and make alliances with racist parties. The organisation that is needed must show how all sections of the working class are weakened by oppression. Unfortunately for Black Sections, the Labour party is not the organisation that can play this role. Therefore, within the Labour Party, Black Sections pursues representation and amelioration rather than mobilisation and social transformation. This is not a tactical discussion but, rather, the nub of their problem.

Conclusion

From the late seventies both black activists and central government sought change. Whilst black activists were concerned that black people had been consistently voting Labour with little to show for it, central government feared social unrest. Consequently, black activists began to demand representation through the Labour party, local authorities and parliament while the state produced concessions that would tie black activists more closely to the existing political and economic process.

The result has been that Black Sections activists and the four black MPs are totally committed to the Labour party. They endure suspensions, expulsions, deselections, opposition from the Labour leadership and yet continue to campaign for the Labour party. This is because they believe that the Labour party can and must be transformed to reflect the interests of black people. The pressure considered necessary to achieve this is applied through the Black Sections campaign for recognition and representation. In reality, however, the Labour leadership has shown that it controls the Labour party's direction. For black people that means they may participate and pursue anti-racist policies only on the terms acceptable to the Labour leadership. These terms are highly influenced by the potential vote-losing effects of many Black Sections demands. Although the Labour party needs black votes, it must balance this against the possibility of alienating white voters. Consequently, whilst the Labour leadership restricts what black activists may say and do, Black Sections continue to build support for the Labour party amongst black communities. The effect is a campaign for a party which activists themselves have declared 'racist' and a struggle to be formally identified with that party.

The state has encouraged the integration of black people into mainstream politics through black activists in the Labour party. Radical Black Sections supporters have been able to give credence to the ballot box in a way that no government could do alone. The result has not been the provision of equal rights. Black Sections greatest success has been a redirection of anger and militancy away from the streets towards the official political system. Street rebellion creates both social instability and the potential for building mass anti-racist movement whereas integration into the official political system renders dissent harmless.

Bibliography

Afro-West Indian United Council of Churches, 1984. A Handbook, 1984 Edition. London: Centre for Caribbean Studies, Caribbean House

Alderman, G., 1983. The Jewish Community in British Politics, Oxford: Clarendon Press

Alderman, G., 1984. 'Anglo-Jewry: the Politics of an Image', Parliamentary Affairs, Vol. 37, No. 2, Spring

Ali, Arif, (ed.) 1986 & 1988. Third World Impact, 7th & 8th eds., London: Hansib Publishing Ltd.

Allen, S. & Smith, C. 1977. 'Race and Ethnicity in Class Formation: A Comparison of Asian and West Indian workers', in B. Parekh (ed): The Social Analysis of Class Structure, Tavistock Publications

Allen, S. 1971. New Minorities, Old Conflicts, London: Random House

Althshuler, 1970. Community Control : The Black demand for participation in large American cities, New York, Pegasus

Anwar M., 1979. The Myth of Return, London: Heinemann

Anwar, M., 1975. 'Asian Participation in the 1974 Autumn Election'. New Community, III(4)

Anwar, M., 1980. Votes and Policies: Ethnic Minorities and the General Election, 1979, London: Commission for Racial Equality

Anwar, M., 1986. Race and Politics: Ethnic Minoritie and the British Political System, Tavistock Publications

Asian Herald, 22-28 March, 1988

Asian Times, passim

Aurora, G.S. 1967. The New Frontiersmen Bombay:Popular Prakashan

Banton, M. 1974. 'The Definition of the Police role', in New Community, Vol. III, No.3

Barrett, L.E., 1977. The Rastafarians, Kingston: Sangsters' Book Stores Ltd.

Ben-Tovim, G. & Gabriel, T., 1982. 'The Politics of Race in Britain 1962-79: A Review of the Major Trends and of Recent Debates', in Husbands, C. (ed.), Race in Britain: Continuity and Change, London: Hutchinson

Ben-Tovim, G. et al, 1986. The Local Politics of Race, London: MacMillan

Bentley, S. 1970. 'The Structure of Leadership among Indians, Pakistanis, and West Indians in Britain', (Unpublished M.Sc. Thesis) University of Bradford

Bevins, A., 1984. 'Black Members on Collision Course with Labour Leaders', Times, 11.6.

Bourne, Jenny, & Sivanandan, A., 1980. 'Cheerleaders and Ombudsmen: The Sociology of Race Relations in Britain' Race and Class Vol. XXI, No.4 pp.331-52

Bradford Telegraph & Argus, 1984-88, passim

Brown, C., 1984. Black and White Britain:The Third PSI Survey London: Policy Studies Institute / Heinemann

Butler, D. & Pinto-Duschinsky, M., 1971. The British General Election of 1970, Macmillan

Cambridge, A.X. & Gutzmore, C. 1974/5. 'The Industrial Action of the Black Masses and the Class Struggle in Britain', The Black Liberator, Vol. 2, No.3, June-January

Cambridge, A.X. & Pryce, E.A. 1980. 'Race, Class, Culture and Resistance in Lambeth', paper commissioned by and presented to, The Working Party on Community/Police Relations in Lambeth, (Unpublished)

Campbell, H. 1980. 'Rastafari: Culture of Resistance', Race and Class, Vol. XXII, No.I

Cansdale, D., 1983. 'The Development of the Community/Police Consultative Group for Lambeth'. (Unpublished M.Sc.), Cranfield Institute of Technology

CARF, 1988 'Poll-axing the black community' Searchlight 153 March

Caribbean Times, 1/2/85

Carter, T., 1986. Shattering Illusions: West Indians in British Politics, London: Lawrence & Wishart

Cashmore, E. 1979. Rastaman: The rastifarian Movement in England, London: George Allen & Unwin

Castells, M., 1983. The City and the Grossroots. London: Edward Arnold

Catholic Commission for Racial Justice, 1982. Notes & Reports, No.10: Rastafarians in Jamaica and Britain. Catholic Commission for Racial Justice

Cavanagh, T.E., 1984. The Impact of the Black Electorate, Washington DC: Joint Centre for Political Studies

Chandra, Bipan, (ed) 1983. The Indian Left: Critical Appraisals, New Delhi: Vikas Publishing House

Charman, P., 1979. Reflections: Black and White Christians in the City, Zebra Project

Chase, L. 1977. Transcript of Speech to CAC, 24 May

Chase, L. 1978. Notting Hill Carnival: Street Festival, London: Interlink Longraph Limited

City Limits, June 1988 passim

Clark, David 1975. 'Recollections of Resistance: Udham Singh and the IWA' in Notes and Documents, Race & Class Vol 17 No.1

Clarke, S. 1980. Jah Music: The Evolution of the Popular Jamaican Song, London: Heineman
Cohen, A. 1982. 'A Polyethnic London Carnival as a Contested Cultural Performance', in Ethnic and Racial Studies, Vol. 5, No.I, (January), pp.23-41
Cohen, Abner 1980. 'Drama and politics in the development of a London carnival' MAN 15.1
Collins, S. 1957. Coloured Minorities in Britain, London: Latterworth
Commission for Racial Equality, Ethnic Minorities in Britain: Statistical information on the pattern of settlement, Commission for Racial Equality
Commission for Racial Equality, 1984. Ethnic Minorities and the 1983 General Election, Commission for Racial Equality
Commission on Industrial Relations, 1970. Report No.4, Birmingham Aluminium Casting (1903) Company Limited, Dartmouth Auto Castings Limited, Midland Motor Cylinder Company Limited, London: HMSO
Community Relations Commission, 1975. Participation of Ethnic Minorities in the General Election, October 1974, Community Relations Commission
Community Relations Council 1975. Participation of Ethnic Minorities in the General Election - October 1974, London: Community Relations Council
Constant, D., 1982. Aux Sources du Reggae, Paris: Parentheses
Constantine, Learie 1954. Colour Bar, London: Stanley Paul & Co. Ltd.
Crewe, I., 1979. 'The Black, Brown and Green Votes,' New Society 12 April
Crewe. I., 1983. 'Representation and ethnic Minorities in Britain' in N. Glazer and K. Young, Ethnic Pluralism and Public Policy, Heinemann
Cross, M & Entzinger, H. (eds.), 1988. Lost Illusions: Caribbean Minorities in Britain and the Netherlands, London: Routledge
Daily News, 15/10/85
Desai, Rashmi, 1963. Indian Immigrants in Britain Oxford University Press
Duffield, Mark R. 1988. Black Radicalism and the Politics of De-industrialisation, Gower
Edelman, M., 1985. 'Political Language and Political Reality' Political Studies, vol. xxxiii, no. 1, pp.10-19
Edelman, M., 1988. Constructing the Political Spectacle, Chicago: University of Chicago Press
Egbuna, Obi 1971. Destroy This Temple: The Voice of Black Power in Britain, London: MacGibbon & Kee
European Parliament News, June 1984
Evening Mail, 11/12/85
Fitzgerald, M., 1983. 'Are Blacks an Electoral Liability?' New Society, 8 December, pp.394-6
Fitzgerald, M., 1987. Black People and Party Politics in Britain, The Runnymede Trust

Fitzgerald, M., 1988. 'Different Roads? The development of Afro-Caribbean and Asian Political organization in London', New Community, vol. xiv, no. 3
Fitzgerald, M., 1984. Political parties and Black People: participation, representation and exploitation London: Runnymede Trust
Fletcher, K. 1983. 'Notting Hill Starts to Throb', The Sunday Times, (London), 28 August
Foner, N. 1979. Jamaica Farewell: Jamaican Migrants in London, London: Routledge and Kegan Paul
Foot, M. 1977. 'Carnival Splits', Time Out (London), May 27 - June 2
Foot, P., 1965. Immigration and Race in British Politics, Penguin
Friedland, 1982. Power and Crisis in the City. London: MacMillan
Gay, P. & Young, K., 1988. Community Relations Councils: Roles and Objectives London: Commission for Racial Equality
Gilroy, P. 1987. There Ain't No Black in the Union Jack, London: Hutchinson
Gilroy, P. 1982. "Stepping' Out of Babylon - Race, Class, and Autonomy', The Empire Strikes Back: Race and Racism in 70's Britain, CCCS, London: Hutchinson
Glukman, M. 1954. Rituals of Rebellion in South-East Africa, Manchester University Press
Gordon, P. 1983. White Law, London: Pluto Press
Gordon, P. 1985. Policing Immigration, London: Pluto Press
Goulbourne, H. (forthcoming (a)). *Communalism or Community?: The Dr.Martin Luther King, Jr Memorial Lecture, 1989*, Centre for Research in Ethnic Relations, Occasional Papers
Goulbourne, H. (forthcoming). The Communal Option: Ethnicity and Nationalism in Post-Imperial Britain
Goulbourne, H., 1988a. 'The Contribution of Caribbean People to British Society', in, Ali, A. Third World Impact, 8th ed.
Goulbourne, H., 1988b. *West Indian Political Leadership in Britain*, The Byfield Memorial Lecture 1987, Coventry: Centre for Research in Ethnic Relations, University of Warwick, Occasional Papers No. 4
Goulbourne, H., 1988. Teachers, Education and Politics in Jamaica, 1892-1972, London: Macmillan/Warwick Caribbean Studies
Green, J., 1986. 'West Indian Doctors in London: John Alcindor (1873-1924) and James Jackson Brown (1882-1953)', Journal of Caribbean History, vol. 20, no. 1
Gutzmore, C. 1978. 'Carnival, The State, and the Black Masses in the United Kingdom', The Black Liberator, No.I, December, pp.9-27
Hall, S. 1979. 'Cultures of Resistance and moral panics: an interview with Stuart Hall', University of Sussex: AFRAS Review No.4
Hall, S. et al 1978. Policing the Crisis: Mugging, the State and Law and Order, London: Macmillan Press
Harris Research Centre Survey for ITN, 1987
Haskins, W.H., 1988. The Crisis of Afro-American Leadership, New York: Prometheus Books

Heineman, B., 1972. The Politics of the Powerless, Institute of Race Relations/OUP

Hill, E. 1972. The Trinidad Carnival: Mandate for a National Carnival, Austin: University of Texas Press

Hines, D. 1966. Journey to an Illusion, London: Heinemann

Hiro, Dilip, 1971. Black British White British London: Eyre and Spottiswoode

Howard, V., 1987. A Report on Afro-Caribbean Christianity in Britain, Department of Theology and Religious Studies, University of Leeds

Howe, Darcus 1985. On Black Sections in the Labour party, London: Race Today Publications

Immigration, 1961 Published jointly by Indian Workers' Association, Pakistani Workers' Association and West Indian Workers' Association

Jacob, B.D., 1986. Black Politics and Urban Crisis in Britain, Cambridge University Press

John, De Witt, 1969. Indian Workers Association in Britain, Oxford University Press

John, G. 1981 'In the Service of Black Youth: A Study of the Political Culture of Youth and Community Work with Black People in English Cities', (National Association of Youth Clubs Special Report Series) Special Report, No.2, March

Johnson, M. 1988. 'Resurrecting the Inner City: A New Role for the Christian Churches', New Community, vol. 15, no. 1

Johnson, M. & Cross M., 1984. 'Surveying Service Users in Multi-Racial Areas' Research Paper 2, Birmingham: Aston University, Research Unit on Ethnic Relations

Johnson, M., 1985. "Race' Religion and Ethnicity' Ethnic and Racial Studies 8,3 pp 426-437

Johnson, M., Cox, C. & Cross, M., 1989. 'Paying for change: Section 11 and local authority social services' New Community 15, 3 pp.371-390

Jones, C. 1978. 'The Caribbean Community in Britain', The Black Liberator, No.1, December

Katznelson, I., 1981. City Trenches: Urban Politics and the Patterning of Class in the United States, New York: Pantheon

Kavanagh, D. 1982. (ed.), The Politics of the Labour Party, London: George Allen and Unwin

Keith, M. (forthcoming). Lore and Disorder: Policing a Multi-Racial Society in the 1980

Keith, M. 1988. 'Squaring Circles? Consultation and Inner City Policing' in New Community 15 (1) October 1988 63-77

Kensington News and Post 1977. (London), 27 May

Kensington News and Post 1977, 3 June - 17 June

Kettle, M. and Hodges, L. 1982. Uprising: The Police, the People and the Riots in Britain's Cities, London/Sydney: Pan Books

Khan, N., 1978. The Arts Britain Ignores: The Arts of the Ethnic Minorities in Britain, London: Commission for Racial Equality

Kirsch, B. 1988. 'Crisis Comes to Carnival', 7 DAYS (Communist Party Weekly), Vol. 3, No.39, August 13

Labour Party Black Section, 1988 The Black Agenda London: Hansib Publishing

Labour Party Black Sections, 'Campaign Black Links - The Way Ahead for Black Sections - July 1985, as amended May 1987 (Black Sections internal discussion paper)

Labour Party Black Sections, 'National Committee Report of Strategy Consultation,' Feb. 1988

Labour Party Black Sections, 'Rules for the Labour Party Black Section, Draft as amended in March 1987'

Labour Party Black Sections, 1988 Press Release, October

Labour Party Black Sections, 1988. The Black Agenda, Hansib

Labour Party Black Sections, Chair's report to 1988 Annual Conference

Labour Party Black Sections, Newsletter, Autumn 1986

Labour Party Black Sections, Newsletter, Autumn 1987

Labour Party Black Sections, Newsletter, Spring 1985

Layton Henry, Z. & Rich, P.B., 1986. Race, Government and Politics in Britain London: Macmillan

Layton-Henry, Z. & Studlar, D., 1984. 'The Political Participation of Black and Asian Britons' Working Paper, 36, Department of Politics, University of Warwick

Layton-Henry, Z. & Studler, D.T. 1985. 'The Electoral Participation of Black and Asian Britons: Integration or Alienation?' Parliamentary Affairs, Summer

Layton-Henry, Z. 1978. 'Race, Electoral Strategy and the Major Parties', Parliamentary Affairs, XXXI, 3, Summer

Layton-Henry, Z., 1983. 'Immigration and Race Relations: Political Aspects No.9', New Community 11, pp 109-116

Layton-Henry, Z., 1984. The Politics of Race in Britain, London: Allen and Unwin

Le Lohe M., 1987 A Study of Non Registration Among Ethnic Minorities, A Report submitted to the Commission For Racial Equality, May

Le Lohe, M., 1979. 'The Effects of the Presence of Immigrants upon the Local Political System in Bradford 1945-77 in R. Miles and A. Phizacklea (eds.) Racism and Political Action, Routledge & Kegan Paul

Le Lohe, M.J., 1983. 'Voter discrimination against Asian and black candidates in the 1983 General Election', New Community 11, pp.101-108

Le Lohe, M.J., 1984 'Ethnic minority participation in Local Elections', mimeo, University of Bradford

LeLohe, M., 1975. 'Participation in Elections by Asians in Bradford', in Crewe, I. (ed.) British Political Sociology Yearbook, Vol 2: The Politics of Race, Croom Helm

Liberal Party, 1986. Promoting Greater Involvement: report of the Commission of Inquiry into Ethnic Minority Involvement in the Liberal Party Hebden Bridge: Liberal Party Community Relations Panel

Lukes, S., 1974. Power: A Radical View. London: MacMillan

Marxism Today, 1985 'Black Sections: Radical demand...or distraction?' Sept.

McClennan, G., Held, D, Hall, S (eds), 1984. State and Society in Contemporary Britain. Cambridge: Polity Press

McGlashen, C. 1973. 'The Sound System', The Sunday Times (London), (Colour Magazine) February

Messina, A., 1987. 'Mediating race relations : British commmunity relations councils revisited', Ethnic & Racial Studies, vol.10 no.2, pp.186-202

Miles & Phizacklea (eds.) 1979. Racism and Political Action, London: Routledge & Kegan Paul

Miles, R. 1978. 'Between Two Cultures The Case of Rastafarianism', SSRC Research Unit on Ethnic Relations, Bristol University

Miller, W. 'What was the Profit in Following the Crowd: Aspects of Conservative and Labour Strategy since 1970' British Journal of Political Science, 10, 1

Mingione, E., 1981. Social Conflict and the City. Oxford: Blackwell

Moore, R. 1975. Racism and Black Resistance in Britain, Pluto Press

Murji, K. and M. Keith, (forthcoming). "Race', racism and the local politics of policing' in Ball, W. & Solomos, J. (eds.) Race and Local Politics

National Council for Civil Liberties, 1980 Southall 23 April 1979 The Report of the Unofficial Committee of Enquiry

National Council for Civil Liberties, 1980 The Death of Blair Peach, The Supplementary Report of the Unofficial Committee of Enquiry

Nettleford, R., 1978. Caribbean Cultural Identity, Kingston: Institute of Jamaica

Nettleford, R., Smith, M.G. & Augier, R. 1960. The Rastafari Movement in Kingston, Jamaica, I.S.E.R., University College of the West Indies

New Life, 16/10/87

Oppenheim, C., 1988. A tax on all the people London: Child Poverty Action Group

Phillips, M., 1981. 'Flexing the muscles of the ethnic vote', New Statesman, 15 May

Poulantzas, N., 1973. Political Power and Social Classes, London: New Left Books

Pryce, E.A. 1981. 'Jamaican Migration: Colour, Class and status', New Community, Vol. IX, No.1

Pryce, E.A. 1983. 'Black Style', New Community, Vol. IX, No.1/2, Autumn-Winter

Pryce, E.A. 1983a. 'Debating Britain's Election 1983', The West Indian Digest (London), June

Pryce, E.A. 1987. "Currants' in the Bun - New Challenges Facing Whitehall', The Money Index, No.88, September 8, Kingston, Jamaica

Public Service, December 1988

Race and Class, 1985, passim

Race and Immigration, May 1987

Race Today Collective 1977 The Road Make to Walk on Carnival Day: The Battle for the West Indian Carnival in Britain, Race Today Publication
Race Today Collective, 1983 The Struggle of Asian Workers in Britain Race Today Publications
Race Today, 1973. 'West Indian Youth and the Police in Notting Hill', Vol. 5, No.11, December
Race Today, 1987-88. passim
Ramdin, Ron, 1987. The Making of the Black Working Class in Britain, Gower
Report of the General Secretary IWA (GB) Avtar Jouhal 1967
Report of the General Secretary IWA Southall 1974
Retzlaff, Ralph, 1969. 'Revisionists and Sectarians: Indias Two Communist Parties' in The Communist Revolution in Asia Robert A. Scalapino, (ed.) London:Prentice Hall
Rex, J. & Tomlinson, S., 1979. Colonial Immigrants in a British City: A Class Analysis, London: Routledge & Kegan Paul
Rex, J. 1979. 'Black Militancy and Class Conflict', in R. Miles and A. Phizacklea (eds.): Racism and Political Action in Britain
Rex, J., 1988. The Ghetto and the Underclass: Essays on Race and Social Policy, Aldershot: Avebury
Rice, C. & Patel, B., 1988. Last Among Equals Birmingham: West Midlands Low Pay Unit
Rohlehr, G. 1984. 'An Introduction to the History of the Calypso', (Paper 2), in The Social and economic Impact of Carnival-Seminar Papers, ISER, UWI, St. Augustine, Trinidad, April
Salewics, C. & Peel, J. 1983. 'Reggae: The Rhythm of Roots', The Sunday Times (London), (Colour Magazine), 28 August
Schoen, D., 1964. Enoch Powell and the Powellites, Macmillan
Sherlock, Sir Philip, 1980. Norman Manley: A Biography, Macmillan
Sivanandan, A. 1982. A Different Hunger: Writings on Black Resistance, Pluto Press
Sivanandan, A. 1985. 'RAT and the degradations of black struggle' Race and Class Vol XXVI, No.4, pp.1-33
Sivanandan, A., 1983. 'Challenging Racism: Strategies for the '80s', Race & Class, xxv, 2
Sivanandan, A., 1986. *From Resistance to Rebellion: Asian and Afro-Caribbean Struggles in Britain*, Race & Class Pamphlet No. 10, Institute of Race Relations
SMASH RACIALISM AND FASCISM 1976. IWA (GB) Avtar Jouhal
Solomos J., 1986. 'Riots, Urban Protest and Social Policy: The Interplay of Reform and Social Control' Warwick:Centre for Research in Ethnic Relations, Policy Papers in Ethnic Relations No.7
Solomos J., 1988. Black Youth, Racism and the State The Politics of Ideology and Policy, Cambridge University Press
Southall Rights, 1980 23rd April 1979, Crest Press

Studlar, D., 1986. 'Non-white Policy Preferences, Political Participation and the Political Agenda in Britain', in Z. Layton-Henry and P. Rich (eds.) Race, Government and Politics in Britain, Macmillan

Studlar, D.T., 1983. 'The Ethnic Vote 1983: problems of analysis and interpretation', New Community 11, pp.92-100

Studler, D.T., 1978. 'Policy Voting in Britain: The Coloured Immigration Issue in the 1964, 1966 and 1970 General Elections', American Political Science Review, No.72

Sunday Telegraph, 1978-85, passim

Taylor, S. 1981. 'Riots: Some Explanations', in New Community, Vol. IX, No.2

The Birmingham Post, 1985-6, passim

The Guardian, 19.11.88

The Guardian, passim

The Harris Research Centre, 1987. National Pol III, 27-28 May

The Independent, 2/10/87

The Times, 1983, Guide to the House of Commons, London

THE VICTIMS SPEAK: (N.D) IWA (GB) Avtar Jouhal

Times, 1984-5, Passim

Todd J. & Butcher B., 1982. Electoral Registration in 1981, London: Office of Population Census and Surveys

Toynbee, P. 'Lambeth's walk on the wild side', Guardian, 11/5/87

Travis, A., 1983. 'Ethnic minorities hold a major stake in battle for Ladywood', Birmingham Post, 31 May

Voice, 2/11/85

Voice, 28/1/86

Wadsworth, 1988. 'The Fight for black political recognition', Ali, Arif (ed.) Third World Impact 8th ed.

Wainwright, H. 1987. Labour: A Tale of two Parties, London: The Hogarth Press

West Indian Digest, 1988. 'London Carnival Wins European Solidarity', No. 156, August, pp.42-43

West Indian Standing Conference, Constitution (1981)

West Indian Standing Conference, T am Work (passim)

West Indian World 1977 (London), 3 June - 9 June

Wrench, J., 1986. 'Unequal Comrades: Trades Unions, Equal Opportunity and Racism' Policy Paper 5, Warwick University: Centre for Research in Ethnic Relations

Index

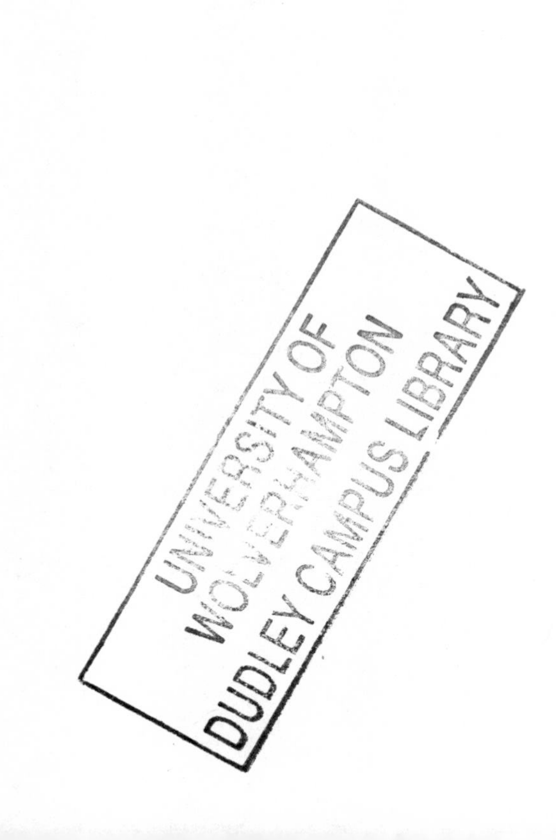
UNIVERSITY OF
WOLVERHAMPTON
DUDLEY CAMPUS LIBRARY